T0208622

Aid, Trade and Development

'This is a very well written book, technically sound, and a great source of material for anyone who wants to understand the factors that have shaped much of international economics for the past half a century. More tellingly, Michalopoulos writes with passion on developments that he knows very well and cares deeply about.'

—K.Y. Amoako, *President of the African Center for Economic Transformation, Ghana*

'It is salutary in these unsettled days to recall Frederic Bastiat's warning of 175 years ago: when goods cannot cross borders, armies do. Constantine Michalopoulos' review and analysis of the realities of globalization over the past half century is perfectly timed to counteract the resurgence of know-nothingism, intolerance and isolationism. With his unique combination of extensive research experience and personal participation in a leading capacity in the major international events in aid and trade, Constantine Michalopoulos is one of just a handful of persons who could possibly have attempted to write such a book. And he has succeeded in full. Thoroughly documented, insightful, interesting, lucid, *Aid, Trade and Development* is a major contribution to the debate on the great and delicate issues facing the world economy in the years to come.'

—Salvatore Schiavo-Campo, *former Senior Adviser at the Asian Development Bank, the Philippines*

'This book makes a unique contribution in documenting an important chapter of the history of development cooperation.'

—Heidemarie Wieczorek-Zeul, *former Federal Minister of Economic Cooperation and Development, Germany*

'This book is a fascinating history of 50 years of the most salient and interesting issues concerning aid, trade and development as seen from a seasoned practitioner's viewpoint. Over these years Michalopoulos played important roles in two key organizations—USAID and the World Bank—and is able to bring this story to life with many examples drawn from his personal experience. He is clearly very comfortable with the many complexities of his subject matter but he writes in terms that the lay reader will easily be able to grasp. In short, I highly recommend this book for anyone who wishes to understand the many stages of global development we have experienced in recent decades and how they may shape the future.'

—Alexander Shakow, *former Senior Official at USAID and Deputy Secretary of the World Bank, USA*

'In a broad sweep of the modern economic history underpinning aid, trade, and development, Michalopoulos manages to capture the most salient trends and does so in a thorough, perceptive, and compelling fashion. This is a great read for those following globalization and for those wanting to know more. A tour de force!'

—Danny Leipziger, *George Washington University, USA*

'Michalopoulos' chapter on the Greek crisis is very elegant and well written, covering the ground comprehensively and fairly.'

—George Papaconstantinou, *former Greek Finance Minister and author of Game Over: The Inside Story of the Greek Crisis*

Constantine Michalopoulos

Aid, Trade and Development

50 Years of Globalization

Constantine Michalopoulos
School of Advanced International Studies
Johns Hopkins University
Washington DC, USA

ISBN 978-3-319-88118-8   ISBN 978-3-319-65861-2   (eBook)
https://doi.org/10.1007/978-3-319-65861-2

Cover illustration: Miro Kovacevic / Alamy Stock Vector

Printed on acid-free paper

This Palgrave Macmillan imprint is published by Springer Nature
The registered company is Springer International Publishing AG
The registered company address is: Gewerbestrasse 11, 6330 Cham, Switzerland

To Development professionals in public service working tirelessly for a better tomorrow

Preface

The idea about writing this book first came to me about a decade ago. At that time I had written *Migration Chronicles*, a semi-autobiographical volume, and a number of my friends had said: 'Nice book, but what did you actually do in those jobs you had?' So, I thought that at some point I would write something which focused on the various development policy issues involving aid, trade and development with which I grappled in various positions with US AID, the World Bank and WTO.

I was lucky that one way or another I was involved in a small way in policy making on the major issues of the period from the late 1960s to the early twenty-first century: addressing the impact of the OPEC oil price rise in the early 1970s, the development of a basic human needs aid strategy in the late 1970s, the debt crisis, the 'Washington Consensus' and 'Adjustment with a Human Face' of the 1980s, the collapse of the Soviet Union and the birth of the WTO in the 1990s; and later in the decade 2000–2010 with continued involvement on these issues as a consultant. I also had kept a lot of notes, letters and other material from all these years. So, in the fall of 2015 when, after 50 years, I basically finished my professional career teaching a course on International Trade and Development at the School of Advanced International Studies (SAIS) of Johns Hopkins University, I thought I may take up the idea of writing a book detailing my professional experience.

Very soon it became clear that the material I had collected plus my own publications would not do justice to the complex issues that I had to address. Much more research was needed. Palgrave Macmillan was gracious enough to offer me a contract in the summer of 2016. Laura Pacey, Commissioning Editor, has been extremely supportive from the very beginning and I am grateful for her help and guidance. But as I started to write, the world around me started to change: Brexit, the result of the US elections, the rise of populism, protectionism and anti-globalization required that my work focus more explicitly on the forces of globalization and its impact on those left behind. The result is this volume.

It would never have been done without the help of a large number of friends and former colleagues and especially Eveline Herfkens, my long-time partner in life and in work, to all of whom I express my deep gratitude. I am also grateful to three economists who taught me a lot as their student: Alan Batchelder, my first economics professor, Albert O. Hirschman and Peter B. Kenen.

Many friends and colleagues influenced my thinking about aspects of aid, trade and development, but were not involved in the writing of this book. I mention in particular Peter Allgeier, Misha Belkindas, Philip Birnbaum, Esperanza Duran, James Hanson, Bernard Hoekman, Paul Isenman, Keith Jay, Anne Krueger, John Mellor, Lorenzo Perez, Riordan Roett, Sylvia Saborio and Ernie Stern. There were tens of others who also helped me over the years and who should forgive me for not mentioning them explicitly for lack of space.

Special thanks are reserved for a group who devoted a lot of effort, some to provide material, others to correct my mistakes, add perspectives, and actually change my views by reading and commenting on one or several chapters or the whole of this book. These include Masood Ahmed, K.Y. Amoako, Michael Crosswell, John Eriksson, Ruth Jacoby, Hilde Johnson, Danny Leipziger, Ira Lieberman, James Michel, John Nellis, Donal Donovan, George Papaconstantinou, Salvatore Schiavo-campo, Alexander Shakow, Clare Short, David Tarr, George Tavlas, and Heidemarie Wieczorek-Zeul.

I am grateful to Gordon Bodnar, Morris W. Offit Professor of International Finance and Kelley Kornell, Associate Director of the Master of International Economics and Finance Program (MIEF) at Johns

Hopkins SAIS for their support and financial assistance for this project. The volume could not have been done without the contributions of Zhangrui Wang (MIEF'17), who did an excellent job in developing all the statistical work and tables for the volume as well as provided invaluable assistance with the references. Thanks are also due to Regina Monticone for helping with translation of materials from German.

I reserve my greatest thanks to Eveline Herfkens, who read and commented on the whole book; contributed her own valuable experience, speeches, publications and other materials that were critical to developing the story about aid and development in the two decades 1990–2010, which she and her soul mates in the Utstein group had a hand in making; and forgave my temporary dereliction of some of my household duties during the period of writing another book.

Thanks are also due to the IMF for permitting me to reproduce certain passages of my article 'World Bank Programs for Adjustment and Growth' in Vittorio Corbo, Morris Goldstein and Mohsin Khan *Growth Oriented Adjustment Programs*; to the World Bank for letting me reproduce Table 1.8 from *Global Economic Prospects* 2002; and to FAO, UN and the World Bank for letting me reproduce a table that they prepared which was published as Table 2.7 in the World Bank's 1988 *Report on Adjustment Lending: Ten Years of Experience*. All remaining errors are my responsibility.

Constantine Michalopoulos

Contents

xii   Contents

List of Acronyms

ACET	African Center for Economic Transformation
ACP Countries	African Caribbean and Pacific Countries
ADB	Asian Development Bank
AFT	Aid for Trade
AGOA	African Growth and Opportunity Act
AID	Agency for International Development
AIIB	Asian Infrastructure Investment Bank
AITIC	Agency for International Trade Information and Cooperation
AMS	Aggregate Measures of Support
BHN	Basic Human Needs
BRICS	Brazil, Russia, India, China, South Africa
BWI	Bretton Woods Institutions
CEE	Central and Eastern Europe
CFC	Common Fund for Commodities
CGD	Center for Global Development
CIEC	Conference for International Economic Cooperation
CMEA	Council for Mutual Economic Assistance
COMESA	Common Market for East and Southern Africa
DFQF	Duty Free, Quota Free
DSM	Dispute Settlement Mechanism
EAC	East African Community
EAEU	Eurasian Economic Union
EBA	Everything But Arms

EBRD	European Bank for Reconstruction and Development
ECB	European Central Bank
EIF	Enhanced Integrated Framework
EMENA	Europe, Middle East and North Africa
ESM	European Stability Mechanism
EU	European Union
FDI	Foreign Direct Investment
FSU	Former Soviet Union
FTA	Free Trade Agreements
GATS	General Agreement of Trade in Services
GATT	General Agreement on Tariffs and Trade
GSP	Generalized System of Preferences
IDA	International Development Association
IDB	Inter-American development Bank
IDS	International Development Strategy
IDT	International Development Targets
IFAD	International Food and Agriculture Development
IFC	International Financial Corporation
IFI	International Financial Institutions
IMF	International Monetary Fund
ITA	Information Technology Agreement
ITC	International Trade Center
LDC	Least Developed Countries
MDBs	Multilateral Development Banks
MDG	Millennium Development Goals
MEBO	Management–Employee Buyouts
MFN	Most Favored Nation
MSA	Most Seriously Affected
NAC	National Advisory Council
NAFTA	North-American Free Trade Agreement
NAMA	Non-Agriculture Market Access
ND	New Democracy
NGOs	Non-Governmental Organizations
NTMs	Non-tariff measures
ODA	Official Development Assistance
OECD	Organization for Economic Cooperation and Development
OPEC	Organization of Petroleum Exporting Countries
OPIC	Overseas Private Investment Corporation

PRSPs	Poverty Reduction Strategy Papers
PSI	Private Sector Involvement
PTAs	Preferential Trade Agreements
RCEP	Regional Comprehensive Economic Partnership
RTA	Regional Trade Agreements
SADEC	Southern Africa Development Community
SAL	Structural Adjustment Loan
SDG	Sustainable Development Goals
SDR	Special Drawing Rights
SDT	Special and Differential Treatment
SECALs	Sectoral Adjustment Loans
SPS	Sanitary and Phytosanitary Measures
TBT	Technical Barriers to Trade
TFA	Trade Facilitation Agreement
TPP	Transpacific Partnership
TPRM	Trade Policy Review Mechanism
TRIMS	Trade Related Investment Measures
TRIPS	Trade Related Intellectual Property Rights
TTIP	Transatlantic Trade and Investment Partnership
UK	United Kingdom
UN	United Nations
UN ECOSCO	United Nations Economic and Social Council
UNCTAD	United Nations Conference on Trade and Development
UNDP	United Nations Development Program
UNICEF	United Nations Children Fund
USAID	United States Agency for International Development
USSR	Union of Soviet Socialist Republics
WTO	World Trade Organization

List of Tables

1

Aid, Trade and Development: 50 Years of Globalization

Introduction

Developing countries have made tremendous progress in reducing poverty over the last 50 years. More open societies and more open economies have contributed to this progress as has international cooperation in support of development. This volume traces the evolution of thinking and practice of developed and developing country policies on trade and foreign aid which have shaped the external environment within which development has taken place this past half-century. The concluding section provides some answers to the challenges presented by anti-globalization forces in the developed world that question the principles on which international cooperation has been based and threaten to undermine future progress.

The narrative is roughly chronological but with many recurrent themes. The mid-1960s, the beginning of the analysis, were turbulent years for the developing world. In 1965, India was fighting a war against Pakistan. Indonesia had a bloody coup in which tens of thousands lost their lives and resulted in Suharto's dictatorship. Brazil was run by another dictator, General Castelo Branco, who had come to power months before. China's Mao was preparing his Cultural Revolution to be launched the following

© The Author(s) 2017
C. Michalopoulos, *Aid, Trade and Development*,
https://doi.org/10.1007/978-3-319-65861-2_1

1

year. The US was in the middle of the Vietnam War. The Arab world was two years away from war with Israel, while Mobutu had just consolidated his control of Zaire through another coup.

In the mid-1960s, the starting point of this book, the world was in the middle of what some called the second phase of globalization in the modern era, with the sum of exports and imports around 20% of world Gross Domestic Product (GDP) (European Commission 2017). Developing country attitudes toward international trade and foreign investment, important aspects of globalization then and now, were mostly negative. Demand prospects appeared dim for primary commodities that constituted the bulk of developing country exports. The predominant view was that development required import substitution industrialization behind strong protective walls of tariff and non-tariff barriers. Foreign direct investment was eyed with suspicion as developing countries were seeking to establish a 'code of conduct' for multinationals. Other private capital flows were virtually non-existent. The US and the Soviet Union were using foreign aid in competing for the hearts and minds of the public in the so-called Third World, while Europeans were channeling most of their aid to former colonies; the World Bank was only financing infrastructure and UN assistance was in its infancy.

The oil price increases in the 1970s led to increasing debt burdens for many oil-importing countries combined with demands for the establishment of a 'New International Economic Order' based on the increased economic power of commodity and energy exporters joined through international agreements. Little came of the latter efforts. But the oil price increases left a large debt burden for many developing countries, which, combined with lack of international action to provide relief, doomed their economic prospects in the 1980s. A new international economic order did come about of a very different kind later on through the breakup of the Soviet Union and the rise of China as a world economic giant and the largest trading nation.

Over time, stronger growth performances of export-oriented developing countries, especially in Asia, led to a generally positive view of the impact of trade on development, though concerns continue to linger about its impact on poverty alleviation. At the same time, the end of the Cold War permitted a greater focus of economic assistance on development and eliminating poverty, as well as on ways of making assistance more effective.

The rise of China and other emerging powers posed significant challenges for the international financial institutions (IFI) such as the International Monetary Fund (IMF), the World Bank, the regional development banks and the General Agreement on Tariffs and Trade (GATT) which had been established after World War II to promote monetary stability, development and international trade. The 15 new states that emerged from the former Soviet Union had to become members of these institutions in order to receive much needed assistance. China, an aid recipient from multilateral institutions for many years, was growing so rapidly that it soon became a donor itself. A new trade institution, the WTO was being established in which China was not a member. And as the relative importance in global trade and general economic power of these emerging economies rose, the balance of power in the IFIs had to be reconsidered to reflect the new economic realities and China as well as Russia and the other countries of the former Soviet Union had to become members of the WTO.

Rapid technological change combined with expansion of trade and private capital flows in the 1990s and the early years of the twenty-first century resulted in the massive spread of globalization throughout the developing world with trade reaching and exceeding 50% of global GDP.

Globalization has many dimensions: economic, technological and cultural with many interconnections between the three. On the economic side it involves the integration of national economies into the international economy through trade in goods and services as well as flows of capital and labor. Capital flows include foreign direct investment and other private capital flows as well as official capital flows through aid from bilateral or multilateral donors. For a long period of time, official aid was the main source of capital flows to developing countries and thus of great importance to development and links to the global economy. But no longer, as private capital flows and private philanthropy have expanded pari passu with globalization.

Globalization has been called many names: sudden, unavoidable, uncontrollable, kaleidoscopic, problematic, evil, ugly. Discourse about it has been mostly fearful: some have thought that it reflects policies of malign intent, while others simply believe its effects have been negative, especially on the poor. There is a general unease that globalization will benefit only a few countries, while moving forward at a faster pace than the institutions in most others can cope with. At the same time, there is awareness that exogenous forces involving technological change are pushing globalization and growth inexorably forward, and hence there is fear of being left behind—of becoming further marginalized.

Attitudes toward globalization have shifted. In the 1960s, the developing world was much more fearful. Following the 2008 financial crisis, reactions are most negative in the developed world. Anti-globalization sentiment has given rise to populist movements in developed countries with agendas to raise trade protection, reduce foreign aid and limit migration. These developments pose serious dangers for the future of the world economy and the prospects for reducing poverty.

The overall theme that will hopefully emerge from this retrospective is that both trade and aid can benefit development, but whether they do depends very much on the presence of other coherent supportive policies in both developed and developing countries. In particular, there is a need for coherence between developed country aid and trade policies; there is a need for overall coherent strategies for development in developing countries for trade and aid to have a beneficial impact on reducing poverty and promoting sustainable development; and there is a need for effective international collaboration to achieve these objectives. Such collaboration has to take into account the new economic reality of a large and dynamic China and the political reality that in the absence of effective systems to support those left behind by globalization, the world will become vulnerable to protectionist, isolationist movements that undermine the liberal principles on which the world has relied to lift billions out of poverty in the last 50 years.

The policy review by necessity will be selective in coverage, and broadbrush in approach. The enormity of the task prevents many details and nuances. Some important issues such as the environment and gender and the recent advances in artificial intelligence are not addressed at all. Longterm demographic changes also have a bearing on patterns of development and migration but are discussed only briefly. Only the income dimension of poverty is considered. In this broad canvas, there will be a few light sprinkles of paint regarding my own personal involvement, especially in the first half of the volume. In part the selection of themes will be guided by my experience of working on aid and trade issues in two major aid-giving agencies: the US Agency for International Development (AID) and the World Bank as well as the World Trade Organization (WTO).

The first chapter that follows this introduction discusses the early thinking about the role the volume of aid can play in development, including the idea that aid makes a contribution by providing access to foreign exchange, which was thought to be in scarce supply at early stages of development. The popularity of this notion is explained in part by the early pessimism about the prospects for developing country exports, the topic of the following chapter.

Over time there was a reaction to both of these early notions. On the aid side, there was increasing concern that the focus on aid volume ignored questions of aid effectiveness and in particular questions about who benefited from the assistance programs. In turn, this led to a discussion of how to use aid to address more explicitly the needs of the poor. On the trade side, it became increasingly clear that developing country trade policies played a significant role in determining foreign exchange availability, and that countries whose trade policies did not discourage exports tended to have a stronger growth performance. These considerations led many developing countries to reevaluate their trade policies and adopt more outward looking strategies involving greater integration into the global economy. The chapter also raises for the first time the issue of incoherence between developed country aid and trade policies.

Chapter 4 starts by looking at the impact of the successive oil crises in the early and late 1970s on developing country prospects and their implications in raising their international debt burden, another less attractive aspect of globalization. The chapter then analyzes the long and tortuous efforts of the international community to come to grips with the problems of two groups of countries: the highly indebted middle-income countries whose international indebtedness was primarily to commercial banks in the developed world and the highly indebted poor countries, mostly in Sub-Saharan Africa whose debt was primarily to official bilateral and multilateral aid agencies. The muddling through approach in the end produced the Brady bond and HIPC (Highly Indebted Poor Country) schemes which, however, did not prevent stagnation for many countries for long periods.

The following three chapters address three key developments of the 1990s: Chap. 5 analyzes the breakup of the Soviet Union and the troubled transition from plan to market which resulted in more open societies and economies but at great short-term costs—despite large international assistance. Chapter 6 discusses the birth of the WTO, a new multilateral trade organization whose establishment has had significant implications for the conduct of international trade in both goods and services as well as intellectual property rights and 'behind the border' regulations which impact all countries' trade. Chapter 7 focuses on poverty and globalization: it assesses the performance of different developing country groups in reducing poverty and the attitudes of their public toward the onset of globalization; it also discusses the changing attitudes and practices toward foreign assistance and its increasing focus on poverty reduction.

Chapter 8, perhaps the most hopeful of all chapters, looks at aid and trade in the first few years of the new millennium, a period of rapid growth of trade and GDP, the emergence of China as a global power, large reductions in poverty and many international agreements aimed at improving the effectiveness of economic assistance and liberalizing trade. The period ends with the developed world's financial crisis of 2008 which casts a pall on future global prospects.

Chapter 9 analyzes the prolonged economic crisis in Greece—not a developing country by income standards but with many 'developing country' weaknesses in policies and institutions—whose problems were precipitated by the 2008 financial crisis. Chapter 10 reviews global policies toward development post-2008. It rejoices about the achievement of most Millennium Development Goals, but points to a worrisome trend of increasing protection, only modest achievements in further trade liberalization, back-tracking on commitments to increase aid effectiveness and, most disturbing, the rise of anti-globalization populism in the US and Europe which threatens the core principles on which international cooperation on trade and economic assistance has been based for the last half-century. The last chapter looks to the future and attempts to provide some answers to the challenges that threaten the future of international cooperation for development and undermine efforts to reduce global poverty.

References

European Commission (2017) *Reflection Paper on Harnessing Globalization,* (Brussels: European Commission).

2

Growth Constraints, Aid Targets and Basic Needs

Introduction

Government to government economic assistance programs on concessional terms that aim to promote the development of the recipient is a post-World War II phenomenon, although there were occasional official loans and other assistance in earlier periods. Most consider that aid started with the US Marshall Plan in 1947.[1] In 1960, the Development Assistance Group of the Organization for European Economic Co-operation (OECD, which included European recipients of Marshall Plan aid and the US) was set up to exchange information on members' aid activities in developing countries. In 1961, upon the establishment of the OECD, the Group became the OECD Development Assistance Committee (DAC). Its mandate is 'to consult on the methods for making national resources available for assisting countries and areas in the process of economic development and for expanding and improving the flow of long term funds and other development assistance to them' (Fuhrer 1996, p. 10).

During these early years, the US provided the bulk of foreign aid from the OECD countries: about 55% of $3.8 billion in 1957 and as much as 57% of $6.3 billion in 1965, the beginning of this study. But 15 other OECD countries were also providing assistance in the late 1950s, with

© The Author(s) 2017
C. Michalopoulos, *Aid, Trade and Development*,
https://doi.org/10.1007/978-3-319-65861-2_2

France and the UK being the major other donors primarily to former colonies and territories. The Netherlands also launched a technical assistance program early, in 1949. But for a long time it provided assistance only through the UN or other multilateral agencies. The Soviet Union and other socialist countries were also providing economic assistance to developing countries during this period, whose amount was hard to quantify but was estimated at roughly a tenth of the OECD total (OECD 1969, p. 294).

Aid comes in different forms and on different terms. The definition used in this book includes Official Development Assistance, (ODA) which is defined to include assistance from the donor's public sector for developmental purposes, net of repayments of capital with a grant element of at least 25%.[2] It will also include flows from the World Bank's International Development Association (IDA) and other Multilateral Development Banks (MDBs) 'soft' windows which are extended on ODA terms. Other official flows (OOF) from these institutions which are on harder terms (interest rates and maturities) than ODA but softer than what can be obtained in the private capital markets as well as other official flows from bilateral donors which do not qualify as ODA are measured separately and exclude credits from the IMF.

Developed country aid objectives have always been very complex. Political/security objectives and pursuit of domestic economic and commercial interests, sometimes very narrowly defined often combine and dominate the promotion of development or global humanitarian objectives. In earlier periods, US agricultural commodity assistance under the so-called Public Law 480 had as much the objective of disposing of US agricultural surplus commodities as it did to help feed poor people in the developing world. New donors' assistance, especially from China, is often closely linked to projects aimed at increasing China's access to raw materials. And even today almost 20% of bilateral aid programs are tied to procurement in the donor reducing substantially their value to the recipient.

Multilateral assistance which is usually untied by source tends to be less dominated by narrow commercial considerations of the major donors. Some donors nevertheless include procurement staff among their representatives at the World Bank in order to help them obtain a 'fair share' of the procurement. Political/security objectives were explicitly paramount in certain bilateral US programs until the collapse of the Soviet Union, but also today in the Middle East and elsewhere. The allocation of bilateral aid in the UK and France has been tilted in favor of former colonies. And the Dutch aid program, though originally channeled through the UN technical assistance program, was viewed as an 'excellent source of employment for the many tropical experts who risked losing their jobs as a result of decolonization' (Nekkers and Malcontent 1999, p. 12). Albert Hirschman in a classic early paper called 'Foreign aid as Janus-faced an institution as can be found. In a world of sovereign nations, rich and poor, it is an instrument of national policy which can be used by the rich to acquire influence and to increase their power. At the same time, foreign aid redistributes income from the rich to the poor and can thus serve to speed the latter's development' (Hirschman and Bird 1968, p. 3).

The complexity of donor policy objectives and the multiplicity of actors make an assessment of the effectiveness of aid in promoting development extremely difficult. A great deal depends on the individual donor and recipient. Still, over the last 50 years, enough experience has been accumulated on what works and what does not to develop some consensus about the basic principles of aid's development effectiveness.[3] This chapter will attempt to trace the evolution in this thinking starting with the very simple notions of the 1950s and 1960s to about 1980. Considerable attention will be paid to US and World Bank assistance programs partly because of my greater familiarity with the programs of these two institutions and partly because of their relative importance in the early years both in the evolution of thinking about aid and in the volume of their assistance: in 1975, US net ODA was still almost 30% of the total ODA. In 1980, World Bank Loan and Credit Commitments were more than 60% of total multilateral commitments.

Development Constraints

Early thinking about economic development stressed the role of accumulation of physical and human capital. Thus, the role of aid focused on its potential in helping recipients address constraints on capital accumulation that inhibited their development. In terms of physical capital, aid could help countries break the vicious circle of poverty: their low real incomes were thought to result in a low capacity to save; 'their low real income is a reflection of low productivity, which in turn is due largely to the lack of capital. The lack of capital is a result of the small capacity to save, and so the circle is complete' (Nurkse 1967, p. 5). There was also awareness that weaknesses in institutions and infrastructure create limits in the capacity of the recipient to absorb capital efficiently (Nurkse 1967, p. 95). Thus, the absorptive capacity constraint and its impact on the productivity of investment and hence its relation to the savings constraint was identified as an important issue (Little and Clifford 1966).

On the human capital side, aid could help developing countries strengthen their educational systems as well as set up institutions that would develop and adopt appropriate technologies that would enhance productivity, especially in sectors such as health and agriculture. Very little attention was initially paid to recipient's policies, how the aid will be used or who will benefit from it. The bulk of aid was devoted to financing individual projects or the provision of bilateral technical assistance through experts usually provided by the donor.

In the early 1960s, continued pessimism about developing-country-export prospects (see below Chap. 3) and recognition of the importance of raising imports needed to finance additional domestic capital formation led to the development of the so-called two gap model. In the basic Harrod-Domar model (Hicks 1965), growth depends on the rate of savings and a measure of capital productivity. Hollis Chenery, his colleagues in the US Agency for International Development (USAID) and others (Chenery and Strout 1966; Adelman and Chenery 1966; McKinnon 1964) showed that under assumptions of fixed production coefficients, a fixed supply of foreign exchange inadequate to meet a technologically given volume of capital and intermediate goods imports will subject the growth of a developing economy to a constraint arising from the structure of its foreign trade (Michalopoulos 1968, p. 296). This constraint could be more or less limiting a developing country's growth than a constraint arising from the availability of domestic savings. Foreign assistance can address both of these constraints—whichever is more limiting—and thus enhance the recipient's growth.

These so-called two-gap models were used to project foreign aid needs in a number of developing countries—first in connection with AID programs and later at the World Bank. Indeed, the attractiveness of the model for projecting foreign aid needs made it almost indispensable to international organizations such as the UN and the World Bank. Partly because developing countries felt that their trade concerns were not being effectively addressed in GATT (see below Chap. 3) and partly because of the perceived link between trade performance and financing needs, they successfully lobbied for the establishment of a separate organization to deal explicitly with problems of trade, finance and development. This organization, the United Nations Conference on Trade and Development (UNCTAD) came into being in 1964, and was the main institution through which developing countries pursued their international trade and finance agenda during the next 15 years or so. UNCTAD produced several early studies using a variety of such models to determine developing country foreign assistance needs under different assumptions about desirable growth objectives (see UNCTAD 1966, 1967a, b). The World Bank used variants of this model for country aid projections well into the 1990s (World Bank 1996).

I used such a two-gap model to explore constraints to the growth of the Greek economy during 1952–1962 and concluded that a foreign exchange constraint was limiting growth in the earlier part of the period and less so later; and that foreign official and private transfers were important in helping raise Greek growth substantially during the period (Michalopoulos 1968).

I spent the years 1965–1969 teaching and doing research exploring the policy implications of the rigid assumptions underlying the two-gap models, especially the assumptions regarding the fixed supply of foreign exchange, as it appeared that it was unreasonable to assume that the balance of payments could not be affected by government trade and foreign exchange policy (Michalopoulos 1970). In early 1969, I applied to AID for a research grant to continue this research. I was turned down, but instead was offered a position with the Agency in its Policy and Program Division, which I accepted in the fall of that year.

When I arrived in Washington, the IMF had just established the Special Drawing Rights (SDR), Chenery had left for the World Bank and AID was still burdened with supporting the continuing war in Vietnam. But Ernest Stern, the new Assistant Administrator for Policy and Program

Co-ordination (PPC), was keen to continue the analytical and research work of the Agency and quite relaxed about his staff taking positions at variance with official US policy.[4]

Stern was fresh in this job from a position as Deputy Staff Director of the Pearson Commission, a high-level group appointed by World Bank President Robert McNamara and headed by former Canadian Prime Minister Lester Pearson to make proposals to the international community on aid and development. As developed countries dominated the decision making of the World Bank, the McNamara initiative could be seen as their response to emerging pressure from developing countries to develop international targets for the volume of assistance provided by developed countries.

Aid Targets

At the first ministerial meeting of the G-77 in Algiers in 1967, they called for 'a separate minimum target … for the official component of aid flows, net of amortization and interest payments' (OECD 2002). At the second ministerial UNCTAD meeting in 1968, its Secretary General Raul Prebisch proposed that 'a minimum figure of 0.75% of Gross National Product (GNP) of developed countries could be established for net official aid' (OECD 2002). This was based on work by Jan Tinbergen who, using a foreign exchange constraint model, came up with estimates of foreign aid needed to achieve the desired GNP target of 6% per annum for developing countries until 1975 (OECD 2002).[5] The target grew out of an earlier suggestion first made by the World Council of Churches in 1958 to transfer 1% of donor country incomes to developing countries. But as private capital flows could not be the subject of government commitments, the focus was shifted to official assistance. The Pearson Commission Report recommended that ODA be raised to 0.70% of donor GNP by 1975 and in no case later than 1980. But interestingly, its first recommendation had nothing to do with aid. Instead it proposed 'To create a framework for free and equitable international trade' (see Box). Many of its recommendations were clearly ahead of its time and became issues with which the international community would have to grapple many decades later. Included in these were the problems of mounting developing country debts, improving the coherence of aid efforts and the effectiveness of aid administration, as well as addressing population growth and increasing aid to education.

> **Partners in Development**
> Recommendations
>
> 1. Create a framework for free and equitable international trade
> 2. Promote mutually beneficial flows of foreign private investment
> 3. Establish a better partnership, a clearer purpose, and a greater coherence in development aid
> 4. Increase the volume of aid
> 5. Meet the problem of mounting debts
> 6. Make aid administration more effective
> 7. Redirect technical assistance
> 8. Slow the growth of population
> 9. Revitalize aid to education and research
> 10. Strengthen the multilateral aid system
> Partners in Development (1969, pp. 14–22)

The aid volume question became central to UN discussions in 1970 in connection with the International Development Strategy (IDS) for the Second UN Development Decade. The UN General Assembly adopted a resolution calling, inter alia, for 'each economically advanced country will progressively increase its official development assistance to the developing countries and will exert its best efforts to reach a minimum net amount of 0.7% of its GNP at market prices by the middle of the decade.' Practically all developed countries, with the exception of the US have, over time, accepted this target, although very few have consistently achieved it (see Table 2.1).

The Nixon administration also commissioned a task force on international development whose report to the President on March 4, 1970 echoes many of the same themes as the Pearson Commission (Task Force

Table 2.1 ODA performance of DAC countries 1965–2015

DAC Countries	$ million[a]							% of GNI						
	1965	1970	1980	1990	2000	2010	2015	1965	1970	1980	1990	2000	2010	2015
Original DAC														
Australia	1,255.8	1,846.9	2,032.3	2,029.0	2,383.2	3,971.6	3,896.6	0.53	0.62	0.48	0.34	0.27	0.32	0.27
Austria	133.3	107.9	484.5	281.7	807.9	1,297.7	1,424.3	0.11	0.07	0.23	0.11	0.23	0.32	0.32
Belgium	933.1	915.2	1,346.6	1,514.6	1,511.9	3,196.4	2,256.9	0.60	0.46	0.50	0.46	0.36	0.64	0.42
Canada	749.6	2,020.7	3,084.0	4,248.7	3,183.6	5,263.0	4,965.3	0.19	0.41	0.43	0.44	0.26	0.34	0.28
Denmark	133.1	556.1	1,340.9	2,055.8	3,205.2	3,036.6	3,027.9	0.13	0.38	0.74	0.94	1.06	0.91	0.85
Finland	17.6	57.2	279.1	1,102.4	681.9	1,470.1	1,540.6	0.03	0.06	0.22	0.65	0.31	0.55	0.56
France	6,077.6	5,317.1	6,358.1	11,111.5	7,298.8	13,390.2	10,919.1	0.76	0.52	0.44	0.60	0.31	0.50	0.37
Germany	4,585.6	4,560.2	8,164.7	9,710.2	8,606.2	13,866.3	20,854.9	0.40	0.32	0.44	0.42	0.27	0.39	0.52
Italy	628.0	1,303.7	2,076.0	5,317.7	2,612.8	3,154.6	4,576.5	0.10	0.15	0.15	0.31	0.13	0.15	0.21
Japan	2,361.6	3,333.9	7,275.8	10,836.3	11,848.6	9,002.8	10,418.2	0.28	0.23	0.32	0.31	0.28	0.20	0.22
The Netherlands	799.0	1,733.8	3,799.9	4,463.8	5,797.7	6,610.3	6,932.4	0.36	0.62	0.97	0.92	0.84	0.82	0.76
New Zealand	98.4	142.8	254.3	212.1	289.4	424.1	514.9	0.18	0.23	0.33	0.23	0.25	0.26	0.27
Norway	158.1	391.3	1,630.0	2,806.3	2,954.9	4,776.1	5,527.7	0.16	0.33	0.87	1.17	0.76	1.05	1.05
Sweden	295.2	730.4	1,956.1	2,750.1	3,022.5	4,989.5	8,526.6	0.19	0.35	0.78	0.91	0.80	0.97	1.41
Switzerland	201.5	422.6	829.4	1,414.4	1,792.3	2,602.6	3,758.5	0.09	0.14	0.24	0.30	0.32	0.39	0.52
UK	4,502.6	4,138.9	4,539.4	4,456.5	6,805.2	14,968.4	19,919.5	0.47	0.39	0.35	0.27	0.32	0.57	0.71
US	23,383.3	15,032.1	17,475.2	18,540.8	13,212.4	31,854.2	30,764.8	0.58	0.32	0.27	0.21	0.10	0.20	0.17
Later DAC														
Czech Rep. (2013)	–	–	–	–	–	–	236.4	–	–	–	–	–	–	0.12
Greece (1999)	–	–	–	–	412.9	486.8	343.3	–	–	–	–	0.20	0.17	0.14
Iceland (2013)	–	–	–	–	–	–	41.6	–	–	–	–	–	–	0.24
Ireland (1985)	–	–	–	97.0	398.6	930.2	830.9	–	–	–	0.16	0.30	0.52	0.36

DAC Countries	$ million[a]							% of GNI						
	1965	1970	1980	1990	2000	2010	2015	1965	1970	1980	1990	2000	2010	2015
Korea (2010)	–	–	–	–	–	1340.7	2010.5	–	–	–	–	–	0.12	0.14
Luxembourg (1992)	–	–	–	–	258.3	451.8	418.1	–	–	–	–	0.70	1.05	0.93
Poland (2013)	–	–	–	–	–	–	527.7	–	–	–	–	–	–	0.10
Portugal[b]	–	–	–	–	519.5	666.3	360.8	–	–	–	–	0.26	0.29	0.16
Slovak Republic (2013)	–	–	–	–	–	–	102.6	–	–	–	–	–	–	0.10
Spain (1991)	–	–	–	–	2313.6	5971.6	1905.0	–	–	–	–	0.22	0.43	0.13
Slovenia (2013)	–	–	–	–	–	–	74.5	–	–	–	–	–	–	0.15
Total DAC Countries	46,313.4	42,610.8	63,592.8	84,989.1	80,346.0	134,497.1	146,676.1	0.48	0.33	0.35	0.32	0.22	0.31	0.30

Source: OECD

[a]At current prices and exchange rates

[b]Portugal joined DAC in 1961, withdrew in 1971 and re-joined in 1991

1970). For example, it recommends (a) a more sensible approach of coping with debt than rescheduling only when a country is in imminent default; (b) the establishment of a high-level council within the US government to promote greater coherence of aid programs; (c) greater reliance on multilateral aid; and (d) the coordinated untying of bilateral aid from donor country procurement. The report pays the same tribute to the importance of private investment flows as the Pearson Commission and recommends the establishment of a new US government agency (Overseas Private Investment Corporation (OPIC)) to promote such flows.

With the exception of the establishment of OPIC and a relative increase of the role of multilateral institutions, none of its other institutional recommendations was followed at the time. Eight years later, the Carter administration killed an effort to untie procurement of bilateral aid on a coordinated basis (see Chap. 3) but implemented the recommendation to establish a high-level council to coordinate aid which, however, was undone by Reagan in 1980. The task force report is also very interesting because unlike the Pearson Report, it contains a very explicit statement on an issue that would be central to aid programs in the next decade. It states: 'Development is more than economic growth. Popular participation and the dispersion of the benefits of development among all groups of society are essential to the building of dynamic and healthy nations. US development policies should contribute to this end' (p. 4). At about the same time, the role of 'social factors' as explanatory variables of economic growth started to receive recognition (Schiavo-Campo and Singer 1970, p. 79).

In retrospect, these international discussions highlight the many links between North and South, the developed-country commitment to promote development in the South and recognition of rising interdependence, where events in one part of the world are central to the welfare of many in distant places—whose distance is rapidly diminishing by technological progress in communications. Increasing trade, capital flows and aid for development, combined with increased access to information, are key elements of a process which later was called globalization but whose essential elements were present in the late 1960s and early 1970s.

Soon after Pearson Commission report and the adoption of the IDS, the world was hit by a number of events which had little to do with the lofty objectives of the IDS but changed the picture of international finance and aid through much of the following decade and underscored the rising importance of global interdependence. First, in 1971 came the US decision to float the US dollar followed in 1973 with the establishment of a floating exchange rate system for the major currencies—which modified the fixed rate system adopted in Bretton Woods almost 30 years earlier. Then, later in 1973, following the Arab-Israel war, the members of the Organization of Petroleum Exporting Countries (OPEC) cartel colluded to raise the price of crude oil by about 400%.

The Oil Crisis and Its Aftermath

The OPEC action had two main impacts on developing countries: on the one hand, it emboldened them politically to emulate OPEC and attempt to organize commodity agreements aimed at regulating supplies and raising primary commodity prices; on the other, it resulted in significant balance of payments difficulties for oil-importing countries. A number of low-income countries, the so-called most seriously affected (MSA), faced increasing difficulties to import essential fuels and foodstuffs.

To address these difficulties, a variety of proposals surfaced, in particular proposals to link the allocation of the newly established SDR with development aid. The SDR was originally conceived as a new reserve asset aimed at expanding global liquidity and distributed on the basis of IMF quotas. The motivation for the SDR link was to augment the amount of resource flows to the developing countries at a time when tight budgets limited prospects for regular aid appropriations to meet increased developing country financing needs.

Many felt that linking SDR creation to development assistance would have changed its role and undermined its value as a reserve asset (Johnson 1972). Some thought that it would be inflationary. Others thought it would not result in additional resources. On the other hand, there was nothing sacrosanct about the distribution formula used by the IMF, which resulted in 69% of the new reserve asset being allocated to developed countries, while 93 developing countries that were then experiencing greater balance of payments problems only received the remaining 31%.

I wrote several papers advocating an SDR link. A paper, jointly done with R.W. Warne from the State Department (Warne and Michalopoulos 1971), explored various alternative link proposals and suggested that providing for a different SDR distribution formula that favored the developing countries was the simplest solution. In another paper, I came out in favor of a link designed to support food imports to low-income food-importing countries. There was little novel about these papers except for the fact that I was permitted to present positions totally contrary to the official US position on SDRs as determined by the US Treasury (Michalopoulos 1973).

In April-May 1974, the UN Sixth Special Session endorsed a Declaration and Program of Action on the establishment of a New International Economic Order calling for, inter alia, increased prices for commodity exporters, greater food aid and food reserves, establishment of the SDR-aid link, achieving the ODA/GNP target and special programs for the least developed countries. The developing country efforts to establish a New International Economic Order culminated in the convocation of a Conference on International Economic Co-operation (CIEC) in Paris in 1975. The Conference was intended to reflect the emerging tripolar global power structure: the developed countries, the developing countries and OPEC. The demands of the developing countries focused on setting up a Common Fund to finance commodity trade agreements, increased aid flows from both OPEC and the developed world, and generalized debt relief. The developed countries and OPEC discussed commitments on energy supplies and pricing.

In the end, very little came of these efforts. At the conclusion of CIEC in 1977, there was agreement to establish a Common Fund but the Fund was not established until much later without significant effect on commodity trade (see Chap. 3). There also was agreement in principle to provide $1 billion of additional aid to the most seriously affected developing countries, but with no concrete mechanisms to make it operational. Four bilateral donors (Denmark, the Netherlands, Norway and Sweden) however, were able to exceed substantially the 0.7ODA/GNP target by 1980.

There was no agreement on generalized debt relief or on energy. In practical terms, the only concrete international action taken during this period was to establish several new facilities in the IMF, including the Buffer Stock Facility, the Oil Facility, the Extended Fund Facility and the Trust Fund as well as to liberalize the IMF's Compensatory Financing Facility—all of which were intended to provide additional financing to developing countries on improved terms but all on a case-by-case basis and subject to the usual IMF conditionalities. The main contribution of the OPEC members came in the form of the establishment of a new International Food and Agriculture Organization (IFAD) that operates much like an MDB and funded to a significant extent by OPEC members.

But the effects of the oil price increase and the balance of payments difficulties would linger. Developing countries were able to run very large current account deficits by increasing borrowing from the private sector especially commercial banks, often on hard terms. The debt burden of oil-importing developing countries increased fourfold from 1972 to 1976 and led to subsequent debt servicing difficulties, which will be discussed in Chap. 4.

Aid Effectiveness

What is most remarkable about the late 1960s was the very strong developing country and international focus on the level of aid as a determinant of developing country growth. There was little discussion of the use aid was being put to, who would benefit from it or its relationship to other donor or recipient policies.

There were always opponents of aid from both the left and the right. P.T. Bauer (1972) was an early and persistent opponent from the right. His early criticism was that aid tended to strengthen the role of the public sector and to support public sector enterprises which were inefficient. Later, he would argue that 'External donations have not been necessary to achieve development for any country anywhere' (Bauer and Yamey 1981). Others argued that aid tended to tilt the investment patterns of recipients toward sectors with longer term or lower payoffs, thus reducing the productivity of investment (Griffin and Enos 1970). On the left, Teresa Hayter argued that 'aid can be explained only in terms of an attempt to preserve the capitalist system in the Third World … But inso-far as it is effective its contribution to the well-being of peoples of the Third World is negative, since it is not in their interest that exploitation should continue' (Hayter 1971, p. 9).

Cross-country statistical analyses to explore various aspects of the aid-growth relationship yielded mixed results. Griffin and Enos (1970, p. 318) using analysis from 15 countries in Latin America in 1957–1964 concluded that the greater the capital inflows, the lower the rate of growth of the receiving country. Similar conclusions were reached by Weisskopf (1972) using a two-gap model for 17 countries. Papanek (1973a, b), on the other hand, while finding a negative relationship between aid and domestic savings, also found a strong link between foreign capital inflows and GNP growth.

There are both conceptual and statistical problems with many of these studies (Cassen and Associates 1986; Krueger et al. 1989). For example, it is not appropriate to use the current account deficit as a proxy for foreign aid as Weisskopf did. The savings-capital inflow relationship in a cross-country sample may reflect simply donor allocation decisions that favor lower income countries with lower savings rates. Absorptive capacity is difficult to define. Similarly, the two-gap model is difficult to test in practice, as ex-post there is equality in the observed savings and foreign exchange gaps. Country studies are needed in order to explain the role of aid in GNP growth. In some cases such studies have shown foreign aid to have made an important contribution as in the case of Greece as well as Korea and Taiwan. Asian countries appear to have made better use of aid than Latin America (Cassen and Associates 1986).

Aid is typically a small portion of domestic capital formation, savings and other macroeconomic variables in many countries. Domestic policies and institutions and in some cases exogenous factors such as developments in the international economy are likely to be far more important determinants of long-term sustainable growth. Thus, it is not surprising that cross-country analyses produce inconclusive results. But, as experience with aid giving increased, another more serious criticism of aid started to gain acceptance in the early 1970s. The problem was not, some argued, that aid was not contributing to growth. Rather that whatever growth occurred did not 'trickle down'. The problem with aid was not so much its lack of impact on growth but that such growth did little to alleviate poverty. This criticism had a lasting effect on aid programs of the major donors in the 1970s and formed the basis for assessing aid effectiveness for the next several decades.

Who Benefits

The lead in addressing the question of the impact of aid on poverty was taken by the World Bank and USAID in 1973. Before that, in 1969—perhaps following the Pearson Commission report—McNamara at the World Bank started to have concerns that rapid population growth would undermine development prospects. 'Population control was a likely first approach to poverty alleviation' (Kapur et al. 1997, volume 1, p. 235). Over the next few years, he focused increasingly on problems of absolute poverty and income distribution in developing countries and in finding ways that World Bank could help address them. In 1973 McNamara announced a drastic expansion of the Bank's program of lending to small farmers as the main World Bank instrument of attacking poverty. From $2.2 billion or 19% of total lending in FY 1970–1973, it grew to $13.2 billion or 31% of total lending in FY 1978–1981 (Focus on Poverty 1983, p. 10). The Bank also started to increase the poverty focus of urban projects, provided about 5% of its lending to education—mostly benefiting primary schools—and started a small program of health, nutrition and population.

In 1974, following Hans Singer who had developed the theme of redistribution with growth in work he did for the ILO in Kenya, Chenery and World Bank associates in collaboration with the Institute of Development Studies at the University of Sussex produced a pathbreaking study on a development strategy that would combine redistribution with growth (Chenery et al. 1974). While the main novelty in the book was the argument that it would be possible to develop a strategy that would result in both growth and income redistribution, a lot of proposals focused explicitly on programs and policies that would raise employment and incomes of the absolutely poor in rural and urban settings. 'Our rural strategy therefore focuses on increasing the productivity of the small farmer and the self-employed farm through better access to land, water, credit market and other facilities' (Chenery et al. 1974, p. xviii).

In 1981, a Task Force on the World Bank's Poverty Focus concluded that 'The evidence suggests that poverty oriented projects met their primary objective of increasing the incomes and productivity of the small farmers', though they did little to help and in some cases may have hurt the landless poor (pp. 12–13). Whatever the actual results may have been, by the middle of the decade the World Bank took steps to reorient its overall priorities to address concerns about poverty alleviation and not simply focus on project efficiency and overall growth of the economies it was assisting.[6]

The US aid programs shifted in the same direction. In 1973, the US Congress based on an initiative of the House Foreign Affairs Committee but having bipartisan support in a Congress controlled by the Democratic Party, passed new aid legislation which, inter alia, required the following:

> Future United States bilateral support for development should focus on critical problems in those functional sectors which affect the lives of the majority of the people in the developing countries: food production; rural development and nutrition; population planning and health; and education, public administration, and human resource development.
>
> United States bilateral development assistance should give the highest priority to undertakings submitted by host governments which directly improve the lives of the poorest of their people and their capacity to participate in the development of their countries. (US Congress 1976)

This new thrust of the US assistance program reflected in part growing dissatisfaction with the continued drain of resources to support the Vietnam War but also the influence of writers like Edgar Owens (Owens and Shaw 1972) who stressed participatory processes for development and wanted to reduce the use of aid to achieve foreign policy goals. The Nixon administration initially complained that this so-called New Directions legislation reduced flexibility, but over time USAID responded with the establishment of a policy that concentrated aid in three key sectors: food and nutrition, population and health and education and human resources, aiming 'to help developing countries increase their capacity to meet the basic needs of their people' with 'projects and programs especially directed toward reaching the poor majority' (US AID 1978). To be sure the projects and programs involved only about a third of total bilateral US aid, as the Economic Support Fund continued to provide aid in support of foreign policy objectives to countries like Vietnam and Israel; and the PL 480 programs continued to serve US agricultural policy objectives. But at least for about a third of the projects and programs the key question of 'who benefits' was being asked.

In 1976, concerns about poverty and income distribution were heightened by the publication of the ILO report on *Employment Growth and Basic Needs: A One World Problem* (ILO 1976). The Report argued that the way to address poverty is to develop ways that address basic human needs (BHN) in food, shelter, health and education. The World Bank and several developed countries, including the US, the UK, the Netherlands and Sweden, moved quickly to support the principle that aid should focus on addressing BHN. McNamara in his 1976 and 1977 annual addresses to the Board of Governors of the World Bank stressed that 'developed and developing nations alike establish as one of their major goals the meeting of the basic human needs of the majority of the absolute poor within a reasonable period- say by the end of the century.' The Bank's work was spearheaded by Mahbub ul Haq, head of the Bank's Policy Planning and Program Review Department who together with his colleagues produced a series of papers focusing on various aspects of a BHN strategy.[7]

The Carter administration also quickly espoused the approach. A key question on which there was a lot of discussion in the summer of 1977 was whether the new strategy would focus on direct transfers that would raise the consumption of services by the poor and thus permit them to meet their basic needs in nutrition, health, education and shelter (the 'income transfer' approach) or would it address basic needs through approaches that raise their incomes and thereby permit them to meet needs (the 'resource augmenting' approach). A presidential directive was issued in late 1977 mandating that concessional assistance would be provided to meet the basic needs of poor people primarily in low-income countries, but without describing the means.

Finally, in March 1978, AID issued a policy paper to provide guidance as to how to implement the Presidential directive (US AID 1978). A central theme was the recognition that a sustainable basic needs strategy 'requires broad based economic growth in which the widespread productive participation and benefit of the poor is an essential feature ... Unless basic needs is considered an integral part of development to be built into rather than "added onto" growth, a massive and unrealistic welfare transfer program would be needed to meet the needs of the poor.' Key to the attainment of BHN objectives would be increased employment and incomes of the poor which 'can only come about from increased investment in and production of both basic needs related and other goods and services—for both domestic consumption and, for many counties, exports' (pp. 10–11). Further in testimony before the US Congress, Alexander Shakow, AID Assistant Administrator for Program and Policy, stated: 'A basic human needs development strategy requires broad based economic growth in which the widespread participation of the poor is an essential feature' (Shakow 1978).

Evidence accumulated that in many low-income countries poverty resulted from long-term economic stagnation. Leipziger and Lewis (1977) showed that 'at lower levels of income per capita, it is growth that matters most in improving social indicators, while at higher levels of income it is distribution that is more relevant to improve BHN-related indicators' (Leipziger 1981, p. 117). There followed additional analyses of the developing country policy implications of a BHN strategy especially to address the question whether a BHN strategy was 'anti-Growth' (Crosswell 1978). In 1979, a Development Co-ordination Committee paper (US AID 1979) stressed that there is no BHN/growth dichotomy.[8] Thus, the Foreign Assistance Act of 1979 stated that 'development assistance shall be concentrated in countries which will make the most effective use of such assistance to help satisfy human needs of poor people through equitable growth.'

The international community as reflected in the views of other bilateral donors in the DAC was not fully or easily convinced. 'There appears to be a gradual shift in the development priorities of Third World countries to give more attention to problems of mass poverty and unemployment under the pressure of rapid population growth. And many are according increased priority to agriculture. However, the resource "crunch" is severely limiting, particularly for low income countries… Without a stepped-up pace of economic investment, particularly in the poorer countries, Third World leaders regard many of the suggestions for social development of Western development specialists as quixotic' (OECD 1976, p. 21). In the following year, under pressure from the US, and with the support of countries like the UK and the Netherlands (National Advisory Council 1977), DAC members adopted a statement in support of a BHN strategy which was annexed to their High-Level meeting communique in 1977 (OECD 1977). The paper stated that 'member governments wish to work with developing countries in further defining the implications of a more determined basic-human needs oriented approach for development efforts and policies.' But the UK in a separate paper issued in May 1978 made it explicitly clear that for them BHN meant 'increase the output and incomes of the poor as a means of meeting basic needs through self-sustaining growth', not programs with a 'welfare bias' (Basic Needs: the British Position 1978).

Developing countries supported the thrust of the ILO report both for the promotion of basic needs objectives and for domestic and international policies that would support their achievement.

But in subsequent UN and UNCTAD meetings, many were vocal in their opposition. Some suspected the US intended to sidetrack discussion of issues of the international distribution of income in favor of issues relating to the internal distribution of income. Others considered the initiative to reflect a developed country desire to force them into an essentially rural and backward production structure at the expense of industrialization and modernization (Michalopoulos 1982, p. 242). In many respects, this was a demonstration of differences in the perspectives of the Bretton Woods institutions dominated by the OECD and the UN institutions dominated by the developing countries—which in many cases resulted from policy incoherence within individual governments. But there were also OECD members who seemed to go along with the new US policy thrust only because Congressional support for it would have resulted in significant US aid volume increases.

In early 1980, the Brandt Commission report was produced. The Commission (formally the Independent Commission on International

Development Issues), originally launched by McNamara in 1977, was chaired by Willy Brandt and consisted of a large group of leaders from both the North and the South. Its report *North-South: A Programme for Survival* contained a massive number of recommendations on a variety of topics ranging from Hunger and Food, Commodity Trade, the World Monetary Order, a New Approach to Development Finance to issues such as Disarmament and Development.

On the issue of development finance, the recommendations called for a substantial increase in the transfer of resources to developing countries in order to finance projects and programs to alleviate poverty and expand food production as well as exploration and development of energy and mineral resources and stabilization of prices and earnings and commodity exports. In addition, there were recommendations to adopt timetables that would result in an increase of the ODA/GNP target from 0.7% to 1% by the end of the century; introduction of revenue reserves through international levies on trade, arms production or exports; consideration for the establishment of a new World Development Fund that would seek to satisfy the unmet needs for program lending; as well as a recommendation to developing countries to improve their policies. Overall there was little in the report about addressing basic human needs. As the DAC Chairman's report stated: 'the Dutch held a remarkable rally of the Queen, the whole government and thousands of citizens with the reassembled Brandt Commission to celebrate and analyze the report. But compared with their initial unofficial reactions, governments generally while remaining unfailingly polite, put increasing distance between themselves and the report as an action document' (OECD 1980, p. 20).

This ending was most unfortunate. It was not that the recommendations lacked substantive merit, although some were very ambitious and did not have the support of many developed countries. It was that the new oil shock which started in mid-1979 created a totally new adverse situation in oil-importing countries both of the North and of the South. Growth was being threatened, so the issue of growth not reducing poverty was becoming moot. At the same time, considerable evidence was accumulating that contradicted the notion that growth was failing to reduce poverty (Crosswell 1981).

A number of initiatives that had been previously started like the World Bank capital replenishment and a new IDA agreement were concluded in 1980. But what was not known at the time was that the developing world was entering a decade of lost growth as well as a change in the development priorities that had emerged in the late 1970s, a topic that will be addressed in Chap. 4. Chapter 3 will provide an interlude that addresses the evolving attitudes toward international trade and its impact on development.

Notes

1. George Marshall's speech occurred on June 5, 1947. The assistance legislation authorizing the Marshall Plan passed the US Congress in 1948.
2. This is the traditional calculation, which results in overestimating the aid contribution for countries such as Japan which traditionally provided a lot of ODA in the form of loans on relatively hard terms (Leipziger 1983). In 2014, going in the direction suggested by Leipziger some decades earlier, DAC changed the definition and starting in 2018 the grant element will be differentiated by recipient with ODA to LDCs and low-income countries requiring a 45% grant element to qualify, while for other countries the threshold will be reduced to 10%. At the same time, the commercial interest rate against which the grant element will be calculated was reduced from the traditional 10–5%. (OECD, *Why Modernize Official Development Assistance*, Third International Conference on Financing for Development, Addis Ababa, 2015).
3. As a lot of bilateral aid is not given for development objectives, one has to be careful in assessing this aid's effectiveness: if it is given for foreign policy objectives, its effectiveness should be judged in achieving those objectives. We have learned a lot about what is required for developmentally effective aid by observing and analyzing the weak developmental impacts of aid driven by commercial or strategic or other goals and objectives.
4. Other AID superiors in later years such as Philip Birnbaum, Alexander Shakow and Peter McPherson were equally supportive.
5. According to Jagdish Bhagwati, this 'was the idea of Sir Arthur Lewis, a Jamaican economist who was adviser to Hugh Gaitskell, leader of the

Labor Party, who wanted a target for his political platform in the 1950s (OECD 2002).

6. How much of a shift had occurred by the 1970s is open to some discussion because of problems in measuring what is a 'poverty'-oriented activity or project, see Chap. 4.
7. See, for example, papers by M. Haq (1977), S.J. Burki and J. Voorhoeven (1977) and P. Streeten (1977).
8. This was US government committee that was used in the 1970s to coordinate US aid policy.

References

Adelman, I. and H.B. Chenery (1966) "Foreign Aid and Economic Development: the Case of Greece", *Review of Economics and Statistics,* XVVIII (February, 1966), 1–19.

Bauer, P.T. (1972) *Dissent on Development,* (Cambridge, Mass.: Harvard University Press).

Bauer, P.T. and B. Yamey (1981) 'The Political Economy of Foreign Aid' *Lloyds Bank Review,* October.

"Basic Needs: The British Position" (1978) Overseas Development Paper No. 11, London: Her Majesty's Stationary Office.

Burki, S.J. and J. Voorhoeven (1977) "Global Estimates for Meeting Basic Needs" Basic Needs Paper No. 1, (processed) World Bank, Washington DC.

Cassen R. and Associates (1986) *Does Aid Work?* (Oxford: Clarendon Press).

Chenery, H.B. et al. (1974) *Redistribution with Growth* (London: Oxford University Press).

Chenery, H.B. and A. M. Strout (1966) "Foreign Assistance and Economic Development" *American Economic Review* LVI (September 1966), 679–733.

Crosswell, M. (1978) *Basic Human Needs: A Development Planning Approach,* AID Discussion Paper No. 38, (Washington, DC: USAID).

Crosswell, M. (1981) "Basic Human Needs" in D. Leipziger Ed. *Basic Needs and Development,* (Cambridge, Mass: Oelgeschlager, Gunn and Hain).

Focus on Poverty (1983) Report of the Task on the World Bank's Poverty Focus, ('Shakow Report'), revised edition, February (Washington, DC: World Bank).

Fuhrer, H. (1996) *The Story of Official Development Assistance* (Paris: OECD).

Keith L. Griffin and J.L. Enos (1970) "Foreign Assistance Objectives and Consequences" *Economic Development and Cultural Change,* 18 April, 313–337.

Mahbub ul Haq (1977) "Basic Needs: A Progress Report" (processed), (Washington, DC: World Bank).

Teresa Hayter (1971) *Aid as Imperialism*, (Harmondworth, Middlesex: Penguin Books).

Hicks, John (1965) *Capital and Growth*, (New York and Oxford: Oxford University Press).

Albert O. Hirschman and Richard M. Bird (1968) *Foreign Aid-A Critique and a Proposal*, Essays in International Finance, No. 68, (Princeton: Princeton University).

ILO (1976) *Employment, Growth and Basic Needs*, (Geneva: ILO).

Johnson, H. (1972) "The Link that Chains', *Foreign Policy*, fall.

Kapur, D., J. P. Lewis and R. Webb (1997) *The World Bank Its First Half Century* (Washington DC: Brookings Institution Press).

Krueger, A.O., C. Michalopoulos and V. Ruttan (1989) *Aid and Development* (Baltimore: Johns Hopkins University Press).

Leipziger, D.L. (1981) *Basic Needs and Development*, (Cambridge, Mass: Oelgeschlager, Gunn and Hain).

Leipziger, D.L. (1983) "Lending versus Giving: The Economic of Foreign Assistance" *World Development*, 11 (4) pp. 329–335.

Leipziger, D.L. and M. Lewis (1977) *A Basic Needs Approach to Development*, Paper presented at the Western Economic Association Meetings, Honolulu, Hawaii.

Little, I.M.D. and J.M. Clifford (1966) *International Aid*, (Chicago: Aldine Publishing Company).

McKinnon, R.I. (1964) "Foreign Exchange Constraints in Economic Development and Efficient Aid Allocation" *Economic Journal* LXXIV (June) 388–409.

Michalopoulos, C. (1968) "Imports, Foreign Exchange and Economic Development: The Greek Experience" in P. B. Kenen and R. Lawrence *The Open Economy*, (New York: Columbia University Press).

Michalopoulos, C. (1970) "The Foreign Exchange Constraint Tariffs and Import Substitution" *Kyklos* XXIII, (2) pp. 315–331.

Michalopoulos, C. (1973) *Financing Needs of Developing Countries: Proposals for International Action* Essays in International Finance No. 110, (Princeton: Princeton University).

Michalopoulos, C. (1982) "Basic Needs Strategy: Some Implementation Issues of the U.S. Bilateral Assistance Program" in M. Crahan Ed. *Human Rights and Basic Needs in the Americas*, (Washington, DC: Georgetown University Press).

National Advisory Council for Development Co-operation (1977) *Recommendation on Bilateral Development Co-operation,* 55, The Hague.

Nekkers, J.A. and P.A.M. Malcontent Eds. (1999) *Fifty Years of Dutch Development Co-operation 1949–1999* (The Hague: Jdu Publishers).

Nurkse, R. (1967) *Problems of Capital Formation in Underdeveloped Countries and Patterns of Trade and Development,* (New York: Oxford University Press).

Papanek, G.F. (1973a) "Aid, Foreign Investment, Savings and Growth in Less Developed Countries" *Journal of Political Economy* 81 January-February 120–130.

Papanek, G.F. (1973b) "The Effect of Aid and Other Resource Transfers on Savings and Growth in Less Developed Countries", *Economic Journal* 82 (September) pp. 934–980.

OECD (1969) *The Flow of Financial Resources to Less Developed Countries,* (Paris: OECD).

OECD (1976) *DAC Chairman's Report,* (Paris: OECD).

OECD (1977) OECD Development Assistance Committee "Communique" Sixteenth Annual High Level Committee Meeting Press/A (77) 47, 27th October, Paris.

OECD (1980) *DAC Chairman's Report,* (Paris: OECD).

OECD (2002) *DAC Journal* Vol. 3, No. 4, (Paris: OECD).

OECD (2015) *Why Modernize Development Assistance* Third Finance for Development Forum, Addis Ababa.

Owens E. and R. Shaw (1972) *Development Reconsidered,* (Lexington, Mass: D.C. Heath and Company).

Partners in Development (1969) Report of the Commission on International Development (London: Pall Mall Press).

Schiavo-Campo, S. and H. W. Singer (1970) *Perspectives on Economic Development,* (Boston: Houghton Mifflin Company).

Shakow, A. (1978) Statement of the Honorable Alexander Shakow, Assistant Administrator for Program and Policy, Agency for International Development, before the Subcommittee on International Development, House International Relations Committee, (US Congress, Washington DC).

Streeten, P. (1977) "The Distinctive Features of a Basic Needs Strategy" (processed) World Bank, Washington DC.

Task Force on International Development (1970) "U.S. Foreign Assistance in the 1970s: A New Approach" Report to the President of the United States (processed) Washington DC.

UNCTAD (1966) "Alternative Projections of the Foreign Assistance Gap: A Reconciliation" TD/B/C.3/30 29 November.

UNCTAD (1967a) "Consideration of the Adequacy of the Rates of Growth Achieved by the Developing Countries: Growth and External Development Finance" TD/B/C.3/34 February 17.

UNCTAD (1967b) "Growth and External Development Finance" TD/7/Supp. 1, October 17.

US AID (1978) "A Strategy for a More Effective Bilateral Development Assistance" An A.I.D. Policy Paper, Washington, DC: US AID).

US AID (1979) "Basic Human Needs Strategy" Development Coordination Committee, Washington, DC: US AID).

U.S. Congress (1976) "New Directions in Development Aid, Excerpts from Legislation" Committee on International Relations (Washington, DC: US Government Printing Office).

Warne, W.R. and C. Michalopoulos (1971) "Study of SDR-Aid Link" (processed) (Washington, DC: Department of State and US AID).

Weisskopf, T.E. (1972) "The Impact of Foreign Capital Inflow on Domestic Savings in Underdeveloped Countries" *Journal of International Economics* 2 February pp. 25–38.

World Bank (1996) "Issues in Adjustment Lending" (processed) Development Economics, January 10.

3

Export Pessimism and the Neoclassical Revival

Export Promotion and Import Substitution

In the early post-World War II period, developing country voices especially in Latin America started to articulate concerns about the special challenges they faced in international trade. Their basic premise was that sustainable increases in income and output could only be brought about by increased industrialization. In most countries, there was a consensus that liberal trade policies would not promote industrialization and development because of the prevailing patterns of international specialization. Developing countries tended to specialize in raw materials and primary commodity exports and were dependent on imports of manufactures, especially the capital goods and intermediate inputs needed for investment and industrialization. It was felt that liberal trade policies would stymie the development of infant industries, while the continued dependence on primary commodity and raw materials exports would result in volatile export earnings and deteriorating terms of trade (Prebisch 1950; Singer 1950). The latter was thought to be the result of inelastic demand with respect to both price and income for primary product exports and led to widespread pessimism about their export prospects.

© The Author(s) 2017
C. Michalopoulos, *Aid, Trade and Development*,
https://doi.org/10.1007/978-3-319-65861-2_3

Moreover, there was a strong belief that the development process was inherently associated with balance of payments difficulties, which could be addressed, in the short term through trade controls. Myrdal in his classic *Asian Drama* (Myrdal 1968, Vol. III, p. 669) says: 'It should be stressed that in South Asia import substitution is less a free policy choice than a necessity. If industrialization is the goal, it has to be directed to the home market since export expansion in the field of manufacturing industry meets with such great difficulties.'

The trade strategy that emerged from this thinking and was practiced by most developing countries 50 years ago had three main strands: first, the promotion of industrialization through import substitution behind protective tariff and non-tariff barriers; second, the promotion of manufactured exports in order to diversify the export structure, in part through export subsidies, which were perceived as necessary to offset the advantages enjoyed by established developed country producers; third, the use of trade controls in response to actual or potential balance of payments difficulties.

The trade strategies pursued by developing countries during this early period gave rise to demands for improved market access for their exports of manufactures to developed markets, through the provision of trade preferences, to overcome the disadvantages developing countries faced when attempting to break into these markets and to stabilize, and if possible increase, commodity prices, through supply management.

The GATT had been established in 1947 to provide a forum for rule setting and negotiations to liberalize trade on a multilateral basis. Originally, it contained no explicit provisions for development. Though about half of its original membership consisted of developing countries, they did not participate actively in its deliberations and negotiations to liberalize trade. Still, over time the developing countries members succeeded in incorporating several provisions into the agreement designed to address their special needs (Michalopoulos 2001).

In 1964, GATT adopted a specific legal framework within which the concerns of developing countries could be addressed: Part IV dealt specifically with trade and development and consisted of three new Articles: Article XXXVI stated that Contracting Parties should provide 'in the largest possible measure' more favorable and acceptable market access conditions for products of export interest to developing countries, notably primary products and processed or manufactured products. Article XXXVII called for the 'highest priority' to be given to the elimination of restrictions that served to 'differentiate unreasonably' between primary and processed products. Article XXXVIII called for joint action by the Contracting Parties through international arrangements to improve market access for products of export interest to developing countries. The Committee on Trade and Development was established and mandated to review the application of Part IV provisions, carry out or arrange any consultations required for the application of these provisions, and consider any extensions, and modifications of Part IV with a view to furthering the objectives of trade and development (Michalopoulos 2001, Chap. 3).

A pattern appears to have evolved during these early years: the GATT Contracting Parties accommodated the developing countries' desire not to liberalize their import regimes, partly on infant industry grounds and partly for balance of payments reasons, but on the question of improved access to developed country markets and commodity price stabilization, no action was taken or legally binding commitments made. The establishment of UNCTAD in 1964 gave the developing countries an institution in which they could pursue their trade priorities. The establishment of a system of preferences for developing country manufactured exports in developed country markets and the stabilization of commodity trade were important topics on the agenda of the new institution during the 1960s and 1970s.

In 1968, the developing countries succeeded in establishing a Generalized System of Preferences under the auspices of UNCTAD. The system was established on a voluntary basis by the developed countries, meaning they were not legally bound under GATT to maintain it; but a GATT waiver from Most Favored Nation (MFN) obligations was granted in 1971, initially for a period of ten years (GATT 1972).

While the international community was busy modifying international trading rules regarding manufactures in response to developing country pressure, two problems emerged: First, access to developed country markets was far more difficult than one might suspect, given the existence of generalized system of preferences (GSP) and the extensive reductions of tariffs on manufactures negotiated among developed countries in previous GATT Rounds. Second, as the developing countries appeared to have successfully secured a set of trading rules that would be beneficial to their development, the intellectual underpinnings of these rules started to be extensively questioned.

There were many serious problems with market access. Both the Kennedy Round of GATT negotiations, which ended in 1967, and the Tokyo Round, which ended in 1979, resulted in cuts on tariffs on industrial goods based on an agreed formula. However, the average reduction in tariffs following each Round was less favorable to developing countries than to developed ones: 26% compared with an average of 36% on goods of export interest to developed countries after the Kennedy Round (UNCTAD 1968) and 26% compared to 33% after the Tokyo Round (GATT 1979). This was because many such goods were either exempt from formula cuts or subject to lower than formula cuts. On the other hand, several developed countries extended to developing countries non-reciprocal reductions in the duties on tropical products.

The relatively less favorable outcome of the two GATT Rounds for the developing countries was in part attributable to their limited participation in the negotiating of concessions (Hudec 1987). The basic formula having been agreed, it was the developed countries that negotiated exceptions to the cuts specified in the formula. Final concessions were then extended to all GATT Contracting Parties by virtue of the MFN provisions of GATT.

While the tariffs on manufactured imports from developed countries had been reduced considerably, non-tariff barriers had tended to increase, especially on products of interest to developing countries. This was especially true in the case of textiles and clothing (under the Multi-Fiber Arrangement, MFA) and in respect of the so-called voluntary export restraints imposed by developed countries on emerging developing country suppliers in such products as shoes, iron and steel, and non-ferrous metals.

Despite the tariff reductions, tariff escalation was substantial, restraining developing country entry into the processed goods markets and thereby inhibiting their industrialization efforts. Finally, the agricultural sector remained essentially outside GATT, permitting developed country exporters to constrain imports and subsidize exports at will, including on several products of export interest to developing countries.

The GSP turned out to be less than it had been touted to be at its inception. It was important for some products, for some countries and for some of the time. But it was not serving to strengthen the integration of developing countries into the world trading system. Because it was a voluntary scheme, it meant that developing country suppliers were less certain about market conditions than under the contractual arrangements involving bound tariffs in GATT. At the same time, the benefits of preferences seemed to be accruing primarily to the more advanced developing countries, which needed them the least. According to Karsenty and Laird (1987), early on, four beneficiaries—Brazil, Hong Kong, Korea and Taiwan—enjoyed more than 50% of all GSP benefits. But, perhaps most importantly, several products of great export interest to developing countries, such as textiles, were either excluded from preferential treatment or severely limited. In addition, the margin of preference was eroded because of the MFN tariff reductions agreed in successive multilateral trade negotiations.

Recourse by developed countries to 'graduating' higher income or more competitive developing countries from the GSP (along with occasional recourse to political or non-trade-related graduation criteria) increased the relative importance of reciprocal liberalization with 'bound' concessions. Over time other preferential systems also emerged and were applied to different developing country groupings in various developed country markets, such as the so-called Lome preferences extended to Asian, Caribbean and Pacific (ACP) countries in the EU markets. These systems offered deeper and more secure preferences than the GSP. Indeed, it appeared that developed countries saw measures such as the GSP as a substitute for thoroughgoing action to liberalize trade (Leutwiler et al. 1985).

Neoclassical Revival

At the same time, a serious rethinking of trade policies appropriate for development was taking place. There were several strands to this rethinking. The first questioned the export pessimism associated with the early post-World War II writings, found extensive empirical evidence linking developing country income growth to the growth of their exports and tried to identify policies that would enhance their export prospects (Emery 1967; Maizels 1968). The second involved several country studies analyzing in depth developing country experience with trade liberalization.

I was promoted to Chief of AID's Trade and Payments division in 1972 and started a decade-long effort in this and other positions to promote a better integration of US trade and aid policy for development as well as a better understanding of how developing country trade policy can promote development. The position had responsibilities in setting the terms of USAID loans, determining USAID policies regarding procurement of goods and services financed by US assistance and coordinating with other US agencies, primarily the Departments of Treasury and State and to lesser extent Agriculture, Commerce and the Export-Import Bank. As AID was and is a subcabinet Agency with very limited bureaucratic muscle, with a few exceptions (see below and Chap. 4) I had very little success in promoting a more coherent US aid and trade policy. However, I was fortunate enough to have an able staff interested in research and a substantial research budget that permitted useful research by outside consultants.

With respect to the link of export growth to GNP, a study using a neoclassical model with data from 39 developing countries over the period 1960–1969 found the usual strong correlation between the growth of GNP and exports, but more interestingly it showed that export growth explained a significant portion of the variance in income growth rates left unexplained by the growth of primary inputs (labor, domestic capital, imported capital). In this model, export growth was strongly related to productivity growth. Moreover, 'the divergent export performance of less developed countries had almost no relationship to differences in the international demand conditions for their commodities; rather export performance was primarily determined by less developed countries' own policy, particularly with respect to export diversification and the openness of their economy' (Michalopoulos and Jay 1973, pp. 22–23).

In the early 1970s, many had begun seriously to question the effectiveness of infant industry protection, supported by trade controls and foreign exchange restrictions—as a vehicle for industrialization and long-term sustainable development. Various potential perils in persisting with import substitution strategies had been identified. Trade barriers designed to protect infant industries created disincentives to export, since high rates of effective protection distorted relative prices in favor of import-competing production. As a result, many infant industries remained inefficient and failed to achieve export competitiveness. The first of these studies was a five-volume series sponsored by the OECD and summarized in Little et al. (1970).

AID sponsored the second of these, a massive 12-volume series, headed by Jagdish Bhagwati and Anne Krueger, under the auspices of the National Bureau of Economic Research. The authors of the country studies included a very large number of world-known trade economists, such as Robert Baldwin, Carlos Diaz-Alejandro, Albert Fishlow, Michael Michaely and T.N. Srinivasan from both developed and developing countries. When the original project manager Michael Roemer left AID in 1971, I was fortunate to take over and see the project to its conclusion in 1978. The main findings of the individual country studies are summarized in Bhagwati (1978) and Krueger (1978).

The studies showed that the use of quantitative restrictions and exchange controls increased the scope for rent-seeking activities. The inefficiency and waste implicit in some import substitution policies led to increased vulnerability to external shocks, even in countries that had achieved rapid rates of growth in real income in the earlier stages of import substitution. Moreover, the use of fiscal and monetary instruments was far superior to trade and exchange control measures to address external imbalances as the former do not entail the resource misallocation costs typically associated with latter. Consequently, there seemed to be little justification for the use of trade restrictions to address balance-of-payments difficulties (Bhagwati 1978).

The experiences of the 1960s and 1970s also seemed to suggest that countries that had pursued more open trade policies—for example, those that broadly balanced incentives for import substitution production with incentives for export manufacturing—enjoyed strong growth in both exports and per capita income as demonstrated by the 'Four Tigers' in East Asia. Balanced incentives do not imply free trade. Only Hong Kong and Singapore have had essentially free trade policies. Both Taiwan and Korea protected industry and agriculture but offset the protection with duty drawbacks and targeted fiscal and credit subsidies. Balanced incentives mean that the effective exchange rate defined as the nominal exchange rate adjusted for export subsidies and import and other taxes and charges is roughly equal for exportables and the home market. On the other hand, countries that had persisted with import substitution behind high trade barriers had broadly experienced slow growth or a decline in per capita income. Table 3.1 shows the export performance of different developing country groupings by region for the past half century.

Following the shift in the focus of US assistance policy in the early 1970s to emphasize projects and programs that increase employment and more directly impact on addressing the basic needs of the poor, AID sponsored another project of 12-country studies to address the question of the implications of alternative trade strategies for employment in developing countries. The results of the project, summarized in Krueger (1983, pp. 185–186), showed that, despite data limitations regarding conditions in developing country factor markets, (a) developing country exports were intensive in the use of unskilled labor; (b) the scope for increasing developing country demand for labor through both trade policies and realignment of domestic factor market incentives was sizable and (c) that there were gains to be made in employment from shifting to an outward-oriented strategy, but that the extent of the potential gain depended a great deal on how well the labor markets worked.

Despite substantial cross-country evidence (Dollar 1992; Edwards 1993), not everybody has been convinced of the neoclassical argument. Dani Rodrik has been a long time and effective critic especially of some of the cross-country statistical evidence relating liberal trade regimes to GNP growth (Rodrik 1992; Rodriguez and Rodrik 1999). He has basically argued that the direction of causality between exports and GNP growth is unclear; that the main role exports play is to finance imports, which themselves are critical to development; and that the main determinants of GNP growth are the nature of domestic investment and institutions. It is quite clear that, indeed, liberalizing trade without the necessary institutional infrastructure is not likely to be very productive; also, as noted earlier, export growth has been shown to be linked to total productivity gains, not simply to the volume of investment. But at the end, even Rodrik agrees (Rodrik 1999) that an economy's openness is critical to development and it is hard to visualize an open economy with a restrictive trade regime.

Table 3.1 World merchandise exports by country group and region, 1965–2015

Country group	1965 Export ($ bill)	1965 Share in %	1975 Export ($ bill)	1975 Share in %	1980 Export ($ bill)	1980 Share in %	1990 Export ($ bill)	1990 Share in %	2000 Export ($ bill)	2000 Share in %	2010 Export ($ bill)	2010 Share in %	2015 Export ($ bill)	2015 Share in %
By income level														
Developed economies	127	66.8	579	66.0	1,314	66.6	2,653	76.4	4,418	68.4	8,909	58.5	9,227	56.0
Developing economies	38	19.8	205	23.4	597	30.3	837	24.1	2,035	31.5	6,268	41.2	6,838	41.5
LDCs			3	0.3	15	0.8	18	0.5	36	0.6	162	1.1	154	0.9
By region														
World	190	100.0	877	100.0	1,973	100.0	3,473	100.0	6,456	100.0	15,228	100.0	16,482	100.0
Developing economies	38	19.8	205	23.4	597	30.3	837	24.1	2,035	31.5	6,268	41.2	6,838	41.5
Asia	12	6.3	54	6.1	165	8.4	459	13.2	1,285	19.9	4,005	26.3	5,137	31.2
China	3	1.6	8	0.9	18	0.9	62	1.8	249	3.9	1,578	10.4	2,275	13.8
India	2	1.1	4	0.5	9	0.5	18	0.5	42	0.7	226	1.5	267	1.6
Latin America and Caribbean	10	5.3	38	4.4	104	5.3	145	4.2	362	5.6	576	3.8	516	3.1
Europe, Middle East and North Africa	8	4.2	84	9.6	250	12.7	165	4.8	293	4.5	1,035	6.8	900	5.5
Sub-Saharan Africa	8	4.1	29	3.3	78	4.0	68	2.0	94	1.5	341	2.2	285	1.7

Source: UN COMTRADE, WTO

Coherence

Throughout the 1970s I tried to promote better coherence between US aid and trade policies. At the end of the day, I scored a few minor victories and suffered several major defeats.

The Tokyo Round

Early in 1977, our analysis in AID showed that in the ongoing discussions for the Tokyo Round of Multilateral Trade Negotiations, the US had tabled a proposal which would have resulted in less formula cuts for imports from the developing countries than for developed countries. I complained to the State Department about this, stating that the proposal went contrary to numerous US public pronouncements that it will pay special attention to the liberalization of trade barriers on developing country products (Michalopoulos 1977a) but I had no way of influencing the discussion directly as AID did not participate in the US interagency committees that formulated trade proposals. One small victory was that late in 1977 AID for the first time was allowed to participate in the interagency meetings chaired by the Office of the Special Trade Representative (STR) in the preparations for the Tokyo Round (Strauss 1977). But I doubt that this participation had a material impact on the positions taken by the US negotiators in Tokyo.

Aid Untying

Tying of bilateral aid to procurement in the donor country was estimated to reduce the value of overall OECD assistance by as much as 20%. In 1970, consistent with the recommendation of the Peterson Commission (see Chap. 2), the US initiated negotiations in the DAC aimed at the multilateral untying of bilateral aid programs. Substantial progress was made in these discussions despite French opposition. But in the summer of 1971 following the floating of the dollar, the US requested a suspension of the negotiations. In 1976, the US proposed the resumption of the negotiations at the UNCTAD IV meeting in Nairobi. Throughout 1976 and 1977, I led the US team negotiating the agreement in the DAC and made considerable progress based on a proposal to untie significant parts of the US bilateral program excluding food shipments under PL 480, technical assistance and security assistance to Israel and Egypt. The total amount of US assistance to be untied would have been about $800–$900 million. Under certain assumptions about the amounts of other donor aid that would have been untied under the agreement, it was estimated that the package would have resulted in a net gain in US exports of about $250–$350 million. This would have been a win-win situation: developing countries would get more value from the aid, while the US trade balance would not suffer but possibly gain.

The new Democratic administration was slow to focus on the deal. But when it did, in the fall of 1977, it again requested an indefinite postponement of the negotiations. Their main concern was that while the agreement would have resulted in a net benefit to US exports and jobs, it may have resulted in the loss of exports to a few uncompetitive industries that relied on tied aid for their sales abroad. These exporters were bound to contact their representatives in Congress who would then reduce their support for the aid program. The new administration promised instead to work to increase the volume of US economic assistance. Regrettably, this did not materialize until several years later. Nor was there any other effort to untie bilateral aid on a multilateral basis. Instead, several donors have voluntarily increased the amount of their bilateral aid untied over time.

Textiles

The US provided a major increase in economic assistance to Sri Lanka following the establishment of a new reform-oriented government in 1978. One of the main focuses of the reforms encouraged and supported by AID was the stimulation of non-traditional exports such as textiles through the reduction of trade barriers and the adoption of a market-based exchange rate. The reforms succeeded in increasing textile exports to the US by 250% in 1978 and 1979 at which point the US Department of Commerce was considering to impose quota restrictions under the

MFA. I made a personal plea to the then Assistant Secretary of Labor Arnold Packer to at least not reduce the levels of imports from those attained in 1979 (Michalopoulos 1980). The negotiations did result in the imposition of quotas to US textile imports from Sri Lanka for some of the products which had shown very large increases, but in all cases the quotas did not involve a roll back from 1979. The Sri Lankan press indicated 'relief that quantity restrictions were imposed on only seven out of seventeen items imported by the US; and that the terms were more favorable than those extended to most other Asian textile exporters' (Claude 1980). Overall this was a small victory, in the sense that the restrictions were not that limiting, but a major defeat as quotas were imposed on a country that had just started to diversify their export base following the advice of the international community.

Commodities

As noted in Chap. 2, the oil price increases in 1972 precipitated by the OPEC cartel led to increased interest in other developing countries to establish international agreements in other commodities ostensibly to stabilize fluctuations in their prices, although in fact in order to attempt to raise prices through supply management.

The developing country demands were an elaboration of the earlier Prebisch position. They argued that (a) as demand for primary commodities is inelastic at the relevant price ranges, for any given level of demand, producers would maximize total as well as per unit rents and enhance their development prospects by offering lower rather than higher levels of supply; (b) global demand for commodities grows less rapidly over time than demand for manufactures leading to a deterioration of developing country terms of trade; (c) inelastic demand and inelastic supply lead to fluctuations in commodity prices, export earnings and producers' incomes and inhibits investment by creating uncertainty; and (d) producing countries derive too low a share from the exploitation of raw material production and trade.

To address these concerns, in 1976 UNCTAD proposed a major international initiative called the Integrated Commodity Program (ICP).

Under the program, negotiations were to take place aimed at concluding agreements in at least ten commodities[1]; the establishment of a Common Fund, of up to $6 billion, to finance buffer stocks in support of the commodity agreements as well as diversification and assistance to developing countries hurt by the agreements.

These efforts were resisted by developed countries, most notably the United States. It was said at the time that, in principle, the US did not oppose commodity agreements but that it was prepared to examine them, one at a time, on a case-by-case basis, and reject every single one of them on a case-by-case basis. In addition, the US dreamed up a proposal to establish an International Resources Bank (IRB) aimed at (a) increasing supplies of raw materials and (b) increasing investment in raw materials by compensating multinationals against possible expropriation and other risks. The proposal was presented at the Nairobi UNCTAD IV Ministerial by Secretary Kissinger and went nowhere fast as it was too transparent an effort to promote US and other developed country interests.[2]

I wrote two papers at the time in a futile effort to put a development spin on the discussions (Michalopoulos 1977b; Michalopoulos and Perez 1978). In these we argued that while the developing country rhetoric was focusing on stabilizing commodity prices, the emphasis in practice was on trying to raise prices through supply restrictions; the Common Fund was not a good vehicle for providing development assistance as its benefits would not in any way be linked to recipient needs; it was not appropriate to create a Fund in advance of the negotiations for individual agreements; and the US should support agreements truly aimed at price stabilization but should drop support for the IRB.

After extended discussions in CIEC and following a series of negotiations in UNCTAD, the Common Fund for Commodities (CFC) was established in 1980 and went into effect in 1989. The CFC comprises two accounts each with different objectives: the first was intended to finance international buffer stocks and internationally coordinated national stocks and the second account to finance measures for commodity development, and promote coordination and consultation on commodity issues. At present the CFC continues to function providing primarily technical assistance to developing country commodity producers. It has 103 member states (excluding notably the US and France) and ten international organizations with annual disbursements for projects in the range of $10 million with substantial voluntary contributions especially from Japan, Germany and the OPEC Fund. No funds from its first account were ever used to support buffer stock management of commodity agreements. According to its own web page, direct interventions to dampen fluctuations in commodity prices 'are no longer considered a viable option. Alternatives are not to mitigate the fluctuations but to reduce the impact they have on the lives of poor producers and consumers' (www.common-fund.org/commodity-topics//the-future-role-and-mandate-of-the-common-fund).

Looking Back, Looking Forward

In retrospect, except for the political dynamics generated by the OPEC action and the resulting North-South dialogue, it is hard to visualize why so much effort was spent on discussing commodity agreements and the Common Fund. For commodity agreements aimed at stabilizing prices to work, it is necessary to meet two conditions: first, determine the level at which prices (and in the case of quotas, quantities) should be set to equalize supply and demand in the long run as well as continuously adjust prices and quantities in light of changing market conditions; and second, create effective enforcement mechanisms in order to avoid smuggling and free riding as well as dealing with the producers outside the agreement. Both have proven very difficult if not impossible partly for technical reasons and partly because of incompatibility of interests between participating consumers and producers. Efforts to use such agreements to reverse or slow the deterioration in terms of trade through supply management failed. The collapse of the International Tin Agreement in 1985 and the International Coffee agreement in 1989 were due in large part to the setting of too high intervention prices and free riding. By 1996, the economic provisions in all the major commodity agreements had either lapsed or failed and new market-based approaches to guard against price fluctuations started to be explored and used (Claessens and Duncan 1993).

On the other hand, while the direction of causality between trade and income growth continues to be controversial, there is no doubt that many developing countries opted for more open trade regimes in the 1980s and many countries undertook autonomous trade liberalization involving fewer trade restrictions in the belief that such regimes were more conducive to the attainment of their development objectives. Many developing countries introduced stabilization and adjustment programs during this period (supported by the World Bank and/or the IMF), which frequently involved the conversion of quantitative restrictions into tariffs, tariff reductions, the phasing out of selective export subsidies and the liberalization of foreign exchange markets. This is a story that will be discussed in Chap. 4.

As the developing countries were moving to de facto accept the teachings of the neoclassical revival in the 1980s, the economics profession moved on with the development of new hypotheses which could be classified as 'strategic trade policy'. These focused on the optimum trade policy under assumptions of oligopolistic market structures and profit shifting. There is some doubt about the relevance of these hypotheses for developing countries as they involve government policies to affect the strategic behavior of oligopolistic firms competing in international markets (Corden 1990). And it is important to remember Krugman's (1989) admonition: 'New Trade theory offers some subtle arguments for sophisticated government policy, but it could be all too easily used as a cloak for crude protectionism' (cited in Corden 1990, p. 27), a good political economy advice that applies to the 'new trade theory' as much as it does to century-old arguments for protection. Little of this discussion was reflected in the mid-1990s establishment of the World Trade Organization (WTO), a successor of the GATT which will be reviewed in Chap. 6.

Most recently, the arguments about trade policy have again shifted: anti-globalization forces in the US and Europe have focused attention not on the overall gains and losses from trade but on the plight of individuals and communities both in developed and developing countries which for a variety of reasons have either failed to adjust or not received adequate support to compensate for job losses resulting from import competition. These legitimate issues which involve the links between trade and poverty, which were not at the forefront of the debate in the 1970s and 1980s, will be discussed in later chapters.

Notes

1. The ten commodities were coffee, cocoa, tea, sugar, hard fibers, jute, cotton, rubber, copper and tin.
2. Kissinger was not especially interested in development. But whenever the State Department bureaucrats convinced him to participate in discussions on economic development, he had to have some kind of an initiative to present. These initiatives were cooked up quickly and frequently made little development sense. Thus, whenever it was announced that the Secretary was going to be involved in a developing country issue, AID economists typically cringed about what would be coming down from the 'seventh floor' where the Secretary's office was located.

References

Bhagwati, J. (1978) *Anatomy and Consequences of Exchange Control Regimes* (New York: National Bureau of Economic Research).
Corden, W.M. (1990) "Strategic Trade Policy, How New? How Sensible?" *Working Paper #396*, Policy, Research and External Affairs, (Washington, DC: World Bank).
Claude, C. (1980) "Outcome of US- Sri Lankan Textile Negotiations" Memorandum to C. Michalopoulos.
Claessens, S. and R.C. Duncan (1993) "Overview" in Claessens, S. and R.C. Duncan Eds. *Managing Commodity Risk in Developing Countries*, (Washington, DC: World Bank).
Dollar, D. (1992) 'Outward-Oriented Developing Countries Really Do Grow More Rapidly: Evidence from 95 LDCs, 1976–1985,' *Economic Development and Cultural Change*, 40: 23–44.
Edwards, S. (1993) 'Openness, Trade Liberalization and Growth in Developing Countries,' *Journal of Economic Literature*, 31: 1358–1393.
Emery, R. (1967) "The Relations of Exports and Economic Growth" *Kyklos*, 1967, pp. 470–485.
GATT (1972) *BISD* 18th Supplement (Geneva: GATT).
GATT (1979) *The Tokyo Round of Multilateral Trade Negotiations,* Report to the Director General (Geneva: GATT).
Hudec R. E. (1987) *Developing Countries in the GATT Legal System*, (Hampshire: Gower Publishing).

Karsenty, G. and S. Laird (1987) 'The Generalized System of Preferences: A Quantitative assessment of the Direct Trade Effects and of Policy Options', *Discussion Paper* No. 18, (Geneva: UNCTAD).

Krueger, A. O. (1978) *Liberalization Attempts and Consequences,* (New York: National Bureau of Economic Research).

Krueger, A.O. (1983) *Trade and Employment in Developing Countries: Synthesis and Conclusions,* (Chicago and London: University of Chicago Press).

Krugman, P. (1989) "New Trade Theory and the Less Developed Countries' in G. Calvo et al (eds. *Debt, Stabilization and Development,* (Oxford: Blackwell).

Maizels A. (1968) *Exports and Economic Growth of Developing Countries,* (Cambridge: Cambridge University Press).

Leutwiler, F. et al. (1985) *Trade Policies for a Better Future: Proposals for Action,* (Geneva: GATT).

Little, I., Scitovsky, T. and M. Scott, (1970) *Industry and Trade in Some Developing Countries,* (Paris and London: OECD and Oxford University Press).

Michalopoulos, C. (1977a) "Impact of Proposed Exceptions to tariff cuts on LDCs" memo to William Baraclough, January 13.

Michalopoulos, C. (1977b) "U.S. Commodity Trade Policy and the Developing Countries", *A.I.D Discussion Paper No. 37,* (Washington, DC: US A.I.D).

Michalopoulos, C. (1980) "Sri Lanka Textile Exports to the US" Memorandum to Arnold Packer Assistant Secretary of Labor., February 15.

Michalopoulos, C. (2001) *Developing Countries in the WTO,* (Houndsmills: Palgrave).

Michalopoulos, C. and Keith Jay (1973) "Growth of Exports and Income in the Developing World: A Neoclassical View" *AID Discussion Paper No.28,.* (Washington, DC: US A.I.D).

Michalopoulos, C. and L. Perez, (1978)."Commodity Trade Policy Initiatives and Issues" in F. Gerard Adams and Sonia A. Klein Eds. *Stabilizing World Commodity Markets,* (Lexington Mass.: Lexington Books).

Myrdal, G. (1968) *Asian Drama,* (New York: Pantheon).

Prebisch, R. (1950) *The Economic Development of Latin America and Its Principal Problems,* (Santiago: UN ECLA).

Rodriguez, F. and D. Rodrik (1999) 'Trade Policy and Economic Growth: A Skeptic's Guide to the Cross-National Evidence' *NBER Working Paper,* No. 7081, April.

Rodrik, D. (1992) 'The Limits of Trade Policy Reform in Developing Countries', *Journal of Economic Perspectives,* 6(1): 87–105.

Rodrik, D. (1999) *The New Global Economy and Developing Countries: Making Openness Work,* (Washington, DC: Overseas Development Council).

Singer, H. (1950) 'The Distribution of Gains between Investing and Borrowing Countries', *American Economic Review, Papers and Proceedings,* 11, 473–485.

Strauss, Robert S. (1977) US Special Trade Representative letter to Ted Van Dyk, Assistant Administrator US AID, July 22.

UNCTAD (1968) *The Kennedy Round Estimated Effects on Trade Barriers,* (Geneva: UNCTAD).

www.common-fund.org/commoditytopics/the-future-role-and-mandate-of-the-common-fund

4

Debt and Adjustment: Muddling Through

The debt crisis of the 1980s officially started in August 1982 when Mexico defaulted on its commercial bank loans. But its genesis was much earlier. In 1970, Charles Frank wrote: 'This alarming rise in debt service payments and the increasing frequency of debt rescheduling negotiations has generated considerable discussion about the desirability of softening the terms of foreign assistance and liberalizing the terms of debt relief for acute problem countries' (Frank 1970, p. 3). The international response early on was to try to soften the terms of ODA. This was contained in the DAC Terms understanding of 1972 which called for countries to achieve 87% grant element in their ODA and to provide assistance to the least developed countries only in the form of grants.

But the problem was not solved and was compounded by the rising financing needs of developing countries following the 1973 oil price rise which also involved increased borrowing from commercial banks on hard terms. In a paper written in mid-1976, Peter Kenen wrote in favor of using debt relief as an instrument of development assistance and that 'unless consolidation is accompanied by the progressive forgiveness of official bilateral loans, there will be no substantial relief for the lower income countries' (Kenen 1977, p. 28).[1] In response to a draft of the

© The Author(s) 2017
C. Michalopoulos, *Aid, Trade and Development*,
https://doi.org/10.1007/978-3-319-65861-2_4

paper which Kenen had sent me for comments, I expressed my concerns that his proposals will face problems in the US Congress as the Foreign Assistance Act explicitly forbids forgiveness and that Congress is keen on providing assistance targeted to lower income groups rather than generalized debt relief. I concluded:

> I am in favor of using debt relief as an instrument of raising development assistance but am concerned about the feasibility of generalized debt relief. An alternative approach perhaps less satisfactory in terms of both equity and volume of transfers might be to proceed on a case-by-case basis. By this I mean an honest case by case basis which does not involve case by case rejection but rather a conscious blending of debt relief with other assistance instruments to obtain particular resource transfer targets for individual LDCs as well as an acceptance that debt relief can, indeed should, be used as a development assistance tool. I submit that given the total state of disarray and negativism prevailing on debt within this government at present, such an approach would indeed be a significant turnabout and one which the LDCs might understand, although it may fall short of their overall debt relief demands (Michalopoulos 1976).

From the very beginning it was quite clear that although developing countries were demanding generalized debt relief, there were two distinct kinds of problems affecting two different groups of countries: low-income countries with per capita income less than $400 and middle-income countries with per capita income between $400 and $3,000 (in 1984 US$).

The first group did not face a debt problem as such, as their debt service payments were relatively small, since the bulk of their debt was in the form of soft ODA credits with long maturities. The problem was 'how to raise the net resource flows to these countries on terms consistent with their debt servicing ability in order to raise their lagging rate of economic growth. The debt issue is whether efforts to increase net resource flows should include the provision of debt relief in the absence of imminent default' (Michalopoulos 1979, p. 299). For the middle-income countries, the issues were derived from the maturity structure of their debt and the unwillingness of private creditors to roll over their loans.

Something like what I proposed in my letter to Kenen regarding debt forgiveness was actually implemented about 20 years later in the Highly

Indebted Poor Countries (HIPC) initiative. In the meantime, these early proposals for debt forgiveness fell on deaf ears.

As late as the end of CIEC in 1977, the developed country position on providing debt relief was pretty rigid. Debt relief was being provided primarily in 'imminent default situations' when for a variety of reasons a developing country finds itself unable to meet its international obligations and seeks relief from its creditors. The concern was that otherwise it would result in serious moral hazard problems. The relief was provided in the form of debt reorganization undertaken under the auspices of a creditor club, usually convened in Paris, by the French Ministry of Finance—hence the so-called Paris Club reschedulings. These covered only official credits, usually for a period of 12 months and they were multilateral in nature in the sense that they involved the participation of all major creditors. In many instances, arrangements were also made for parallel renegotiation of private credits.

Seventeen of the 38 multilateral debt reschedulings that occurred between 1956 and 1977 were in the Paris Club. These agreements were typically conditioned on the developing country obtaining a standby agreement with the IMF. The latter in turn was conditioned on the country adhering to policy reforms which the IMF believed would permit it to restore its debt servicing capacity at the earliest possible. 'The creditors thus use IMF conditionality as a means of assuring that they will get repaid' (Michalopoulos 1979, p. 317). This was as true then as it was in the case of the Greek debt crisis thirty years later (see below Chap. 9).

The creditor club functioned as a rescue operation when the deterioration of a country's financial situation had progressed to such a point that drastic remedial measures would be needed which would compromise long-term development objectives. A related problem was that the 'Club' had tended to focus on short-term relief measures with little concern about long-term developments and plans. The debtor was kept on a short leash which may have been appropriate when the problem was triggered by bad developing country monetary or fiscal policy or overambitious plans. It was not when the problem resulted from exogenous factors such as a drastic decline in key export earnings or a spectacular increase in the cost of oil imports. Of course, to the extent that oil prices were expected to remain high, some reductions in domestic demand were unavoidable, which would have been larger or smaller depending on how readily the *pattern* of production and demand could be adjusted to economize on foreign exchange in general and on oil imports in particular. This would have resulted in some near-term hits to income and growth, in the interests of resumed growth on a more sustainable basis in the medium term.

Over the same 20-year period, another 14 reschedulings occurred in the context of aid consortia chaired by the World Bank or the OECD and the remaining using ad hoc arrangements. Debt relief provided in aid consortia was considered advantageous to the recipient: although there was discussion about appropriate developing country policies, there was no strict IMF conditionality; the atmosphere was cooperative rather than confrontational; the focus was long-term development rather than short restoration of creditworthiness. There was one awkward part to the proceedings: The World Bank, while chairing the proceedings, did not reschedule its own credits as it was considered that this would have adverse effects on its capacity to borrow in the capital markets. In 1976, the US announced that it will not do any further reschedulings in aid consortia.

The US formalized this two-track approach to reschedulings in a proposal submitted in 1977 to CIEC in which it identified two types of situations: (a) default or imminent default; (b) long-term financial and transfer of resources problems where 'an adverse balance of payments hampers development'. In the latter cases the World Bank is supposed to analyze the situation and make recommendations for national and international action. Among the actions to be taken by donors would be the provision of program aid; other flexible forms of quickly disbursable aid would be considered preferable to ODA debt reorganization.

The developing countries rejected the proposal and persisted with their demand for generalized debt relief. But the main elements of the proposal, that is, a case-by-case approach rather than generalized relief, the World Bank role, developing country structural adjustment policies and quickly disbursable aid became the main elements of the international response to the persistent developing country problems in the 1980s. But nowhere was there ever a hint of debt cancellation or reduction, with one exception in which I played a small role, and which in the end did not amount to much.

In the mid-1970s, AID was able to obtain congressional approval to provide all future aid to least developed countries (LDCs) on a grant basis. Subsequently, Congress approved legislation that my office had prepared to provide retroactive terms adjustment (RTA) for the least developed countries. The argument was simple: since we now recognized that the LDCs did not have the capacity to service credits even at the concessional rates charged by AID, it made sense that previous credits to them should be cancelled as they could not be expected to repay them.[2]

The debt issue and the demands for generalized debt relief resurfaced at the UNCTAD Trade and Development Board Ministerial in March 1978. In advance of the Ministerial, as the AID representative at the National Advisory Council (NAC)—the US government interagency group which at the staff level prepared the positions of the US delegation at the UNCTAD meeting—I helped establish a US position that it would be prepared to provide RTA which de facto meant debt cancellation, as long as it was not phrased as debt relief.

Indeed, in a typical all night UNCTAD meeting, it was agreed that (1) developed countries 'seek and adopt measures to adjust terms of past ODA or other equivalent measures as a means of improving the net ODA flows'; (2) the definition of these measures was left vague; (3) the beneficiaries would be 'poorer developing countries and particularly the least developed'; (4) each donor would 'determine the distribution and net flows involved within the context of its own aid policy'; which implied an abandonment of the developing country request for generalized debt relief.[3]

While the above resolution represented a serious break with the traditional US position of not providing debt cancellation, it ultimately had little effect. The total outstanding debt by these countries to the US was at the time about $1 billion. The actual amounts of debt relief provided required congressional appropriation. The US Congress House Authorization Committee approved the authorization of $18.8 million for RTA for FY1980 (Michalopoulos 1978). However, the House Appropriations Committee provided no funds for this purpose. The Carter administration focused very much on obtaining Congressional support for the implementation of the BHN legislation and gave lower priority to other initiatives. In the end, the administration did not request appropriations for debt cancellation in the FY80 because it was afraid that to do so would result in offsetting cuts in other aid programs. Other countries did better: Canada cancelled all aid debt by LDCs. The UK converted into grants all official debts by 20 of the world's poorest countries amounting to $1.85 billion (Crow 1978). In 1990–1993, through various congressional actions, the US finally did cancel debt amounting to $1.1 billion owed by 19 Sub-Saharan African countries, $1.9 billion owed by 11 countries in Latin America and $289 million owed by Bangladesh (CRS 1993).[4]

The 1980s

Starting in 1981, the Reagan administration also gave debt relief a low priority. The new thrust of its assistance policies emphasized the use of aid in support of US foreign policy and economic objectives and the role of the private sector in development. At the same time, it attempted to re-emphasize an economic policy dialogue with aid recipients and restock the Agency with economists, an effort to which I contributed as AID's Chief Economist for 1981–1982.[5] The AID programs in the 1980s focused on the so-called four-pillars: institution building, policy dialogue, private sector development and technology transfer. These were essentially programmatic instruments to be used rather than sectors of emphasis or policies. They resulted in broader interventions, as opposed to targeted, direct-impact poverty programs. To the extent that they were successful in promoting growth, they could reasonably be expected to have favorable impacts on poverty. The programs, with the exception of eliminating population as a sector of assistance, remained pretty much the same in substance as in the late 1970s but the rhetoric on basic human needs all but disappeared.

In the fall of 1982, I moved to a position as Senior Advisor and later Director for Economic Policy and Co-ordination at the World Bank. The Bank was at the time in the process of defining its role in addressing the intensified developing country balance of payments and debt problems under a new President, Thomas Clausen who succeeded McNamara in June 1981.[6]

The oil price increases of 1979 precipitated the developments that were the antecedents of the debt servicing problems of the 1980s. There were the direct adverse effects of the oil price increase on the balance of payments of oil importers. But there were also large indirect effects resulting from developed country, especially US policy shifts. In the early 1980s, developed countries focused on reducing inflation by maintaining a fiscal stimulus but tightening significantly monetary policy with resulting high real interest rates. This policy combination succeeded in curbing inflation but led to a significant recession with very adverse effects on developing countries. The recession decreased demand and prices of primary commodities and hence developing country export earnings. And the historically high real interest rates and an appreciating US dollar led to increasing debt burdens which developing countries could not shoulder. Developing country per capita growth rates plummeted and except in East Asia became on average negative with disastrous effects on the poor (see Table 4.1).

It has been argued that the new Bank leadership steered the institution away from its previous focus on poverty. 'When Tom Clausen succeeded Robert McNamara as the president in June 1981, the poverty theme which had been faltering was abruptly muted in Bank decision making and public statements. Then almost as suddenly it reappeared in 1987' (D. Kapur et al., p. 331). The referenced volume goes on to provide

Table 4.1 GDP per capita annual growth (in % per annum)

Country groups	1965–1970	1971–1980	1981–1990	1991–2000	2001–2010	2011–2015
OECD members	4.08	2.48	2.37	1.86	0.87	0.99
Middle East and North Africa	6.94	3.84	−1.21	1.65	2.67	1.17
Europe and Central Asia[a]	–	–	−2.12	−2.38	4.78	1.74
Latin America and Caribbean	3.04	3.56	−0.52	1.43	1.95	0.96
Brazil	4.19	5.92	−0.32	1.01	2.48	0.10
East Asia and Pacific[a]	4.32	4.51	5.50	6.82	8.22	6.53
China	6.15	4.37	7.77	9.28	9.93	7.34
Sub-Saharan Africa	2.27	0.99	−1.56	−0.64	2.87	1.29
South Asia	1.43	0.71	3.09	3.21	5.18	4.99
India	1.20	0.74	3.25	3.61	5.76	5.40
Least developed countries[b]	–	–	−0.37	0.57	4.15	2.19

Source: World Bank Development Indicators
[a]Excluding high income countries
[b]UN classification

details of the erosion of the focus in the early part of the period and subsequent discussions over several years among Bank managers of what to do or say on the subject during a period when 'poverty' was 'demoted' 1981–1986 and when it was rededicated slowly first after 1987 and then more forcefully in the early 1990s.

My own recollection of the period was stated in a memo to one of the authors of the History study in 1990: 'In the early 1970s there was the work of redistribution with growth. This evolved into the work on basic human needs under the direction of Mahbub ul Haq in the late 1970s. I was not at the Bank at the time, but when I came to the Bank in 1982 I was absolutely astonished to find out that this part of the Bank's thinking—which was quite visible to the outside world had not permeated at all the Bank's operations' (Michalopoulos 1990). In practice, while the Bank talked a lot about poverty in the 1970s, only about a third of its projects (those involving small farmers, water supply rural roads, health, education and population) could be construed to have a poverty focus compared to about a quarter in the period 1982–1987 (Kapur et al., p. 332). And as late as December 1982, a year and a half after Clausen became President, the report of the Task Force on the World Bank's poverty focus endorsed by the World Bank Board and Management stated:

'A balanced strategy of growth combined with poverty alleviation provides the best general framework for development in the 1980s (*Focus on Poverty*, p. 33).'

So it is not at all true that poverty alleviation was not a concern. It is probably true that the Bank rhetoric may have exceeded its loan portfolio in addressing the immense immediate problems faced by a variety of heavily indebted countries- poor and not so poor.

The developing country situation deteriorated further in 1982–1983 when GNP growth for highly indebted developing countries was negative. The result was increasing recourse to debt reschedulings. In 1975–1977, there were on average three developing country reschedulings a year involving $700 million per year. In 1983–1984, there were 77 reschedulings involving a total of $165 billion.[7] The reschedulings, of both official and private credits involved debts already in arrears as well as amounts due in the next 12–18 months and were accompanied by severe retrenchment on imports and low growth. The situation improved in 1984, but in 1985 at least ten Sub-Saharan African countries were seeking Paris Club reschedulings and a number of them were having arrears in repaying the IMF. There was concern that the so-called debt overhang would impede growth in many developing countries for years to come.

The situation seemed to require bold actions, including decisions to actually cancel or somehow reduce the stock of debt. These actions did come much later. For the time being and until 1989, the international community focused on small steps permitting it to muddle through the decade, which for many developing countries proved to be a lost one.

Some of the steps under this muddle-through approach were the increased use of multiyear reschedulings for both official and private credits, the IMF using repayments of its Trust Fund to increase the drawings that members could make and the World Bank's increasing disbursements through the Structural Adjustment Loans (SALs) and Sectoral Adjustment Loans (SECALs) as well as through its Special Action Program for Africa. But even then, these steps did not appear enough.

Speaking at the Fifth Malente Symposium on debt in Lubeck, West Germany in late 1985, I again repeated the two-way breakdown of developing country debt problems which were exacerbated by adverse international developments but also reflected domestic policy deficiencies:

1. The middle countries mostly in Latin America, but also in the Mediterranean (not including Greece!), the Philippines and a few others, whose debt consisted of credits from commercial banks. A few countries in East Asia increased their private borrowing but were able to transform their export structures permitting them to achieve high growth of exports, especially manufactures, and income which permitted them to maintain a reasonable balance between debt, exports and income. However, in many others, debt accumulation resulted from rising budgetary deficits, overvalued exchange rates and a structure of incentives that discouraged export growth.
2. The low-income countries mostly in Sub-Saharan Africa; these countries had not diversified their export structure and continued to be dependent on a few primary commodity exports. Over the 1970s, they had reduced their domestic savings rates and had become more

dependent on foreign capital inflows for the bulk of their investment. I concluded: 'The Sub-Saharan African countries need a fundamental restructuring of the maturity and terms of their external debt. Multiyear rescheduling arrangements would only result in bunching of debt repayments in a few years' time' (Michalopoulos 1987b, p. 82). But being a senior World Bank official, I toed the official line and did not call for debt forgiveness. Instead, I fell back on the already accepted retroactive terms adjustment concept and called for an adjustment of official credits to very soft IDA terms.

Over the course of the 1980s, the international community developed a pattern of responses to the debt problems and broader development strategy for developing countries seeking assistance through the programs of the IMF and the World Bank. The strategy had three components: first, policy reform commitments by the developing countries; second, program support by the IMF and the World Bank; third, somewhat vague commitments by the developed countries regarding their own aid, trade and domestic policies, and general exhortations to the private sector to maintain or increase private capital flows rather than provide debt relief.

Developing Country Policies and the 'Washington Consensus'

The IMF and the World Bank worked together to elaborate policy reform packages that were intended to promote adjustment and restoration of growth in developing countries involved in debt reschedulings. More broadly, these reform packages reflected what was later called the 'Washington Consensus' as perceived and practiced by the two Washington institutions and articulated by local think tanks and others.

The developing country policy packages reflecting the 'Washington Consensus' became quite controversial as discussed below. But they were important for two reasons: first, it was the first time that a comprehensive strategy linking aid, trade and development was being articulated by these institutions; and second, its application affected the growth performance of a significant number of countries for a considerable period of time. It is worth therefore to present it in some detail. I prepared a summary presentation on these policies for a Symposium on *Growth-Oriented Adjustment Programs*, organized jointly by the IMF and the World Bank and held in Washington, DC, February 25–27, 1987, from which the following is broadly excerpted.

I started again with the usual distinction between highly indebted middle-income countries and Sub-Saharan Africa. I argued that the reforms should aim to (a) restore or maintain macroeconomic stability, as many countries had considerable macroeconomic imbalances, resulting in a high rate of open or suppressed inflation and unsustainable rates of domestic absorption; (b) raise overall efficiency and factor productivity, which was often impaired by regulations that distorted factor and market prices, inefficient public sector enterprises and inward-looking uncompetitive industries; (c) undertake banking and financial sector reforms; (d) raise savings relative to consumption, recognizing that this is very difficult to do when per capita consumption is extremely low and stagnant for a long period of time; (e) restructure production toward tradeables so as to increase foreign exchange earnings needed to service debt and to finance additional imports needed for growth.

Macroeconomic stabilization and structural change can generate transitional costs in the form of unemployment. The reduction in absorption needed to reduce inflation and to achieve a sustainable current account deficit will usually be accompanied in reductions in the rate of growth of output and increased unemployment. Similarly, productive resources are not redistributed instantaneously among alternative uses in response to changes in relative commodity and factor prices. The slowdown in the economy and the increase in unemployment will be less pronounced, the greater the downward flexibility of product prices and wages and the greater the availability of external financing. Sub-Saharan African countries faced other additional long-term growth constraints. These included weak physical and human infrastructure, inadequate institutions and a rapid rate of population growth.

In the design of macroeconomic stabilization programs, I argued that to minimize the reduction in total output needed to attain any targeted rate of absorption, it is desirable to have a real exchange rate depreciation to engineer a shift in the composition of output toward tradeable goods. In addition, an increase in the supply of tradeables requires an incentive structure that is neutral as between production for the domestic and the foreign market. This in turn requires at a minimum the elimination of an anti-export bias, lowering and if possible eliminating export taxes, removal of quantitative restrictions on imports and eventually attaining relatively uniform tariffs on inputs and outputs. The experience of 1970s and 1980s had shown that countries with trade regimes characterized by a balanced set of incentives toward exports and import competing activities have been far more resilient to external shocks.

Recognizing the difficulty of raising savings, it would be desirable to introduce tax reforms aimed at broadening the tax base and lowering tax rates. Also, public savings could increase by better targeting of government support programs, for example, food subsidies to those that truly needed them. Finally, I discussed ways to improve the productivity of public enterprises, and in some cases privatizing or closing down inefficient public enterprises and deregulating product and factor markets—especially labor market restrictions that impeded labor mobility.

I asserted that there is broad agreement on the nature of the reform packages needed for adjustment and growth. Uncertainties become more prominent at the implementation stage because implementation involves the dynamics of reform about which less is known, and which depend partly on initial conditions and partly on political considerations that vary from country to country. This was an important point that cautioned against the application of standard reform packages to different countries irrespective of the specifics of their situation. It was an issue that came to haunt a number of World Bank and IMF programs in the coming years.

The strategy of reform requires judgments about the sequencing of reforms: for example, if domestic factor market liberalization does not occur early on, the benefits of reforms in the product market cannot be realized. Doing both macroeconomic stabilization and trade reform at the same time presents difficulties. For example, trade reforms that reduce tariff rates may result in revenue losses which would be contrary to stabilization objectives. Deregulation of the financial sector needs to be carefully considered taking into account, inter alia, the size of non-performing loans. For various reasons, it is better to liberalize the current account of the balance of payments first and the capital account much later as it 'could result in large capital movements with unwanted consequences for the real exchange rate' (Michalopoulos 1987a, p. 27)—an issue that will become very important in the 1990s.

The speed of reforms is also an issue that has to be determined in the light of the economic and political situation in individual countries.

> A substantial reform which is undertaken within an agreed and reasonably paced timetable offers major advantages. What is reasonably paced would obviously vary by country. But the required reallocation will not occur unless the signal given is strong enough and in clear enough direction to make the reform credible. An unduly slow pace of reform will delay the development of export activities and provide ample time for vested interests to block the realization of its objectives. And the pace of reform will have to differ between sectors: trade reforms can occur rapidly, but a change in agricultural pricing may need to be slower in order to take into account of needed changes in the establishment of safety net for the urban poor whose food costs may rise. (Michalopoulos 1987a, p. 29).

There are strong similarities—indeed identities, between these policy positions and policy and strategy prescriptions made famous by John Williamson in his later presentation to the US Congress in 1989 and subsequently referred to as the 'Washington Consensus' (Williamson 2003).[8] There are a few differences: (a) property rights mentioned by Williamson were not actually an element of the conditions pressed upon by the Bank and the IMF but were important in the discussions involving the GATT multilateral trade negotiations (see below); and (b) liberalizing foreign private direct investment, which I neglected to mention but was discussed in many cases.

Actually Williamson was a discussant of my above paper. In his comments he stated that it 'provides an authoritative exposition of most of the policies the Bank has been advocating and the mechanisms it has been using to promote adjustment and growth'. But he felt that I did not adequately focus on the existence in most countries of a foreign exchange constraint, though he agreed with my statement that 'additional external finance in the initial years of reform could be an essential component of a strategy designed to restore long-term growth while also maintain per capita consumption in the interim' (Williamson 1987 in Corbo et al., p. 99).[9] Of course, there was a foreign exchange constraint in the short run. But the structural adjustment programs of the Bank focused on the medium term. And over time, as I had argued many times in the past, exchange rate and trade policy can impact on the availability of foreign exchange.

What is important to note in the above summary is the recognition that we did not have all the answers. There were no standard prescriptions. There were serious doubts about liberalizing the capital account of the balance of payments. There was little triumphalism about the role of private enterprise. Privatizations were only one of many approaches to deal with inefficient public enterprises. There were no arguments about the superiority of economic liberalism. In sum, many elements of the so-called neoliberal agenda that were subsequently attributed to the 'Washington Consensus' were not actually part of it at the time (Kanbur 2008). But the concept became the lightning rod for critics for several decades. It will not be possible to do justice to all the arguments and the immense literature pro and con surrounding the concept in this volume. In this chapter, I will only review the early discussion—and the comments on World Bank programs until the mid-1990s. A later chapter will address the debate as it evolved in the 1990s and beyond.

World Bank Programs

These were the broad outlines of the reform packages that the World Bank supported. Their effectiveness in achieving their detailed objectives depended very much on how the programs were actually implemented in individual countries.

Starting with a SAL to the Philippines in 1979, the World Bank shifted substantially its programs in favor of fast disbursing policy-based loans, both SALs and SECALs. Whereas in FY 1979–1980 such loans amounted on average to $403 million or 4% of total World Bank lending, in FY 1986–1987 they had reached $3,099 million or 19% of the total lending. Trade policy reform was probably the most common of the conditionalities attached to these loans, appearing in about 28% of the loans, compared to

15% for public enterprise reform and 11% for agricultural policy. Similarly, about 25% of all SECALs were focused on trade reform (World Bank 1986).

Individual programs emphasized different policy issues depending on country priorities. Macroeconomic policy reform was part of most programs, but the Bank deferred to the IMF on monetary and exchange rate policy. On budget policy, macroeconomic aggregates were typically negotiated by the IMF while the Bank focused on public expenditure reviews as well as tax reforms. Improving the efficiency of public sector investment and the operation of public sector enterprises were a common objective in many loans, while financial sector reform was the target of many sector loans. Regarding the structure of incentives, two sets of policy issues received the greatest attention: (a) trade regime reforms designed to reduce the bias against exports and to lower the level and rationalize the pattern protection; (b) price system reforms in agriculture, and in some cases energy focusing on production and distribution incentives. Finally, institutional strengthening was an objective in all aspects of the programs.

There are problems in assessing the impact of these loans on the performance of the recipient. For one thing the counterfactual is not available. It is impossible to determine what the policies of the recipient would have been in the absence of the assistance. In addition, as the programs of assistance were usually combined with IMF programs, it is difficult to disentangle the impact of each—although an effort was done in some cases with respect to specifically trade-related loans (see below).

The need and objectives of adjustment were well understood in most countries. But countries faced daunting constraints and dilemmas in designing effective policies. It was well known that primary exporters needed to diversify in order to expand exports. But it is virtually impossible to develop a rapid supply response of new export products in traditional low-income one- or two-crop economies. It is well known that it is necessary to expand the tax base in order to improve the revenue potential of the fiscal system. But it takes time for reforms to start yielding results. The temptation may be to raise rather than lower trade taxes which would hurt the external adjustment. When price controls inhibit efficient resource allocation, at what pace should prices be liberalized? What groups will be hurt? Should they be protected? And how? How much reduction in consumption can be politically tolerated and for how long? These are not easy questions, yet all had to be answered by countries in adjustment programs.

> Perhaps the most general conclusion … is the importance of the recipient's commitment to a particular course of reform for the ultimate success of the policy package. The most successful cases of reform supported by the World Bank have involved countries (e.g., Korea and Turkey) that have adopted a series of reforms over time and stuck by them. The least successful were those where for a variety of reasons policies were reversed after a time and the direction and purpose of reform was confused and uncertain (Guyana, Bolivia and Senegal in the early eighties). (Michalopoulos 1987a, p. 41)

There were a number of studies of the effectiveness of these programs in attaining their objectives. Most of the studies concluded that the programs were effective in most cases in improving macroeconomic performance, especially in raising GNP and export growth (Berg and Batchelder 1985; Balassa 1988; Conway 1990; Corbo and Rojas 1990), even after taking into account the counterfactual and different international conditions.

Finally, a major study of the issues raised by policy-based lending by the World Bank in the 1980s authored by a number of economists not associated with the Bank (Mosley et al. 1991) concluded that 'policy based lending represents an imaginative response by donor agencies to the global economic crisis of the early 1980s and that the problems which remain are design problems susceptible to reform rather than problems which undermine the entire original concept.' In a book review of the volume (Michalopoulos 1992, pp. 283–284), I praised the authors on a number of points they made, in particular that the governments of aid recipients with whom the Bank negotiated policy-based loans are not monolithic and the 'benefits' in the form of credits provided by Bank loans accrue to the Ministries of Finance and the Central Bank which are generally supportive of the agreed reforms while the political costs of the adjustment have to be borne by sectoral ministries, often kept out of the negotiations. This internal conflict in aid recipients was often at the root of many aid recipient failures to meet policy commitments made to the Bank. But I did not agree with their recommendation that the Bank adopt a policy of punishing recipients who fail to comply with loan conditionality by *random* withholding future support.

World Bank Programs in Support of Trade Reform

In 1992, the World Bank Operations Evaluation Department assessed the effectiveness of 35 trade-oriented World Bank Adjustment Operations in nine countries (Colombia, Ivory Coast, Ghana, Indonesia, Jamaica, Mexico, Morocco, Pakistan and Turkey) over the decade of the 1980s (World Bank 1992). It is worth summarizing its findings as they are relevant not only about the general topic of this volume but also about the overall assessment of World Bank adjustment operations over this period.

The initial conditions in all nine countries, except possibly Pakistan, involved substantial inflation and significant fiscal deficits. The adjustment programs involved macroeconomic stabilization, exchange rate adjustment and trade policy reform. The trade policy reform involved conversion of quantitative restrictions (QRs) to tariffs, equalization of tariff rates and reduction of tariffs. In some cases, these reforms were also accompanied by price liberalization of public enterprises.

The evaluation concluded that five of the countries (Ghana, Indonesia, Mexico, Morocco and Turkey, the 'intensive adjusters') were more successful than the other four: their rate of growth was faster than before the loans—though there was an initial contraction; in practically all nine cases exports grew much faster than in earlier periods, especially so for the 'intensive' adjusters who also were able to diversify their exports more. The programs achieved less overall in improving domestic regulatory policies which proved to be a handicap in the case of Mexico and Indonesia. The analysis noted that some countries (Ghana, Jamaica) introduced measures to mitigate the social costs of adjustment; but that more information about these issues should be developed in order to assess the impact of such programs in the future

Its main conclusions the programs design and effectiveness are worth highlighting:

1. Trade reform is more effective when complemented by domestic regulatory and institutional reforms.
2. Loan conditions should emphasize a few key variables that are easy to monitor.

3. Broadly based acceptance within a country of a trade adjustment program—'borrower ownership' greatly increases the probability of program success.
4. Often a bottom-up approach is needed if consensus is to be reached within a country's administration.
5. Several countries launched extensive efforts of consensus building to mitigate the adverse costs of adjustment and to avoid policy reversals.

Adjustment and Poverty Alleviation

Despite the fact that most studies concluded that structural adjustment operations on the whole had positive effects on the recipients economy, provided the recipient had ownership of the policies on which the loans were conditioned, the programs were subject to various criticisms from both inside and outside the Bank and the IMF. Inside the Bank, there was concern that the loans were too risky. Traditional project managers felt uncomfortable with project design and implementation.

Some IMF staff were concerned that the World Bank programs were not based on a consistent medium-term macroeconomic framework linking inputs in the form of policies, such as trade or pricing reforms, to outputs in the form of medium-term macroeconomic performance or to the contrary that the programs were too standardized, ignoring country differences. They felt more comfortable with the short-term macroeconomic model which they used to base their policy recommendations for budgetary and monetary policy and exchange rate adjustment, but were not able to crank into such a model variables involving structural or institutional change which the World Bank programs targeted. No such model was available then and even today; when medium-term program magnitudes are projected in IMF programs (see Chap. 9), they do not appear to incorporate in any meaningful way parameters related to structural changes. Indeed, it could be argued that it is best not to rely too heavily on such models because of the different circumstances present in different countries.

A widespread criticism which deserves detailed consideration involved concerns that the SALs lacked sufficient attention to distribution issues. There are several different issues that have been raised with respect to the impact of the World Bank/IMF adjustment programs on the poor which are as relevant today as 30 years ago. First is the question of whether the programs undertaken produced a short-term decline in output and incomes which was somehow excessive in the sense that given the amount of financing available, alternative programs would have permitted a more gradual adjustment over time and thus resulted in smaller declines in the absolute levels of income of the poor—which indeed did decline during this period in many countries including several with World Bank programs. Second is the question whether the poor had suffered disproportionately in the adjustment process and/or the absolute incomes of the poor had fallen below a poverty line. Third, whether government budgetary and expenditure policies associated with the loans had disproportionately affected the poor. And finally, what could be done about it.

The Bank had introduced concerns about these issues into several adjustment loans that it had made in the early 1980s. In 1986, it launched a study aimed at reviewing the impact of structural adjustment on poverty alleviation (Addison and Demery 1986) whose findings are worth summarizing. The study did not assess the success or failure of the loans. Rather the authors surveyed the issues raised, the policy responses given and the role played by the World Bank. The study noted that in cases of macroeconomic disequilibria, some form of adjustment is inevitable; and that disorderly adjustment is likely to hurt the poor more. But assuming orderly adjustment, the following were issues that were being addressed in World Bank loans to several countries. In many countries poverty is concentrated in the rural sector. Raising agricultural product prices would tend to improve incomes of the rural poor provided they have adequate infrastructure to benefit from the price increase (Ivory Coast). If food prices are raised and the rural poor benefit, urban poor may be hurt. To address that problem, there is a need to provide targeted food subsidies, which may be administrative complex to implement without significant leakages to the non-poor (Jamaica). Structural change may require retrenchment of government workers. They are not easily employable in the short run and may require retraining (Gambia). It is important throughout to maintain expenditures in the social sectors, especially education (Indonesia).

A second Bank policy paper in early 1987 (World Bank 1987) stated that because in Sub-Saharan African countries large portions of the population are below or close to unacceptable poverty levels and in view of the unfavorable long-term growth prospects, the need to protect the poor during the adjustment process is all the more important (p. v). It recommended that the Bank (a) increase the efforts to address social costs issues in adjustment loans particularly through increasing the effectiveness and poverty orientation of social expenditures—because existing programs are not sufficiently targeting the poor and (b) the development of effective and targeted compensatory programs in adjusting countries (p. 14).

Then in late 1987, the UNICEF produced its famous report *Adjustment with a Human Face* (AHF), whose title just like the 'Washington Consensus' became central to the subsequent debate about the impact of adjustment lending on poverty. The report's focus was almost exclusively on the IMF's programs. The Bank's structural adjustment lending operations were barely even mentioned.

AHF starts with a recognition 'that the primary cause of the downward economic pressures on the human situation in most countries affected is the overall economic situation, globally and nationally, not adjustment policy as such. Indeed, without some form of adjustment, the situation would be far worse' (Cornia et al. 1987, p. 5). The report then proceeds to outline in detail the deterioration in human welfare indicators in ten developing countries for the period 1980–1985.[10] The deterioration was worse in the indicators of nutrition and education where eight of the ten countries showed declining intake of food and school enrolment. The increase or slower decline in child mortality was less generalized but still present in seven of the ten countries (all except South Korea, Sri Lanka and Zimbabwe). More general research findings suggested similar deterioration of living conditions in more than 30 countries, over half of which were in Sub-Sahara Africa (SSA). The results with respect to the welfare of children were unambiguously worse in all countries studied (Cornia et al. 1987, pp. 34–35).

The main criticism of the IMF programs was that they (a) imposed too large and too rapid an adjustment; a more gradual correction of imbalances was needed—which, however, would have required more medium-term financing; (b) ignored policies which would have resulted in better outcomes for the poor within the context of the existing envelope of resources and macroeconomic stabilization.

With respect to the size and pace of adjustment, similar criticisms have been raised by many. The IMF emphasis on demand management in order to promote macroeconomic stabilization assumes that in the short run prices and wages adjust and markets clear—assumptions that were hardly present in developing countries—especially low-income ones in Sub-Saharan Africa. The inference is that the macroeconomic stabilization effort resulted in excessive contraction in income and employment given the amount of financing available with adverse effects on poverty (Bruno 1987; Sengupta 1987).

With respect to policies that would have resulted in better outcomes for the poor, AHF recommends a series of steps which together amount to an 'alternative approach'. In summary, these include: (a) government policies such as taxation, credit allocation, asset distribution which affect the incomes of the poor; (b) promoting opportunities, resources and productivity for the small-scale sector, in agriculture, industry and services; (c) redirecting public sector effort and resources from high-cost areas that do not contribute to basic needs toward low-cost basic services and by improving the targeting of interventions; and (d) compensatory programs to protect living standards, health and nutrition of the poor. 'The policies of adjustment with a human face need to be designed to achieve both growth-oriented adjustment and to include specific actions directed towards human needs' (Cornia et al. 1987, p. 149).

A final concern with the IMF programs during this period was the increased frequency of its recommendations for exchange rate devaluation. In the case of Sub-Saharan African countries where more than 60% of export earnings come from primary commodities with low demand elasticities, simultaneous devaluations would tend to increase global supplies with adverse results on the producers in devaluing countries.[11]

Following in the heels of the AHF, a World Bank review in 1988 presented some interesting yet disturbing results. It concluded that on average 30 countries with adjustment lending operations performed slightly better on macroeconomic aggregates than countries that did not receive SALs, and that the performance of 12 countries which received more than one SAL was even better. But on the whole the sustainability of the adjustment effort was very much in question. GNP growth was lower than before except for manufacturing exporting countries. Investment ratios declined and budget deficits, debt service ratios and debt export ratios were higher especially in Sub-Saharan Africa. Thus, it could not be said that the debt problems had improved.

Interestingly enough, while per capita private consumption was shown to have declined on average and especially in Sub-Saharan Africa, the performance of countries with adjustment lending in SSA with respect to most social indicators had improved between 1980 and 1985 (see Table 4.2) The data showed that on average infant mortality, life expectancy and primary grade enrollment was better in spite of reductions in public sector spending in many countries. Per capita calorie consumption, however, was lower and fell even more in SSA. The results with respect to the evolution of human welfare indicators, while not strictly comparable, were less dismal than the ones in the AHF. But the recommendations on the poverty issue were similar.

The report's overall conclusions and recommendations are extremely important in the context of the subsequent debate. The main ones in summary were as follows:

* Structural and Sectoral Adjustment Loans must be implemented within the context of an overall strategy agreed with the government.
* The government must own the program, and in whatever way is appropriate must publicly propose and justify the program.
* The program must be realistic: restrictive enough given the financing available but not so restrictive as to prove socially or politically unacceptable;

There are three ways the Bank can help borrowers assist the poor during adjustment: (a) redesign programs to limit hardship on the poor; (b) social expenditures which benefit the poor should be maintained and others better targeted; (c) compensatory programs should be encouraged.

It is desirable to have a government fulfill conditions before a loan is presented for funding:

Table 4.2 Social indicators in the 30 adjustment lending countries

Item	Average 1970–1979	1980	1981	1982	1983	1984	1985	1986
Per capita calories as percentage of daily requirement[a]	101.3	104.5	104.9	104.3	102.9	103.0	104.2	n.a.
Sub-Saharan Africa	94.7	97.2	97.2	95.7	93.0	92.7	95.5	n.a.
Highly indebted countries	107.1	112.3	112.4	112.5	110.7	111.7	111.1	n.a.
Manufacturing exporters	108.8	113.4	113.9	114.1	113.4	113.1	112.9	n.a.
Middle-income	106.7	111.1	111.4	111.6	110.9	111.5	111.1	n.a.
Low-income	93.1	94.6	95.1	93.4	90.8	90.2	94.0	n.a.
Infant mortality[b]	99.5	87.8	86.1	84.6	81.3	79.6	78.0	76.2
Sub-Saharan Africa	126.6	116.0	114.2	112.3	109.8	107.6	105.5	103.3
Highly indebted countries	80.5	68.3	66.5	65.0	60.7	59.2	57.9	56.4
Manufacturing exporters	79.7	62.9	61.2	59.6	53.6	52.2	51.2	49.4
Middle-income	75.3	61.1	59.5	58.1	54.6	53.3	52.1	50.6
Low-income	135.9	125.8	123.9	122.0	120.1	117.9	115.7	113.5
Life expectancy[c]	54.2	56.2	56.5	56.9	57.3	57.6	58.0	58.4
Sub-Saharan Africa	46.8	48.6	48.9	49.3	49.7	50.2	50.6	51.0
Highly indebted countries	59.4	61.5	61.9	62.3	62.7	63.0	63.4	63.7
Manufacturing exporters	60.2	62.2	62.6	62.9	63.3	63.6	64.0	64.3
Middle-income	60.3	62.4	62.8	63.2	63.5	63.8	64.2	64.5
Low-income	45.0	46.8	47.1	47.4	47.8	48.3	48.7	49.1
Primary grade enrollment[d]	83	88	92	90	92	90	97	n.a.
Sub-Saharan Africa	70	79	83	83	85	83	88	n.a.
Highly indebted countries	92	100	103	100	100	98	102	n.a.
Manufacturing exporters	91	94	96	94	96	95	101	n.a.
Middle-income	95	101	105	103	102	102	105	n.a.
Low-income	65	71	74	72	74	73	76	n.a.

Source: World Bank, 1988. The original table was based on sources from the World Bank, FAO and the UN
[a]1977
[b]Deaths before age one, per thousand live births
[c]For newborn infants
[d]Ratio of pupils to population of school age children; may exceed 100% with enrollment of older age children

Loan agreements should contain a few clearly stated, understood and measurable key conditions; the greater the number of conditions the greater the ambiguity about what is expected and the greater the probability that essential conditions will not be carried out. (World Bank 1988, pp. 11–15)

Adjustment in Sub-Saharan Africa

Nowhere were the programs of adjustment and their impact on the poor more controversial than in Sub-Saharan Africa. In the early 1980s, the World Bank started its adjustment lending to SSA on the wrong foot. In 1979, the representatives of SSA at the Bank had asked it to prepare a study of the continent's economic problems and how the international community could help address them. The resulting study, the so-called Berg report after its leader Elliot Berg, proposed significant increases in international support but also highlighted deficiencies in SSA policies that had to be corrected, in particular excessive reliance on the state-led development (World Bank 1981). The study generated considerable opposition and resentment in SSA governments because they felt that they were being unfairly criticized. When at about the same time the Bank started to discuss SALs conditioned on policy reform and especially when these reforms were advocated by arrogant and insensitive Bank officials preaching to African Ministers and Heads of government, relations deteriorated with many African governments.[12]

Still a number of SALs were done these early years in Senegal and in Kenya. The programs were not particularly successful in promoting structural adjustment. Implementation was spotty for two main reasons: (a) they involved a very large number of complex reforms to be undertaken in a rather limited period of time; (b) the reforms taxed the limited implementation capacity of the governments involved. Together this led people to believe that the governments were not committed to implement the program which may have been partly true in the first place but was exacerbated by the complexities of the reform program, the large number of conditions required to be met combined with institutional weaknesses. In addition, these early programs did not appear to pay too much attention to issues of the social cost of adjustment.

There were other problems as well, some real, some because of confused understanding of the role of the Bank and the IMF. The Bank did not get involved in a SAL unless there was a parallel stabilization program by the IMF. The whole idea was that stabilization measures were decided by the IMF and had short-term costs—while the Bank-supported reforms would yield benefits in the longer term. But as the programs came as a package and the Bank was associated with the short-term costs, even though on many occasions it may have argued with its IMF colleagues about the adjustment, seeking, for example, a slower reduction in the budget deficit in order to reduce the expected declines in income.

Adjustment Without Nominal Devaluation: The CFA Franc Problem

In the Francophone area, the Bank was at odds with another strong outside force: The French government. Countries in the area used the CFA franc whose value was tied to the French franc at a fixed rate. The CFA franc was significantly overvalued resulting in uncompetitive exportables—many of them agricultural products yielding incomes to the rural poor—and cheaper imports especially of consumer goods for the relatively better-off urban elite. The Bank was convinced that structural adjustment required a devaluation of the CFA franc. It was opposed by the French government (with J.P. Trichet heading its Treasury) which argued that such an act would relax fiscal discipline. And it was prepared to support its position by providing significant budgetary support to these governments. The IMF was reluctant to push for devaluation: instead, it recommended that competitiveness be improved through what is called 'internal devaluation' which involved domestic deflation designed to reduce prices and wages. The medicine was the same imposed under very different circumstances in Greece 30 years later with similar disastrous results: reduced incomes and higher unemployment for countries at very low levels of income, all in the name of structural adjustment. The Francophone countries continued to muddle through until finally the CFA franc was devalued in 1994. Will Greece eventually follow the same route?

It is not that the Bank's advice was always right. For example, it consistently proposed eliminating export controls for agricultural products as well as food price controls. The argument was that in SSA a lot of tradeables are produced by the rural poor whose incomes would increase from such measures; and that food subsidy programs are not well targeted and hence the poor would not suffer from their elimination. Yet, it has been argued that in several cases the benefits of the adjustment did not materialize: either the supply response did not occur because of deficiencies in the infrastructure or in the operation of the markets or external demand did not rise in response to the devaluation (Mosley et al. 1991).

The Bank seems to have learned from the early failures and improved its performance over time. It recruited a significant number of Africans to staff its African programs—an important element in increasing its capacity to communicate with governments (Amoako 2017). It also increased its training of African officials so that they can play a much greater role in the design of their own programs. This was done through the establishment of the Special Project Preparation Facility in 1984. Finally, the Bank launched a long-term perspective study published in 1989 which relied on background papers prepared by African economists and was used as a consensus building document (World Bank 1989). Perhaps the most important conclusion from this document was its emphasis on improved governance as a key to future growth with equity.

In the 1990s and beyond, there was continued discussion and controversy.[13] There was a lot of discussion about the role of external conditions and the deterioration of the terms of trade faced by a number of SSA countries as a major impediment to adjustment. The debt problem continued to afflict many countries until 1996 before real steps were taken to address it (see below).

Over time, formal Bank policy papers continued to emphasize an increased focus on poverty: The Bank report to the Development Committee in early 1989 stated that it had adopted three strategies to improve its programs on poverty: (a) promote asset creation and redistribution for the poor to involve them in the growth process; (b) ensure that adjustment includes measures to mitigate the costs borne by the temporary new poor; (c) assisting the poor by encouraging social targeting such as through food subsidies, which however, are difficult to administer. But it also noted that in the long run poverty can only be alleviated through a combination of satisfactory overall growth rates, human capital development, asset creation and asset redistribution.

The History of the Bank argues that the appointment of Barber Conable as President in 1987 was critical in restoring the prominence of poverty in Bank operations.[14] I believe that the situation started to change with the publication in 1989 of the report *Sub-Saharan Africa, From Crisis to Sustainable Growth* and did change significantly with the publication of the World Development Report on *Poverty* in 1990 and subsequently with the development of the *Poverty Reduction Handbook* in 1992 (see Chap. 7).

Developed Country Policies

The third component in addressing developing country problems was developed country policies. These had to do with their own macroeconomic policies as well as with their policies on aid and trade. Developing countries would have benefited from a fiscal/monetary balance in developed countries that reduced budget and current account deficits, which absorbed a significant amount of global savings to finance them, and a balance of monetary and fiscal policy that reduced real interest rates, thus easing the debt burden of developing countries. By and large, developed countries did this over the course of the decade, basically because it was consistent with the desirable management of their economies, as both their current account and real interest rates declined.

With respect to aid, developed countries also increased their ODA flows from $40.5 billion in 1980 to $53.8 billion in 1990 (at 1990 prices and exchange rates; Fuhrer 1996), while the ratio of ODA/GNP went from 0.33 to 0.34.

On trade, the key to more liberal developed country trade policies was the reduction of protection in items of interest to developing countries such as textiles and clothing as well as agriculture where developed country export subsidies and domestic support programs undermined development. There was substantial evidence that while developed country tariff rates had been reduced since the 1970s, there was a *significant increase* in non-tariff barriers such as voluntary exports restraints, variable levies and the like (Nogues et al. 1986; Balassa and Michalopoulos 1986). The only way forward on this front was to launch a new round of multilateral trade negotiations under the GATT which hopefully would address developing country concerns.

The IMF and the World Bank strongly favored the launching of these negotiations as demonstrated by the Development Committee communique in the spring of 1984 and I worked hard to bring this about. I felt that it would be important to promote closer links between the World Bank and GATT in order to develop greater coherence between aid and trade policies. Until that time the Director General of the GATT had never participated in the Development Committee meetings. Nor for that matter had the President of the World Bank ever attended the launch of a new round of trade negotiations. Using my contacts with the office of the US Trade Representative, I helped bring about both changes (Michalopoulos 1986). GATT Director General Arthur Dunkel was invited to attend the World Bank/IMF Development Committee meeting of 1984 apparently over the objections of the European Community— which was not represented at this forum (Michalopoulos 2001, p. 236). And World Bank President Barber Conable was invited to address the Punta Del Este GATT Ministerial Conference which launched the Uruguay Round in 1986.

I also tried to promote policy coherence in a more substantive way by linking the trade liberalization developing countries were undertaking unilaterally, 'autonomous liberalization' under World Bank/IMF adjustment programs to the upcoming negotiations in the GATT. A way had to be found to permit developing countries which had liberalized their trade regimes autonomously to obtain 'credit' in the Uruguay Round multilateral negotiations. There was also a fear that if some form of 'credit' proposal was not put in place in advance of the negotiations, incentives may be created to postpone or not undertake urgently needed reforms for adjustment in anticipation that trade concessions could be extracted from industrial countries at some future date (Balassa and Michalopoulos 1986).

There were a variety of problems to address: most important was the question of bindings. GATT negotiations involved the exchange of commitments about legally 'bound' tariffs, whereas under World Bank/IMF programs, the reductions in trade barriers, including tariffs, involved actual 'applied' rates charged, not legally bound ones. A way around that problem could be to give credit to liberalizing countries in the form of extending the period over which they would bind their tariffs in the future. But before I did anything, I thought I would consult with developing country representatives in the GATT. A lunch was arranged for me to meet with the GATT Ambassadors from Brazil and India in Geneva in the spring of 1985. The Ambassadors poured cold water on my hot idea: they were politely but definitely opposed to the 'credit' idea, as they felt that this would put pressure on their countries to liberalize.

During the Uruguay Round discussions, the 'credit' idea was taken up but no formal action was agreed in the area of trade in goods. On the other hand, the credit principle received explicit recognition in Article XIX: 3 of the WTO General Agreement of Trade in Services (GATS) which states that 'For each Round ... negotiating guidelines should establish modalities for the treatment of liberalization undertaken autonomously by Members since previous negotiations.' No rule was set during the Uruguay negotiations or subsequently, and given the difficulties of establishing 'restrictiveness' or 'liberalization' in services, it would be very difficult to design such a rule in the future.

In any case, the Uruguay Round negotiations lasted for more than a decade and their successful conclusion in 1995 and the subsequent establishment of the WTO had little bearing on the prospects of heavily indebted countries in the late 1980s. The international community continued to muddle through until finally, in late 1989, developed countries realized that the muddling through approach could not deal with the problems of the heavily indebted middle-income countries and something more drastic, like actual reductions, in the outstanding debt was needed. This led to the launching of the Brady Plan. Debt reductions for the poorer developing countries would wait even longer, until 1996, when the HIPC initiative would be launched—almost 20 years after the idea was first proposed by developing countries and the Kenen proposals.

The Brady Plan

In March 1989, US Treasury Secretary Nicholas Brady announced a new scheme aimed at reducing the debt burden of middle-income developing countries heavily indebted to commercial banks and other private entities. The basic elements of the scheme involved asking creditors in the private sector to take a loss either by reducing the outstanding value of the debt or the cost of servicing it in exchange for increasing the security of being repaid. This was accomplished by exchanging existing developing country non-performing loans for new dollar denominated bonds, issued by the developing country called 'Brady Bonds' either at below par or at par but with lower interest rates. The new bonds would be collateralized by the developing country purchasing US Treasury bonds of similar maturities and/or with cash. These were the two basic options but details of the restructuring and the securities would differ in different countries. A key objective was to ensure that creditors would be given many options to give up the old debt and that their vast majority would participate in the scheme. In addition, each participating country was expected to agree to a stabilization program with the IMF which would certify the viability of the resulting debt profile, and sometimes with the World Bank, with both institutions as well as other donors, for example Japan, putting up new money in support of the debt reduction program.

Mexico, the first to declare default in 1982, was the first to issue Brady Bonds. Costa Rica and others mostly from Latin America (Argentina, Brazil, Equador, Panama, Peru, Uruguay, Venezuela) followed. Over the next decade, all 17 countries obtained debt relief, including Russia in 1998—which of course did not exist as a country when the initiative started. A total of $160 billion of bonds were issued.

In retrospect, it would seem that the program was successful in the sense that it resulted in significant reductions in the face value of the restructured debt and debt service in the range of 30%–50%, but considerably less in total outstanding debt. It helped restore the restructuring country's creditworthiness and access to the private capital markets. Only Equador and Argentina defaulted on its Brady Bonds and many countries had fully retired them by the early 2000s.

Heavily Indebted Poor Countries

After considerable pressure from NGOs, especially Oxfam, the international community finally established a program to reduce the debt burden of poor developing countries in 1996. Eligibility was limited to low-income countries which met the per capita income criteria for borrowing from the World Bank's International Development Association (IDA) and the IMF's Poverty Reduction and Growth Trust that provide grants and interest-free or heavily subsidized loans. The countries also had to have an unsustainable debt burden, had exhausted the possibilities of rescheduling of official credits through the Paris Club; had a good track of reforms under IMF/World Bank programs and had prepared a Poverty Reduction Strategy Paper (PRSP), the World Bank's new vehicle for defining the strategy of collaboration and lending with its developing country members (see Chap. 7).

The most important major breakthrough for this initiative was the opportunity for eligible countries to reduce debt not only for commercial creditors—which they had little, but also for official creditors as well as multilateral institutions such as the World Bank, the IMF and the African Development Bank. The World Bank was originally objecting to having its debt forgiven because of the potential impact on its own capacity to borrow from the capital markets. But President Wolfenson became a strong supporter and ultimately persuaded the IMF Managing Director, the US and others to go forward.[15]

The original initiative was modified in 1999 in two major ways: first to permit the IMF to participate more fully as well as to design mechanisms that would ensure that countries receiving debt relief would increase their spending in social support programs. It was expanded again in 2005 under the so-called Multilateral Debt Relief Initiative to permit 100 debt reliefs from the three multilateral institutions. In 2007, the Inter-American Development Bank also started to provide expanded debt relief on its loans to HIPC eligible countries in Latin America.

About half of the funding for HIPC comes from the multilateral institutions and the rest from official donors. The funding for the multilateral institutions is in turn provided in part from their own profits and in part from official donors, mostly OECD members. The total value of the write-off in 2014 net present value terms was $75 billion.

Extensive conditionality is imposed on HIPC countries before a final debt write-off. Countries must complete the reforms they have agreed to at the beginning of the program; and they have to have at least one year of successful implementation of the PRSP. Indeed, the conditionality is far more onerous and intrusive than that associated with the Brady Plan. As of this writing, 36 countries had their debt written off. Of these, 30 are in Sub-Saharan Africa. The other six are Afghanistan, Bolivia, Guyana, Haiti, Honduras and Nicaragua. The Ivory Coast has had relief under both the Brady Plan and the HIPC initiative. Three more African countries, Eritrea, Somalia and Sudan, have been judged eligible for HIPC but have not received debt relief yet. The World Bank at the end of 2015 discontinued reporting on the implementation of HIPC considering it to have been completed in substance.

It is difficult to make judgments about the effectiveness of HIPC in promoting development in general and poverty reduction in particular, as debt relief is only one of many aid instruments provided to the recipients. The recipient government policies are critical to the achievement of development priorities and objectives and the international environment also has played a role. Still some encouraging results are being reported: First, of course their debt service relative to GNP has declined. But perhaps more important, before the HIPC initiative, eligible countries were spending on average slightly more on debt service than on health and education combined. In 2014, their total spending on such social services is five times their debt service (www.imf.org/external/np/exr/facts/hipc. htm). Second, a number of these countries, for example, Senegal, Ivory Coast, Zambia and Ghana, have sold government bonds in the international market.

Thus, after almost 40 years of effort, it would appear that debt problems of poor developing countries have been by and large brought under control. Some problems still remain in individual countries. The IMF has identified 7 of the 36 countries as being again at 'high risk' for default. What will happen to these countries if they again need relief is unclear, especially as some of the new creditors are not members of the Paris Club (Kaiser 2016). And, as we will discuss in later chapters, new donors, from outside the OECD, such as China, are becoming progressively more important sources of external finance for HIPC countries and their credits have so far not been reduced to the same extent as debts to other official creditors.

Conclusions

The trigger of the development problems of the 1980s was the oil price increases in 1979 and the subsequent developed country policies which increased the burden of servicing debt. Some developing countries exacerbated the problem by not adjusting to the changing international situation. For others, in particular in Sub-Saharan Africa, the problems were exacerbated by falling commodity prices and extreme poverty and rigid production structures.

Structural adjustment is not easy. It is a slow and sometimes frustrating process. It requires from developing country governments policy stability, continuity and predictability. It can only succeed if everybody, the developing countries, the international institutions and the developed countries do their part.

The international community dragged its feet for decades to address the debt problem in a meaningful and systematic way. When it did, it approached it, correctly in my view, on a case-by-case basis rather than as part of a generalized political solution demanded by the developing countries early on. And it gave a lead role to the IMF and the World Bank, institutions dominated by the developed countries. The institutions on balance did a reasonable job in delivering on the mandate given to them. They made mistakes but they tended to learn from them. And a lot of the successful adjustment assistance programs of the 1980s resulted in good results for a many countries in the 1990s, including in Sub-Saharan Africa.

The main lessons to be learned from the experience are as follows: first, not to try to apply standard solutions but tailor the adjustment programs to the circumstances of individual countries; second, country ownership is critical to program success; third, debt reduction should be done early on so as to avoid long periods of fiscal austerity that are inimical to growth; fourth, it is necessary to take measures to shift resources to the adjusting country's tradeables sector; and finally, particular attention needs to be paid to addressing problems of poverty.

The main costs resulted from the delays in addressing the problem and involved lower growth and more persistent poverty especially for the heavily indebted poor countries. The muddle-through approach did mean that the smaller and weaker countries were hurt more than the rest. But, today with the exception of Zimbabwe and a few HIPC countries, the debt issue that had plagued development for decades has taken the back seat to debt servicing difficulties of members of the euro and to other more complex problems of globalization.

Notes

1. Kenen, who was at the time head of International Finance group at Princeton University, had been my PhD thesis advisor at Columbia University.
2. The recipient would be asked to expend local currencies on worthwhile projects in lieu of repayment to the US in dollars.
3. The head of the UNCTAD secretariat negotiating the text was Gerry Arsenis—later governor of the Bank of Greece.
4. At about that time, the US also forgave mostly Department of Defense debt owed by Egypt amounting to $6.7 billion and about $1.6 billion of exports credits owed by Poland (CRS 1993, p. 15).
5. An AID Policy Paper drafted by S. Schiavo-campo on *Approaches to the Policy Dialogue* issued in December 1982 (USAID 1982) contains valuable advice on the subject of continued relevance today.
6. But his immediate lieutenants in Operations and Finance were old hands Ernest Stern and Moeen Quershi, both of whom had served many years under McNamara. The new Chief Economist Anne Krueger was my direct superior.
7. At the time, the head of the Paris Club was Jean-Paul Trichet who, 30 years later, as head of the ECB was dead set against Greece obtaining a reduction in its private sector debt.
8. Williamson's ten points were Fiscal Discipline, Reordering Public Expenditure Priorities, Tax Reform, Liberalization of Interest Rates, Competitive Exchange Rate, Trade Liberalization, Liberalization of Inward Direct Investment, Privatization, Deregulation and Property Rights (Williamson 2003).
9. Gerard Helleiner (1987) who contributed to AHF was also a commentator on my paper and had many positive things to say, including that 'it is properly humble about our knowledge of the dynamics of the adjustment processes' (see p. 113).

10. The countries were Botswana, Brazil (Sao Paolo State), Chile, Ghana, Jamaica, Peru, Philippines, South Korea, Sri Lanka and Zimbabwe.
11. See Cornia et al., p. 303 which refers to Godfrey M. 'Trade and Exchange Rate Policy: a Further Contribution to the Debate', pp. 168–179 in Rose T., editor, *Crisis and Recovery in Sub-Sahara Africa*, OECD.
12. Lancaster (1997) reports an incident with Nyerere that resulted in strained relations for years (p. 169) as well as an 'African Perceptions' study which talked about insensitive Bank staff behavior (p. 174). See also Amoako 2017.
13. See Van der Hoeven and Van der Kraaij 1994; Husain and Faruqee 1994.
14. I had a somewhat more jaundiced view. In my letter to Lewis (Michalopoulos 1990) I said 'because the interest has come from the top, the issue has been dealt in bureaucratic terms… The Operations complex is being asked to state how many staff years of work and how much lending has been allocated to 'poverty' and other so-called areas of special emphasis. So, all good bureaucrats try to figure out what is a reasonable number which is both substantial and credible so that nobody would question them'.
15. The World Bank Board of Executive Directors put pressure on World Bank Management by arranging a briefing by Oxfam to participate in the debt forgiveness. According to some sources, it is alleged that Managing Director Ernest Stern was dead set against it and it was only after he retired that the HIPC initiative could go forward.

References

Addison, T. and L. Demery (1986) "Poverty Alleviation under Structural Adjustment" (processed) (London: Overseas Development Institute).
Amoako, K.Y. (2017) *A Seat at the Table: An Inside Journey through Five Decades of African Development* (Unpublished Manuscript).
Balassa, B. (1988) "Quantitative Appraisal of Adjustment Lending" Policy Planning Research *Working Paper #79*, (Washington, DC: World Bank).
Balassa, B. and C. Michalopoulos (1986) "Liberalizing Trade between Developed and Developing Countries' *Journal of World Trade Law*, 20 (1).
Berg, E. and A. Batchelder (1985) "Structural Adjustment Lending, A Critical View" CPD Discussion Paper No. 1985-21, (Washington, DC: World Bank).

Bruno, M. (1987) 'Discussion' in V. Corbo, M. Goldstein and M. Khan Eds. *Growth Oriented Adjustment Programs,* (Washington, DC: IMF and World Bank).

Congressional Research Service (CRS) (1993) "Debt Owed to the United States by Foreign Countries: Recent Reschedulings and Forgiveness" CRS Report to Congress 93-1010F, November 19 (Washington, DC: CRS).

Conway, P. (1990) "How Successful is World Bank Lending for Structural Adjustment", (processed) (Chapel Hill: University of North Carolina).

Corbo, V. and P. Rojas (1990) "World Bank Supported Adjustment Programs: Country Performance and Effectiveness" (processed) (Washington, DC: World Bank).

Cornia, G. A., R. Jolly and F. Stewart, (1987) *Adjustment with a Human Face,* UNICEF, (Oxford: Clarendon Press).

Crow, B. (1978) Memo to the files on Retroactive Terms Adjustment July 10.

Frank, C. R. (1970) *Debt and Terms of Aid,* (Washington, DC: Overseas Development Council).

Fuhrer, H. (1996) *The Story of Official Development Assistance,* (Paris: OECD).

Helleiner, G. K. (1987) 'Discussion' in V. Corbo, M. Goldstein and M. Khan Eds. *Growth Oriented Adjustment Programs,* (Washington, DC: IMF and World Bank).

Husain, I. and R. Faruqee Eds. (1994) *Adjustment in Africa,* (Washington DC: World Bank).

Kaiser, J. (2016) 'Back to Square One', *D+C*, 43 (03-04) 2016.

Kanbur, R. (2008) "The Co-Evolution of the Washington Consensus and the Economic Development Discourse" paper prepared for the MacAlester International Round Table, MacAlester College, St. Paul October 2–4. www.people.cornell.edu/pages/sk145

Kenen, P.B. (1977) "Debt Relief and Development Assistance" in Jagdish Bhagwati Ed. *The New International Economic Order: The North-South Debate,* (Cambridge, Mass: M.I.T Press).

Lancaster, C. (1997) "The World Bank in Africa" in Kapur D., J. P. Lewis and R. Webb *The World Bank Its First Half Century* Volume II (Washington DC: Brookings Institution Press).

Michalopoulos, C. (1976) letter to Peter B. Kenen, Princeton University, August 31, 1976.

———— (1978) memo to the files "Retroactive Terms Adjustment" undated.

———— (1979) 'Institutional Aspects of Developing Countries Debt Problems' in David. B.H. Denoon ed. *The New International Economic Order,* New York University Oress, New York.

———— (1986) memorandum to A. O. Krueger, June 13.

——— (1987a) "World Bank Programs for Adjustment and Growth" in Vittorio Corbo, Morris Goldstein and Mohsin Khan *Growth Oriented Adjustment Programs*, IMF and World Bank., Washington D.C.

——— (1987b) "External Debt, Policies of Developing Countries and the International Economy: A Crisis of Growth" in *Die Internationale Verschuldungkrise* Zukunft 10, Nomos Verlagsgesellschaft, Baden-Baden.

——— (1990) Letter to John Lewis, February 20.

——— (1992) Book Review, *The World Economy*, 15 (2) March.

——— (2001) *Developing Countries in the WTO*, Palgrave, Houndmills.

Mosley, P, J. Harrigan and J. Toye (1991) *Aid and Power The World and Policy Based Lending* (London and New York; Routledge).

Nogues, J.J. A. Olechowski and A. Winters (1986) "The Extent of Non-Tariff Barriers to Industrial Countries Imports", *The World Bank Economic Review* 1 (1).

Sengupta, A. (1987) "Discussion" in V. Corbo, M. Goldstein and M. Khan Eds. *Growth Oriented Adjustment Programs,* (Washington, DC: IMF and World Bank).

R. Van der Hoeven and F. Van der Kraaij, Eds. (1994) *Structural Adjustment and Beyond in Sub-Saharan Africa,* Netherlands Ministry of Foreign Affairs (DGIS), The Hague.

USAID (1982) *Approaches to the Policy Dialogue*, Policy paper #1, December (Washington, DC: USAID).

Williamson, J. (1987) 'Discussion' in V. Corbo,. M. Goldstein and M. Khan Eds. *Growth Oriented Adjustment Programs,* (Washington, DC: IMF and World Bank).

Williamson, J. (2003) "From reform Agenda to Damaged Brand Name: A Short History of the Washington Consensus and Suggestions for What to Do Next?" *Finance and Development*, Vol. 40, No. 3, September. http://www.imf.org/external/pubs/ft/fandd/2003/09/pdf/williams.pdf

World Bank (1981) *Accelerated Development in Sub-Saharan Africa: An Agenda for Action*, Report no. R81-211 (Washington, DC: World Bank).

World Bank (1986) "Structural Adjustment Lending: A First Review of Experience" Report no. 6409 (Washington, DC: World Bank).

World Bank (1987) "The Social Costs of Adjustment", (processed) January 13, (Washington DC: World Bank).

World Bank (1988) "Report on Adjustment Lending" (processed) Country Economics Department August 1, (Washington DC: World Bank).

World Bank (1989) *Sub-Saharan Africa: From Crisis to Sustainable Growth* (Washington, DC: World Bank).

World Bank (1992) *Trade Policy Reforms under Adjustment Programs,* Operations Evaluation Department, (Washington, DC: World Bank).

5

The Collapse of Planning and the Troubled Transition

Introduction

In 1989, two political decisions taken by governments, several thousand miles apart, had tremendous and lasting effects on the global economy: first, on June 4, the government of the Peoples' Republic of China decided to suppress with force China's pro-democracy movement at the cost of many lives in the 'Tienanmen square massacre' or the 'June 4 incident' as the events of that day are depicted in the international and Chinese press, respectively. The action permitted the Chinese authorities to proceed—unencumbered by popular dissent—with the continued implementation of their economic program featuring export-oriented development and massive domestic infrastructure investments, in a mixed state/market setting. Over the next decade, success of the Chinese economic programs and policies resulted in the spectacular increase of China's economy and its emergence as a global economic and trading power.

On November 9, 1989, following mass demonstrations, security guards opened the gates of the Berlin Wall leading in a few hours to a vast flow of people from East to West Berlin.[1] The decision of the GDR government and that of the Soviet Union to not use force to oppose and suppress popular demands for freedom of travel signaled the demise of

© The Author(s) 2017
C. Michalopoulos, *Aid, Trade and Development*,
https://doi.org/10.1007/978-3-319-65861-2_5

the authoritarian communist regimes in Eastern Europe and ultimately the collapse of communist party rule in the Soviet Union and its breakup into 15 independent states. In turn, the breakup of the Soviet Union and the transition of the 15 states plus Central and Eastern Europe (CEE) from central planning to market led to massive disruptions in the economies of these countries and huge declines in production and incomes of their people over the next several years.[2]

The Chinese government actions resulted in very limited international reactions. Following June 4, there were some interruptions of bilateral assistance programs, but the international aid institutions in which China was a member, such as the World Bank and the Asian Development Bank, continued their assistance programs with little change in substance.[3] Over time, the Chinese economy was significantly privatized, or quasi-privatized, through opaque procedures, but its momentous growth continued and resulted in the transition of China from an aid recipient to an aid donor.

The economic dislocation and income declines resulting from the transition of Eastern Europe and the former Soviet Union (FSU) from central planning to market induced these countries to seek the assistance of bilateral donors from the OECD and international institutions such as the World Bank of which many were not yet members. Indeed, in several cases, countries of the former Soviet bloc which had been aid donors to developing countries became themselves aid recipients. The collapse of communism led to so great an economic dislocation that in 1990 the European donors and the US combined to set up a new regional institution, the European Bank for Reconstruction and Development (EBRD), charged with the mandate to provide assistance to the private sector in countries of Eastern Europe and the FSU patterned after the International Finance Corporation (IFC), the private sector arm of the World Bank and similar institutions in regional development banks.

At the time of these momentous events, I was enjoying my personal transition in the World Bank from the Economic Policy and Research group to the Operations group, having accepted a position in the office of the Vice President for Europe, Middle East and North Africa (EMENA) following the World Bank reorganization in 1987. At that time, World Bank operations in Europe were limited primarily to projects in what was then Yugoslavia as well as a few projects in Hungary. Romania was a member but there were no projects. Similarly, Poland which had been an original member had left in 1950, was readmitted in 1986 and was in the process of discussing a program of assistance with the World Bank in early 1989, even before the massive win of the Solidarity party on June 4 (the same day as the 'event' in China). The remaining countries in Central and Eastern Europe were not members and neither was the Soviet Union. In the aftermath of the fall of the Berlin Wall all that was to change. This chapter discusses the transition in CEE and FSU. It is by necessity selective as I could not possibly do justice to the vast economic, social and political issues involved in the transition from planning to market. It focuses on two issues in particular which had an important bearing in the future evolution of these countries: privatization and the integration of these countries into the world trading system.

Eastern Europe and the Soviet Union 1989–1991

In 1989–1990, one after the other Albania, Bulgaria and Czechoslovakia applied to become members of the IMF/World Bank[4] and Hungary, Poland and Romania sought to reactivate or expand their programs of assistance. All this posed challenges to the World Bank. A strategy paper prepared for the World Bank Vice President for EMENA in March 1990 warned that 'The scope, complexity and speed of reforms to which governments are committed exceed the World Bank's present capacity to respond effectively to their requests for policy advice, technical assistance and training. The World Bank needs to gear up to support new members or new lending programs.' In discussing the 'Central Development Issues' faced by these countries, the paper went on to state that 'The fact that macro-economic stabilization and systemic reform are both needed more or less simultaneously means that "everything" on the reform agenda is urgent. The main policy choices revolve around the question: How quickly and with what combination and sequence of measures can reforms be implemented which encourage a strong and sustainable market based response of enterprises in all sectors to macroeconomic stabilization. The development challenges facing Eastern European countries are so daunting that government reform alone will not be sufficient to accomplish the transformation and restore sustainable growth. Substantial and diversified external support is needed including flows of public financial assistance to support policy reform and investment not likely to be attractive to private foreign capital in priority sectors: reform of enterprise system, development of new institutions of governance, modernization of infrastructure, strengthening the social safety net and rehabilitation of the environment' (World Bank 1990a).[5]

Standard procedure was that in the case of new members, the Bank, prior to engaging in any lending, undertook a major analytical effort based on the findings of large economic missions that addressed both macroeconomic and other aspects of economic performance. I was chosen to lead the first such mission to Bulgaria in March 1990 with a subsequent mission in July 1990 to discuss our findings and recommendations. The latter mission's aide memoire to the government made detailed recommendations on a number of issues. The specifics of the recommendations are not important but the scope of the challenges faced by Bulgaria and other CEE countries can be gauged by the list of issues addressed by the aide memoire, as follows:

* How to alleviate the foreign exchange shortage and restore equilibrium in the international accounts.
* How to stimulate a supply response in the productive sectors and reorient the structure of production and international trade.
* How to liberalize prices (which is essential for obtaining the needed supply response) without destabilizing the economy and generating an unacceptable rate of inflation.
* How to preserve, consolidate and then extend the substantial social sector achievement of Bulgaria during a period of fundamental transition to democratic pluralism and an open market economy.
* What is the appropriate pace of macroeconomic adjustment and systemic reform that is both socially sustainable and leads to an early resumption of economic growth (World Bank 1990b).

The key question for all planned economy countries was the scope and pace of reform. Poland and to a certain extent Bulgaria and Czechoslovakia were at one end of the spectrum favoring rapid and whole scale reforms to take advantage of what then Polish Deputy Prime Minister and Minister of Finance Balcerowitz called the 'period of extraordinary politics'. This period, which according to Balcerowitz lasts between one and two years, is the interval between the discrediting of the old political elite and the coalescing of new interest groups which are less willing to accept the sacrifices needed for the program to succeed or their distributional implications (Balcerowitz and Gelb 1994, pp. 26–27). Hungary and Romania were on the other end of the spectrum, opting for a slower pace, partly because they did not have to deal with the hyperinflation that was present in Poland which demanded more drastic adjustment.

On international trade, however, the pace of reform was quite rapid throughout CEE. These countries were bound together by the arrangements of the Council of Mutual Economic Assistance (CMEA) which entailed essentially bilateral clearing and barter arrangements that caused various distortions: they permitted specialization and exports by firms and sectors which were totally uncompetitive in world markets; and they resulted in more intensive trade among members than would be justified under market conditions. In the course of 1990, CEE countries abandoned these arrangements and CMEA was formally dissolved in June 1991. However, the CMEA dissolution caused significant losses to individual countries: Bulgaria had built an electronics and computer industry which employed more than 100,000 people and exported the equivalent of $2 billion to CMEA in 1987. The industry had almost disappeared by 1991—although it restarted on a smaller scale later in the 1990s (World Bank 1991).

While all this was happening in CEE countries, the Soviet Union was going through its own half-hearted transition, although at the time it was viewed as radical reform. In 1987, Gorbachev initiated a series of reforms that loosened the existing central planning system but did not introduce full market liberalization. The reforms eliminated centralized annual plans, but retained 'state orders' and controls for strategic products and services. It encouraged small-scale private enterprise activity in a number of sectors, including farming through leases and cooperatives and what was called individual labor. It loosened controls on prices and wages in enterprises which, in theory, now had more autonomy for both domestic and foreign transactions and could actually go bankrupt.

Some of the reforms resulted in significant increases in private enterprise activities as well as the establishment of a large number of new banking institutions which were not effectively regulated. Many of these banks were so-called 'house' banks captive to the enterprises which established them. Also, the reduction of central oversight of enterprises resulted in large rent-seeking activities and huge profits for managers. As enterprise profits could be retained, managers would typically transfer them to private companies or cooperatives that they set up for themselves (Ashlund 2007, p. 59). Payments to the state for the transferred assets were either minimal or nil. Privatization known as 'spontaneous' took place with the best assets being spun out and leased by managers. Also, within the same enterprise you could have socialist production and private production. If the customers wanted the best goods and on-time delivery, they paid a dollar premium with that premium going to the management team.

At the same time, Gorbachev introduced reforms that loosened the controls of the communist party as well as promoted better foreign relations with the West. The former led to free elections which encouraged the return of nationalism for the various ethnic minorities that constituted the Soviet Union and led a number of union republics such as the Baltics to announce their 'sovereignty' in 1990. The Union Republics also set up their own central banks continuing the uncoordinated issuance of credit in rubles.

The improved international environment resulted in several important initiatives and treaties. And in July 1990, the G-7 Summit in Houston commissioned a massive three-volume study of the Soviet Union jointly sponsored by the IMF, the World Bank, the OECD and the EBRD called the 'Joint Staff Study of the Soviet Economy' or JSSE (IMF et al. 1991). Also during 1990, several studies and alternative economic reform proposals were developed by local groups in the Soviet Union. Gorbachev did not choose any of the reform proposals but instead in October 1990 adopted 'guidelines' which in effect let enterprises and local governments to expand expenditures on wages, subsidies and social programs resulting in significant budget deficits and suppressed inflation combined with increasing shortages of many essential goods, particularly consumer products.

The conclusions of the *Study of the Soviet Economy* sponsored by the international organizations were submitted to the Summit countries in December 1990 and the study itself published in February 1991. Not surprisingly, it recommended priority action in three interrelated areas:

> macroeconomic stabilization, price reform and liberalization in an environment of increased domestic and external competition, and ownership reform, including an irrevocable signal of private ownership. In these areas the study advocates a radical approach to reform. Fundamental structural changes would be needed to complement these reforms and measures taken to cushion the effects on consumers and enterprises of price liberalization, unemployment and the transitional costs of restructuring (IMF et al. 1991).

In an internal paper drafted in March 1991 (Michalopoulos 1991a) I wrote:

> With each passing month the news about the Soviet economy is becoming more depressing. Output is going down, prices are rising, queues are lengthening and the ruble's value is eroding. A dizzying series of economic proposals were formulated in 1990 and no less than five major plans were submitted to the Supreme Soviet culminating in the Gorbachev program guidelines in October of last year. Yet little seems to have been implemented. And what was done like the government's withdrawal of 50 and 100 ruble notes in January 1991, was both unpopular and of questionable merit. In the meantime the huge Soviet economy, loosened from its central plan controls but not anywhere close to adopting the discipline of the marketplace is lurching about like a disoriented dinosaur, going nowhere.

In the course of the first part of 1991, the budget situation became untenable as the individual republics started to withhold tax receipts from the central government. According to Ashlund (2007, p. 73), 'In the second half of 1991, the Soviet Union faced financial ruin.'

In July 1991, Gorbachev welcomed US President Bush in Moscow and signed a number of international agreements. A few days later he participated in the G-7 meetings in London amid rumors that he wanted the Soviet Union to become a member of the IMF and that the US was opposed, wanting it instead to agree to an 'associate membership' whatever that may have meant. In any event, the Soviet Union formally applied to become a member of the IMF and the World Bank in late July 1991.

Then in August, while Gorbachev was vacationing in the Crimea, there was the abortive coup to depose him organized by a number of his previous party colleagues and government associates. Following his role in foiling the coup, Boris Yeltsin, the president of Russia, emerged as the leading political figure in Russia and the Soviet Union.

In the fall of 1991, a much-weakened Gorbachev continued his efforts to forge a new Union treaty which would redefine the role of the Union government with the republics. There was also a new plan by an economist named Yavlinski that aimed at drastic reforms at the Union level. The US and the other OECD countries had been accustomed to dealing with Gorbachev, who was generally liked, but were uncomfortable with and unsure of Yeltsin's intentions. They were also concerned about the consequences of a breakup of the Soviet Union with its vast nuclear arsenal scattered in different republics.

The Bank, starting in early 1991, organized a group, which I joined, to work on providing assistance to the Soviet Union. The main focus of its work at the time was to organize a program of technical assistance. Reflecting the attitude of its major stockholders, it focused its main contacts with the Union government. In the summer and fall of 1991, I was in contact with a Canadian-Ukrainian economist, Oleh Havrylyshyn, who was quite certain that Ukraine would like to push for complete independence, and that if that were to happen, the Soviet Union would cease to exist.[6] Thus, on August 27, 1991 I urged Word Bank Vice President Wilfried Thalwitz, that the Bank should chart a new course. In a long memo I argued that: 'The devolution of the Soviet Union and the independence movements in the various Republics means that economic reform cannot be assumed to be pursued at the same pace throughout the Union. This in turn requires a major reassessment of the role of the Bank.

* The implementation of Technical Assistance in the context of devolution will change. The August mission (of the World Bank) focused on

discussions primarily with Union representatives. Any further mission contacts in the Soviet Union will have to be broadened with significant additional resource cost.

* The Joint Study and the Yavlinski proposals assumed a Union government with significant powers and that the reforms would proceed in a coordinated fashion if not simultaneously in the various republics. Both of these assumptions are no longer valid. If the pace and scope of reform varies significantly among various republics this raises questions about the relations between the Union level and the republics. The economic and particularly the trade and payments relations among the republics become very important.

* If the pace of reforms especially regarding systemic issues in which the Bank expects to be involved varies across republics then the Bank should adapt its assistance accordingly and contemplate providing assistance to some republics first then to others as the reform process may move much faster in specific cases' (Michalopoulos 1991b).

In November 1991, the World Bank signed a technical assistance loan amounting to $30 million with the Union government of the USSR.[7] Still, the World Bank and practically everybody else expected the reform process to move faster in the Baltics. Thus, the Bank asked me to lead the first World Bank mission to the three Baltic countries with a scheduled arrival of early January 1992. In order to develop information about the three countries, I went in November 1991 on a mission to Denmark and Sweden, the latter of which had extensive contacts as well as consultants working in the Soviet Union and the Baltics. I was on holidays in late December 1991 when it was announced that as of December 25, 1991 the Soviet Union ceased to exist.[8] Within three days, the World Bank asked me to drop preparations for the Baltics mission and start preparing a mission to Ukraine. The new country requested to become a member of the IMF and the World Bank and wanted a Bank mission, at the earliest, preferably before the end of January 1992. I arrived in Kiev on January 15, 1992, as the head of a 20-person mission to meet with Ukrainian authorities in preparation for their membership in the World Bank.[9]

Aid to Russia and the New Independent States 1992–1998

The paper prepared by the World Bank for the Development Committee Meetings in the fall of 1991 stated that there was an emerging consensus (The Washington Consensus!!??) on the priority objectives for the 1990s which was the achievement of sustainable economic growth and the reduction of poverty and that actions to protect the environment were essential in achieving both. It said little about the CEE and the Soviet Union except to note that the dramatic easing of global political tensions created opportunities to work out issues in a pragmatic way but also produced new demands on the international community with the integration of the Eastern and Central Europe and the Soviet Union into the global market economy.

The states undergoing the transition from plan to market were extremely diverse: There was diversity in size, from the vast Russian Federation to tiny Armenia. There were great differences in standards of living with some of the countries in Central Asia having incomes that were perhaps one quarter the level of CEE and the Baltics. And in 1992, various countries were at various stages in their transformation to market economies, with Poland, Czechoslovakia and Hungary much further advanced than Belarus, Turkmenistan and Uzbekistan. Indeed, one could argue that the greater the commitment to reform, the greater the degree of change from the previous political leadership. Similarly, the farther West the country and the greater its previous integration into the Austro-Hungarian system, the easier to resurrect the institutions of capitalism.

The transition from central planning to market was more complicated in the FSU than in the CEE for several reasons: first, in CEE central planning was of much more recent vintage; second, the establishment of new Central Banks in the 15 new states which proceeded to provide credit in an uncoordinated fashion in a common ruble zone led to huge inflationary pressures—'our ruble zone neighbors had unlimited money-printing capacity' (Gaidar 1999, p. 139); third, creation of rubles by the independent central banks led to the collapse of the system of trade and payments among the 15 countries which had further adverse repercussions on the rest of the new states; fourth, while previous trade among these former republics was artificial in that it did not depend on comparative advantage but on arbitrary planning decisions, the collapse of the payments system led countries to establish export controls to 'keep the goods at home' precipitating further declines in output in importing countries; finally, energy-importing countries suffered a huge terms of trade deterioration as energy exporters started to charge world prices for oil and natural gas instead of the previously heavily subsidized rates.

The decline in output in the FSU was massive and of the order of 40%–50% compared to approximately 15% for the CEE countries and the Balkans. At the same time, income inequality also increased. The combination led to very large increases in poverty, which was different than poverty in developing countries in that the poor had on average much better education and health.

The reversal in the decline in output was typically associated with the introduction of reforms: the faster and the more comprehensive the reforms, the faster the restoration of output. By the end of the 1990s, CEE countries had on average recovered their previous levels of income and output, while countries in the FSU were on average still some distance from restoring earlier levels. Good policies which allowed for faster recovery also have resulted in reduced poverty (World Bank 2000, pp. 122–123). While a few countries, such as Belarus, initiated few reforms and avoided sharp initial declines in poverty, they appear to have been stuck at lower levels of income for lengthy periods.

Whether a country undertook reforms and their effectiveness were obviously affected by the political situation, the institutional capacity and external factors such as conflicts which emerged in countries such as Moldova, Georgia, Azerbaijan and Armenia; they were also affected by the support they received from the international community and the international trade environment they faced.

Russia's reform actually started in late 1991 before the breakup of the Soviet Union. The Yeltsin government liberalized prices—except for energy, eliminated import controls (although it retained export controls—especially for energy), unified the exchange rate and launched a major privatization effort—all measures aimed to establish the fundamentals of a market economy. There was significant resistance to these measures from the Communist Party which had strong support in the Parliament, from the Union of Entrepreneurs (representing the military-industrial complex) and a number of state governors. As a consequence, with the exception of privatization which moved ahead very rapidly, the reform effort stalled from mid-1992 to late 1993.

The conflict between Yeltsin and the Russian Parliament ended on October 4, 1993 with the armed confrontation at the White House. Yeltsin emerged victorious from the confrontation but with the exception of privatization, the reform process lagged as the government continued under the strong influences of enterprise managers and others that took advantage of remaining price distortions and subsidies for private benefit.

Inflation was rampant throughout the ruble zone and was only progressively brought under control with the establishment of national currencies—first by the Baltics and then by others in 1993. In Russia and many other countries, inflation continued through 1994 as a consequence of large budget deficits in part driven by enterprise and farm subsidies and in part because reforms in the tax system were slow to yield results.

Reforms went much faster in the Baltic countries, and to a certain extent in the smaller countries, Armenia, Georgia, the Kyrgyz Republic and Moldova—although all faced a certain amount of disruption because of armed conflicts. Reforms were much slower in Azerbaijan Belarus, Uzbekistan, Tajikistan and Turkmenistan—where there was basically no political change from the old regimes. Reforms in Kazakhstan and Ukraine were on average close to the pace of reforms in Russia, with Ukraine being similar to Russia in the domination of the market by enterprise managers and Kazakhstan's economy being similar to Russia in being dependent on an energy sector with very close ties to the government.

The breakup of the USSR led to massive demands on the IMF and the World Bank as well as on the new EBRD and OECD bilateral donors to assist the new countries. All 15 countries became members of the IMF and the World Bank by the end of 1992 and Bank loans were extended to 8 countries (Russia, Ukraine, Armenia, Moldova, the Kyrgyz Republic and the three Baltics) in FY 1993–1994 with the bulk of the money going to Russia.

World Bank loan commitments to the FSU amounted to $1.6 billion in FY 1993–1994 and rose to $3.5–$3.6 billion in FY 1995–1996. The focus of assistance was broad and varied. It included so-called rehabilitation loans, which were policy-based loans akin to structural adjustment loans with a different name. These large loans were given to Russia in the first instance and later to Kazakhstan and Ukraine and were designed to support IMF stabilization programs. The conditionality in the loans was broadly linked to policies aimed to introduce market reforms, such as with respect to pricing, trade and competition policies.

The transformation from plan to market was the overarching theme. This involved loans providing technical as well as financial assistance in support of privatization, enterprise restructuring, private sector development as well as financial sector reform. With respect to enterprise reform, it was clear from the beginning that while privatization was an important component, it could not be limited to it. A number of enterprises, for example, utilities, may have continued to be in the public sector indefinitely while others had to be restructured. There was also concern about strengthening the social services and the safety net. In the planned economy, a number of these services including health and housing were provided through the enterprises, a function which the enterprises had to shed in order to operate profitably in a market economy.

In addition to the focus on the market, there were loans addressing infrastructure problems such as in transport and roads as well as loans aimed at helping the revitalization of the oil industry. Finally, a number of loans were provided to address environmental problems such as, for example, those for the preservation of the Aral Sea.

It should be recalled that in the early 1990s, the World Bank was shifting its focus to address the problem of global poverty. In this context, the programs in CEE and the FSU presented a major challenge. The international community was faced with the problem of massive and unprecedented reductions in output and income in economies which were thought to have relatively equal income distribution. Such reductions obviously affected the vast majority of the population. It was natural in this context to worry less about targeting the impact of the operations to benefit the poor. The poor were everywhere and the focus simply shifted to trying to establish as fast as possible a market economy which would then lead to a resumption of growth that would raise everybody's income. It was a simplistic approach which did not prove sustainable for long especially after the privatization process resulted in providing great opportunities for rent seeking and the accumulation of vast wealth by a few.

The policy-based lending during this period also presented problems of design and implementation. The operational directives of the Bank at the time said that structural adjustment loans could only be provided to finance current account deficits. There were needs to provide financing, but it was not at all clear that there were actual current account deficits. The problems arose primarily in the need to finance budget deficits in the absence of a domestic capital market or ability to tap foreign private credits. The recipient government structures were in the process of being established and issues of governance were present throughout the economies. So it was not clear what agency was responsible to implement what part of the policies on which the loans were conditioned.

Bilateral donors were initially quite hesitant to be involved in the FSU. In early 1992, they organized a conference which, however, focused only on humanitarian assistance. The donors were also quite eager to ensure that somebody would service the debts of the former USSR and were greatly relieved when Russia offered to do so.[10]

Both of these factors led major shareholders to exert a certain amount of pressure on the Bank to lend, as they pushed the multilateral institutions to lead the international effort of assistance to these countries, especially to Russia whose stabilization was perceived to be of the highest priority. This often led other countries, such as Ukraine, to feel that they were disadvantaged in the allocation of the Bank's human and financial resources.

It was not an easy task to lend to Russia in 1992–1993, given the conflict between Yeltsin and the Parliament and other reactionary forces. Indeed, until late 1993, it was not clear to the outside world that Yeltsin would win the internal battles and that in fact Russia will end up being a market economy, albeit one very different than the model the reformers both inside and outside Russia had in mind. Following a short flurry of projects in 1992 including a rehabilitation loan, only one project was approved in 1993; a fast disbursing oil rehabilitation loan aimed at restoring supply capacity in the oil industry. This operation did not accomplish much and was rated as unsatisfactory by the World Bank's Independent Evaluation Group.

Even in the following years, the pressure to lend—pressure from major shareholders who wished to see a stable Russia, pressure from the client who was desperate to relieve the economic problems entailed in the transition, and pressure from within the Bank, whose staff are strongly incentivized to value action over analysis—resulted in many unsatisfactory results. In the period 1992–1998, the World Bank lent to Russia $11.7 billion in 44 projects. The subsequent evaluation of these projects resulted in almost half of them, amounting to $7.3 billion or 65% of the total amount lent, being rated as moderately, highly or just plain unsatisfactory (see Table 5.1). Two other projects were developed but withdrawn prior to Board approval. By comparison, overall evaluations of Bank projects worldwide show that on average about 20%–25% of projects are rated as unsatisfactory.

Part of my job at the time was to help evaluate the economic justification for projects in Russia and Central Asia. A good number of projects such as the one supporting early Russian privatization efforts or, later, the coal sector adjustment loan, were quite successful. But frequently the projects were wrongly classified as not needing an economic analysis or a poverty assessment. As a result, I lost many battles to the urge to lend (see below).

Table 5.1 World Bank projects in Russian Federation 1992–1998

Outcome ratings by Independent Evaluation Group	Number of projects	Commitment amount $ million
Satisfactory	15	2,323.4
Moderately satisfactory	9	1,701.6
Moderately unsatisfactory	8	2,295.5
Unsatisfactory	10	4,886.0
Highly unsatisfactory	1	85.0
Not rated	1	400.0
Total	44	11,691.5

Source: www.worldbank.org/country/russianfederation/project

A Tale of Two Projects in Russia: Win Some, Lose Some

Housing Project: US $400 million—Economic Analysis not available. Poverty Rating not available

Objectives: (a) Breakup of Government monopoly on supply of land; (b) demonstrate that the private sector can produce housing that is more efficient and appealing than the 'kombinats'; (c) encourage banking community to provide housing finance; (d) encourage the establishment of industries to produce modern and more efficient building materials.

Excerpts from memo from C. Michalopoulos to A. Nassau, May 1, 1994 (Michalopoulos 1994)

'Housing for Whom?'

-'for the project to succeed, it is necessary to put as little restrictions on the land purchasers as possible on the condition that they will build.' This sounds ominously like the land grab of the Wild West except that the richest and those with connections will get the land rather than those with the fastest wagons;

-'the homes will be built for households that can afford $40–60,000 homes;...'building houses even if they are extravagant might be the best possible use of "mafia" money: it creates fixed capital and employment.'

Let us please get serious and try to at least make an effort to pursue the objectives that this institution is publicly committed to.

No changes made. Board Approval date 1995/3/7

Ratings: Completion Report—Unsatisfactory;

Independent Evaluation Group—Moderately Unsatisfactory

Krasnodar Power Generation—$500 million

Objectives: Build a Gas Power Plant to be partly owned by Gazprom

Excerpts from Memo from C. Michalopoulos to Jonathan Brown, April 10, 1996

Krasnodar (Michalopoulos 1996).

...the project should be designed in such a way that the Bank would withhold its support, should the regulatory environment prove to be inadequate.

... this project involves the Bank helping Gazprom, a monopoly, to expand through vertical integration that permits it to own a downstream user of its gas. There are no other suppliers. So the question is how to ensure that gas pricing is OK when Gazprom a monopoly supplier is part owner of the power company that uses its product, a classic situation of conflict of interest.

Project Dropped

Source: worldbank.org/country/Russia/projects

Privatization

Transition to a market economy requires privatization. How much, how fast and in what manner were questions that had to be answered in the first instance by countries in the CEE. Practically every country privatized small enterprises relatively quickly. Some was done by auction, some through so-called spontaneous privatization, meaning the taking over of the enterprises by their managers and employees. Some countries passed laws restituting small enterprises to their previous owners. More broadly, small-scale privatization and liberalization of entry to 'greenfield' enterprises was a critical factor in the successful growth performance of countries like the Czech Republic, Hungary and Poland.

Privatization of medium- to large-scale enterprises presented much more complex challenges. Janos Kornai, a famous Hungarian economist, wrote in 1990 that the state 'is obliged to handle the wealth it is entrusted with… The point now is not to hand out the property but to place it in the hands of a really better owner' (quoted in Nellis 2008, p. 85). To find a proper owner required considerable time and preparation. On the other hand, there was concern that spontaneous privatization threatened to strip enterprises of valuable assets. If one did not act quickly, there might be nothing valuable left to divest.

There was another fear as well—perhaps not well founded in CEE, but a real threat in the FSU—that the communist regime and central planning would be reintroduced unless the millions of citizens get quickly a stake in the new capitalist economy.

In the end, the Czech Republic opted for fast privatization using as a primary instrument a mass privatization scheme with vouchers given to the population and hoping that, subsequently, core owners would emerge—and that they would be the 'better' owners that Kornai was seeking. Hungary opted for a much slower approach involving the restructuring of about 100 enterprises and then selling them—without very good results. Poland used a mixed approach involving both direct sales, management-employee buyouts (MEBOs), IPOs (initial public offerings on the Warsaw Stock exchange) and mass privatization—but its implementation was delayed because of political instability.[11] Other countries used a variety of methods including restructuring enterprises before selling them with a variety of results in terms of the proportion of total production privatized (see Table 5.2).

Table 5.2 Scope of privatization: 1999, 2014 and the method used

	1999[a]	2014	Primary method	Secondary method
Central Europe and the Baltic States				
Czech Republic	4	4	Voucher	Direct
Croatia	3	4−	MEBO	Voucher
Estonia	4	4	Direct	Voucher
Hungary	4	4	Direct	MEBO
Latvia	3	4−	Direct	Voucher
Lithuania	3	4	Voucher	Direct
Poland	3.3	4−	Direct	MEBO
Slovak Republic	4	4	Direct	Voucher
Slovenia	3.3	3	MEBO	Voucher
South-Eastern Europe				
Albania	2	4−	MEBO	Voucher
Bosnia and Herzegovina	n.a.	3	Voucher	Direct
Bulgaria	3	4	Direct	Voucher
FYR Macedonia	3	3+	MEBO	Direct
Kosovo	n.a.	2−		
Montenegro	n.a.	3+	Voucher	Direct
Romania	2.7	4−	MEBO	Direct
Serbia	n.a.	3−	Auction	Direct
Eastern Europe and the Caucasus				
Armenia	3	4−	Voucher	MEBO
Azerbaijan	2	2	Voucher	Direct
Belarus	1	2−	MEBO	Voucher
Georgia	3.3	4	Voucher	Direct
Moldova	3	3	Voucher	Direct
Ukraine	2.3	3	MEBO	Direct
Russia	3.3	3	Voucher	Direct
Central Asia				
Kazakhstan	3	3	Direct	Voucher
Kyrgyz Republic	3	4−	Voucher	MEBO
Mongolia	n.a.	3+		
Tajikistan	2	2+	Direct	Voucher
Turkmenistan	1.7	1	MEBO	Direct
Uzbekistan	2.7	3−	MEBO	Direct

Sources: EBRD Transition Report 1999, EBRD Transition Report 2014
[a]The score is the numerical ranking of the EBRD, its classification system of
  assessing progress of large-scale privatization: (1) minimal progress; (2) scheme
  ready for implementation; some firms divested; (3) more than 25% of assets
  privatized; (4) more than 50% of assets privatized, and substantial progress on
  corporate governance

The process of privatization in Russia was extremely important both because of its massive dimensions—tens of thousands of enterprises, tens of millions of workers—and because of its potential influence as a model in other FSU states. The reformers in the Yeltsin government, supported by experts funded by the EBRD, the World Bank, the European Union and bilaterals such as USAID felt strongly that they had to act with speed: the half-hearted reforms launched by Gorbachev had left enterprises managers and workers with a lot of freedom to launch 'spontaneous' privatizations resulting in the looting of the best assets for private gain; in other cases, government subsidies were posing a burden on the budget and fueled inflation. They were equally afraid that the communists would return to power.

The outsiders advising the government, including those from the World Bank, were heavily influenced by the apparent success of the Czech mass privatization programs using vouchers.[12] Also, after so many years of communist propaganda, it was hard for outsiders to believe that patterns of behavior under central planning would collapse so rapidly and that the main agents retarding reform represented interests that wanted the lack of supervision and rules to continue so that they could continue to loot state assets. But the mass privatization program was equally supported by the main Russian advisers.

Privatization is a necessary but not sufficient condition for creating efficient markets. In Russia there were many issues that needed to be addressed, of which two were critical: the role of corporate governance and the remaining relationships between enterprises and the state. In the rush to turn enterprises over to private hands, these two key concerns were downplayed. Efforts were concentrated on achieving the largest number of transactions in the shortest possible time. The rationale was that a market system needed capitalists to survive, and that mass privatization was the quickest and indeed only way to create them.

On the ground, the problem was that privatization needed to gain political support from both enterprise managers and workers and the population at large. Given the size of the undertaking, implementation required both a central authority—the State Committee for the Management of State Property, GKI—and local level involvement.

Finally, privatization initially excluded a variety of 'sensitive' industries ranging from nuclear facilities, ports, to TV and radio and notably natural resource industries.[13]

The first Russian privatization program ran from 1992 to 1994, although the 1992 program did not get launched until mid-year and was marred by the conflict between Yeltsin and the Russian Parliament. It contained several features needed to address the particular aspects of the Russian situation: (a) it established a system of mass privatization through vouchers, with every citizen receiving vouchers with a nominal value of 10,000 rubles; (b) the system conferred strong preferences to insiders— workers and managers who could acquire up to 51% of the enterprise assets at little cost; (c) it established voucher auctions aimed at promoting the concentration of assets in outside funds that could influence enterprise management and operations. These provisions applied to medium- and large-scale enterprises; small enterprises defined as those with fewer than 200 employees and assets of less than 1 million rubles were owned by municipalities and involved sales by auction or commercial tender, again with significant preferences given to enterprise employees and managers (Nellis 1995; Lieberman and Rahuja 1995).

Small-scale privatization started in the city of Nizhny Novgorod (with considerable assistance from the International Finance Corporation) in April 1992, nine months before the large-scale program began. Nizhny Novgorod was chosen as a pilot city because of the political commitment of the oblast and city authorities (both executive and legislative) to privatization. The approach used transparent procedures, exclusively through auctions without restrictions and was very successful in privatizing the bulk of the enterprises in the city.

It was originally hoped that many of the practices adopted in Nizhny Novgorod would serve as a model for other municipalities. But with few exceptions, this did not happen. Commercial tenders were clearly the favored technique. More than two thirds of auctions and tenders were won by workers' collectives, that is, insiders already running the business. As such, small-scale privatization paralleled the mass privatization program. The GKI estimated that by March 1994, 75% of the 94,300 wholesale and retail networks in the 1992 mandatory privatization category had been privatized. Another 30,000 non-retail enterprises could be added to those estimates, making a total of about 100,000 (Lieberman 2008).

The results of the mass privatization program were impressive in many respects but laid the ground for future problems in others. By the end of the two-year program, perhaps as many as 15,000 medium- and large-scale enterprises were privatized involving perhaps 15 million workers. Sixty percent of Russia's GDP could be considered to have passed to private hands. The bulk of the ownership for enterprises of all sizes went to insiders. In medium-large enterprises, insider ownership ranged from 100% in the steel industry to 40% in department stores with a mean of 69% and with the remaining mostly in property funds. For small enterprises, the information is less certain but over two-thirds of the enterprises were bought at significant discounts by workers cooperatives.

The mechanism of asset transfer to private ownership was inequitable: how much a citizen got depended on the luck of the draw—if you happened to be an employee or manager of a potentially profitable enterprise, you got a lot; if not, very little. As to the incentives for the different owners to operate efficiently, there were many questions: would employees, for whom wages and salaries could be expected to be a far larger share of their income than potential dividends, increase their productivity or push for higher wages? Would the profit incentive be sufficient for managers/owners to increase their productivity or would they revert to lobbying the state for subsidies and other advantages? What was going to be the relationship between the State and the new 'capitalists'? And of course, there was a lot that the first privatization program did not accomplish: a large number of firms of all sizes still remained in non-privatized limbo.

Oligarchs or Kleptocrats

After the initial flurry, in mid-1994 the privatization process lost direction and coherence with disastrous results for the economy. The GKI's initial leadership and staff were dispersed to direct other aspects of the reform with Anatoly Chubais becoming Deputy Prime Minister in charge of all reforms. A second round of privatization started in the fall of 1994

through cash sales or investment tenders. The aim was to generate revenue for the government as well as improve the governance structure of
the privatized enterprises through sales of shares to outside investors. This
effort failed in that it resulted in miniscule revenues and non-transparent
procedures which permitted firms to acquire blocks of shares at nominal
prices. Managers and insiders in the newly privatized Russian firms, act-
ing closely with local authorities, showed considerable reluctance to any
dilution of their dominant share of equity.

In 1995 there was another effort, the so-called loans-for-shares initiative. Under this arrangement, commercial bank consortia would give
loans to the government. The lenders would receive collateral shares in
privatized companies. Full ownership of the shares would revert to the
lending banks in case the government failed to repay the loans. On paper
the scheme looked reasonable. All banks, including foreign banks, were
supposed to be allowed to bid for these blocks of shares, with the winner
being the bank offering the largest loan. In reality, the main result of this
arrangement was to encourage the establishment of so-called financial-
industrial groups or FIGS. The groups would be led by one or more commercial banks which were supposed to bid for blocks of company shares.
The process of bidding was opaque, there was collusion between the bank
groups and between the groups and the government. Foreign banks and
some Russian banks were excluded from the process. Nobody expected
the government to repay and it did not. In effect, by this process the government handed over substantial or controlling blocs in major companies,
at prices far below their real value, to a group of political insiders. Foreign
bidders were kept out, competition was reduced and the real state got little
in return and the beneficiaries were the so-called oligarchs. Through their
acquisition of banks which functioned with little oversight by the Central
bank, they amassed great fortunes.[14] There was also a disturbing increase
in the links between the government agencies and the oligarchs. But after
they helped Yeltsin in the 1996 elections, their political staying power was
short-lived. They should more properly be called kleptocrats as they accumulated their wealth by robbing the state through various shady deals.

Some have argued that the oligarchs only did what came naturally
given the lawless state of the Russian economy in the mid-1990s. They
are favorably compared with America's robber barons of the nineteenth

century and should be praised because 'they salvaged and transformed the giant Russian economy and enabled these companies to lead Russia's economic revival' (Ashlund 2007).

It is undeniable that after 1996, there was no question that the old regime of state planning was dead and private property rights had been established. But the economy that emerged started to look like that of Russia's economy during the Tsarist period: concentration of industry in large blocs with limited economy-wide competition, close links between government and industry at the top and a state prone to arbitrary intervention in the affairs of supposedly private companies. Of course, the rise of Putin in the twenty-first century resulted in the creation of 'Kremlin Inc.', with a very large number of Putin's colleagues and friends being put in charge of many large Russian enterprises (Ashlund 2007, p. 252) has made the Tsarist parallel even more persuasive.

With the exception of the Baltics, privatization in other Commonwealth of Independent States (CIS) has not produced much better results than those that occurred in Russia. In Ukraine, less has been privatized using primarily MEBOs which have not been especially transparent and have led to the emergence of some conglomerates like those in Russia but on a smaller scale. State interference continues. State ownership continues to be predominant in large-scale enterprises in countries like Belarus, Turkmenistan and Uzbekistan.

Criticism of the Russian privatization and elsewhere in the FSU and CEE has been sharp and extensive. Many have argued that the outside advisors from the World Bank and the other international institutions and aid agencies should have known better. Janos Kornai in a blistering attack accused the World Bank of focusing too much on privatization and ignoring the role that new enterprises can play in establishing a properly functioning market economy. He argued, with some justification, that while the World Bank emphasized new entries in ex post publications (World Bank 2002), it did not do enough to promote them during the height of the transition in the 1990s (Kornai 2002).

A lot has to do with the question of sequencing of reforms: it has been argued that market institutions should have been established before privatization took place. This meant the establishment of working capital markets, an effective and independent legal system and an effective administrative apparatus at the center and at the local level, that is, all the essential elements of a functioning capitalist system. And based on this, to undertake a slow, careful and equitable privatization of medium- and large-scale enterprises. In this manner, efficiency would have increased but equity would also have been preserved. Underlying some of the arguments is the notion that somehow Russia should have and could have emulated the pattern of China's privatization —not that that pattern is particularly equitable as we shall see below.

These proposals for a slow, orderly process basically ignore the political realities of Russia at the time. Gorbachev in 1990–1991 destroyed the political power of the communist party at all levels while at same time he loosened controls on the state enterprises. In the absence of the party discipline, there was no alternative political or administrative structure that could maintain control over the enterprises. The mass privatization had to happen when it did or the theft of state property would have been even more massive. In all 1992 and most of 1993, it was not clear whether Yeltsin or his conservative political adversaries would win the battle for Russia. As to the functioning of the judicial system, the proponents of a slow orderly process forgot the tanks in Moscow in the fall of 1993.

The foreign advisors were aware of the problems associated with the loans-for-shares proposals and notified their superiors about the lack of transparency and other aspects of the odious scheme (Lieberman and Veimetra 1996). But the World Bank management and its major stock-holders were not in the mood of being tough on the Russian government at the time. It is not clear whether being tough by, for example, stopping lending at the time would have made any difference; and certainly in retrospect it would have been better to devote more resources and earlier to other aspects of market development. But I have little doubt that doing a fast voucher privatization in Russia at the beginning of the transition was the way to go.

While all this drama was playing out in the former Soviet Union, China was also privatizing, quietly, rapidly and just as inequitably. There was no formal privatization program—the Chinese speak about 'ownership transformation', and hence there are no detailed data. A lot has to be gleaned by looking at the statistics of state-owned enterprises, at the central and local levels. And there were no foreign advisors. All was done locally under the control and supervision of the communist party. In the 1980s, some small enterprises were sold to employees. But insider-led ownership transformation was very extensive after the mid-1990s with more than 100,000 small- and medium-size enterprises were 'let-go' between 1997 and 2003 (Mako and Zhang 2008).

The decentralization of control without providing clear title created opportunities for collusion between enterprise management and party officials at the local level leading to asset stripping, and profiteering, with many cases of corruption being uncovered and many officials and managers being punished. This is not to say that there has not been a spectacular growth of newly established private enterprises at the local level nor that there has not been an improvement in the profitability of some large state-owned enterprises, although information about their finances is hard to come by. Other forms of transformation also resulted in private ownership, for example, through IPOs of state-owned enterprises which itself provided advantages to insiders. Rather, the Chinese privatization under continued Communist Party control also led to inequitable results—perhaps not of the order of the kleptocrats in Russia but hardly an example that could or should be followed elsewhere.

Integration into the World Trading System

Trade Policies in CEE and FSU

Central planning insulated the CEE and FSU economies from the global economy through a formidable array of foreign exchange and trade controls. Integration into the world trading system was essential for the transmission of price signals to domestic producers so that resources could be allocated efficiently. The demise of central planning combined with the political changes resulting from the breakup of the Soviet Union and later Yugoslavia forced tremendous adjustments in the patterns of trade especially among these countries.

In CEE, following the breakup of the CMEA, countries eliminated the state control apparatus and had to adjust quickly to the new situation. As noted earlier, some trade among the countries had to collapse as it was not based on comparative advantage. There were increased demands for protection as international competition led to increased open unemployment. Also, some trade controls (import surcharges) were reimposed temporarily when there was a misalignment of the exchange rates in Poland, Hungary and Slovakia. But the surcharges were later withdrawn and by and large the demands for increased protection were resisted. Some countries were already members of the GATT, became charter members of the newly established WTO and had to abide by its disciplines. Others applied and soon obtained WTO accession. Many signed so-called Europe agreements aimed at association with and ultimately membership in the European Union which was accomplished for all of them in the next decade.

The breakup of the Soviet Union created a much greater disarray and disruption in trade than in CEE. Trade of the 15 new independent states with the rest of the world declined by half between 1990 and 1993 and trade among them collapsed even more. There were many reasons:

* The centralized allocation of resources ended but marketing mechanisms and trade finance were slow to emerge.
* The lack of payments system inhibited so-called interstate trade—trade among each other—as the lack of foreign exchange would have resulted in exporters receiving payment in worthless credit rubles being created by the central banks of the various republics.
* Undervalued exchange rates made import competition very weak in the first couple of years—indeed, Russia subsidized essential imports valued at about 18% of GDP in 1992.

As a result, each of the new states established export controls especially for raw materials and energy. The objective of the controls was twofold: to keep domestic prices artificially low and thus ease the adjustment of domestic producers and consumers; and to shift exports toward the West to buyers that could pay in hard currency—'the strategy of many CIS states was to shift the bulk of their exports overseas to acquire convertible currency' (Gaidar 1999, p. 139). In parallel, they organized barter trade arrangements with the others in order to maintain some trade flows especially of raw materials and energy. Imports were not controlled. But there was severe scarcity of foreign exchange, and the very large depreciation of the ruble provided ample protection to domestic enterprises.

The collapse of the ruble zone led by the end of 1993 to the establishment of new currencies in all countries except Tadjikistan. But as all currencies except those of the Baltics were not convertible, payments difficulties continued. Russia, Ukraine and others established correspondent accounts but because the ruble value fluctuated greatly, trade flows could not be denominated in rubles. Interstate trade continued to be conducted through intergovernmental barter agreements through most of 1994, although by then the agreements contained fewer and fewer products. Still they failed to maintain trade levels with deliveries frequently at half the level of the agreed quantities (Michalopoulos and Tarr 1994).

Over time, the trade regimes of the FSU countries started to diverge significantly. The Kyrgyz Republic, the Baltics, Georgia, Moldova and Armenia adopted liberalized trade regimes. For example, the average tariff for manufactures for the Kyrgyz Republic was 6.7%—much lower than the average for developing countries. In part this is due to the influence of the World Bank which pushed for open trade regimes and membership in the WTO in all the countries in which it had policy-based loans but especially so in the Kyrgyz Republic, Armenia and Georgia, countries heavily dependent on World Bank for external finance. All these countries became members of the WTO by 2003, with the Baltics also becoming members of the EU.

Energy exporters like Russia, Kazakhstan and Azerbaijan also liberalized in the sense that they eliminated formal non-tariff barriers to both imports and exports and adopted moderately protective tariff structures. In the late 1990s, Russia's import-weighted applied tariffs averaged 13.6%, while Ukraine's were 11%. Belarus and Kazakhstan had tariffs similar to or somewhat lower than Russia's. These countries did not impose traditional non-tariff measures but maintained export controls and were prone to arbitrary policy changes in exchange controls. Moreover, trade in practically all these countries was subject to non-transparent trade barriers resulting from the lack of enforcement of contracts and property rights, opaque customs procedures and arbitrary enforcement of standards and safety regulations. The accession of

Kazakhstan, Russia and Ukraine into the WTO was significantly delayed but was finally achieved by 2014. Belarus, Uzbekistan and Turkmenistan, which had not liberalized their market internally, continued with state controls on trade for a long time and are nowhere near acceding to the WTO.

Russia from early on tried to provide leadership in establishing regional trading arrangements. A free trade area (FTA) covering all FSU countries except the Baltics was signed in 1992. But the coverage of the FTA regarding individual products varies and is subject to extensive exemptions between various countries. Belarus, Kazakhstan, the Kyrgyz Republic and Russia signed an agreement to form a customs union in 1996, which intended to use the Russian tariff as the common external tariff for the four signatories. The customs union was not in practice implemented except between Belarus and Russia. Kazakhstan and the Kyrgyz Republic already had duty-free access to the Russian market and a lower tariff schedule with the rest of the world, which in the Kyrgyz case was bound in the WTO in 1998. For these two countries participating in a customs union with Russia simply meant that they had no gain and only losses resulting from giving preferences to (in 1997) efficient Russian suppliers (Michalopoulos and Tarr 1997). For Belarus the arrangement seemed to help it get Russian oil at discount prices. Subsequently, Tajikistan in 2000 and Uzbekistan (briefly) were added to the nominal customs union. The Asian countries apparently applied the common external tariff only where it was low—roughly half of the transactions (Tarr 2016).

This earlier custom union de facto collapsed sometime in the 2000s. But Russia persisted and in 2010 the Eurasian Customs Union was launched with Russia, Belarus and Kazakhstan as members. In 2012, the three countries agreed to closer economic ties and renamed their agreement as the Eurasian Economic Union (EAEU) which in 2015 was joined by Armenia and the Kyrgyz Republic. It is unclear whether these agreements will succeed where the previous failed. The economics of the customs union are similar to those of the earlier arrangements, although the newly bound Russian tariff is lower than the earlier one, thus reducing the costs of trade diversion to the other countries. And unlike the earlier customs union, the EAEU has deep integration (such as the reduction of non-tariff barriers, trade facilitation, services liberalization and the free movement of labor) as part of its objectives. It is unclear whether the customs union would be requested to provide compensation to other WTO members as its common external tariff appears to be slightly higher than the WTO-bound tariffs of Kazakhstan, Armenia and the Kyrgyz Republic (Tarr 2016). The one clear conclusion from these efforts is that regional arrangements among the former economies in transition just as in Sub-Saharan Africa and elsewhere are more an expression of political solidarity than a considered effort to raise the economic welfare of all the participants.

Market Access

Integration into the world trading system also depends on the attitudes and policies of one's trading partners. In the case of the CEE and Balkan countries, this was very supportive from the very beginning. The EU signed association agreements with all these countries and over time, several have become EU members[15] while all the rest—all in the Balkans, are at various stages of association with the EU and as such enjoy preferential treatment in EU markets for their products.

When 15 countries emerged from the dissolution of the Soviet Union, they inherited an adversarial relationship with OECD members; for example, they lacked MFN treatment. This quickly changed for the Baltics, whose relationship with Europe became very similar to that afforded to CEE countries and which have since become EU members. The remaining countries continued to face discrimination in their access to both the EU and US markets. In the EU, they faced significantly higher tariffs than competitors that enjoyed preferential access—for example, the average EU tariff on ethyl alcohol imports from Russia and Ukraine was 30 points higher than the average other exporters faced.

The gravest market access problem these countries faced occurred when the EU and the US invoked trade remedies such as anti-dumping and safeguard measures, the most common legal protection under the WTO. In the 1990s, former FSU countries except the Baltics were subjected to far more protection against their exports relative to the volume of their trade in the form of safeguard and anti-dumping actions in the

EU and the US than other countries (Michalopoulos 2014). Moreover, when protective measures were taken, they were based on arbitrary procedures in determining dumping because both the US and the EU classified these countries (as well as China) as 'non-market' economies. This classification lasted for most FSU countries through the decade of the 1990s and into the next century, notwithstanding the fact that by that time most of these countries had privatized the bulk of their economies. The situation improved for countries after they became members of the WTO. But the practice continued well into the twenty-first century. For China, it was supposed to have ended in late 2016. But it has not, leading to a WTO dispute with the US and the EU.

Aid and Trade Effectiveness

The international community responded quickly and provided massive aid resources to support the very difficult and complex challenges involving the transition from plan to market of the countries in CEE, Russia and to a somewhat smaller extent the other FSU countries and the Balkans. The EU and the US helped build a new institution, the EBRD, directed the reorientation of the programs of the Bretton Woods institutions and provided bilateral aid to help countries with the fundamental changes needed. Aid programs appeared to be most effective in the CEE countries and the Baltics partly because the domestic political environment was more supportive, partly because the planning apparatus was less deeply entrenched and partly because of the commitment of these countries to join the EU.

The transition was less complete in the countries of the FSU other than the Baltics. Russia received large amounts of assistance, significant amounts of which were not well utilized. In part this was because of internal political strife, in part because of the non-competitive market structures that emerged and in part because of the non-transparent links between the private sector and the state apparatus.

With very few exceptions, the transition economies adopted relatively liberal trade policies with few formal barriers to entry for goods and services. However, arbitrary domestic regulation and non-transparent customs procedures have often posed formidable non-tariff barriers to trade in many of the FSU countries, except the Baltics. Transition in the CEE, the Baltics and the Balkans was greatly supported by preferential market access in the EU market. Market access for the FSU countries was less advantageous. But as oil and gas—which are not subject to tariffs—form the bulk of several of these countries exports, the problems these countries faced in the form of anti-dumping were not as damaging to their prospects.

Poverty increased substantially in the beginning of the transition as a result of the disruption caused by the systemic changes from plan to market. Output and income levels were restored faster where reforms were more comprehensive. But poverty persists especially in some of the FSU also because of increased inequality.

Countries entered the transition process with very low levels of income inequality and with substantial safety nets and social services. Inequality has increased tremendously and contributed to the continuation of poverty in countries like Armenia, the Kyrgyz Republic Moldova and Russia. Some of it stems from benign causes: rising returns to education, decompression of wages. 'In the CIS, the partiality and incompleteness of economic and political reforms allowed some power groups, mainly traditional socialist elites in combination with some entrepreneurial newcomers to cement and legalize the power relationships that existed at the end of socialism;...these groups were able to generate concentrated rents for themselves at a high cost in terms of increased inequality and poverty to the rest of society' (World Bank 2000, pp. 16–17).

Could the foreign advisors who were involved in providing assistance have made a difference in this result? The answer has to do with the willingness of governments to take measures that will reduce inequalities. Such measures include better functioning product and financial markets, raising the income of the poor through labor reforms and better targeting of transfers. By and large such measures were included as conditions in the various loans that were made to these governments from the very beginning of the assistance in support of the transition. The differing results achieved in the various transition countries reflect fundamentally different political forces internal to the societies undergoing the process of transformation over which foreign assistance has little impact.

Notes

1. Gorbachev had signaled in late 1988 that force may not be used to prop up Eastern European regimes and Hungary had opened its borders with Austria in September 1989 leading to a large number of East Germans leaving their country. But given past Soviet interventions in Hungary and Czechoslovakia, there was always some fear that the Soviet Union and the German Democratic Republic (GDR) would resort to force.
2. F. W. de Klerk met with Nelson Mandela in December 1989 and released him from prison in February 1990, a momentous event with great repercussions for the future of South Africa and development more broadly.
3. Staff in the World Bank office in Beijing went for a short period to Japan but they returned to continue their contacts with the Chinese authorities to the chagrin of the US.
4. According to the charters of the two institutions, a country first has to become a member of the IMF and then of the World Bank.
5. The redrafting of the legal framework was urgently needed. Every reform needed a new law—privatization, capital markets, corporation law, bankruptcy law, anti-monopoly and so on. The FSU and CEE countries had a legal system based on the Napoleonic Code while most of the World Bank advisors drafting was based on Anglo-Saxon law traditions. Eventually, the Bank sponsored legal reform programs to harmonize the legal codes.
6. Havrylyshyn was prescient: Ukraine voted 90% for independence on December 1, 1991 and the USSR was dissolved at the end of that month. Havrylyshyn joined for a time the Ukrainian government, and later became a Senior Advisor in the IMF.
7. The legal aspects of this agreement are unclear as the World Bank is supposed to make loans only to members which was not the case at the time for the USSR. In practice, this technical assistance loan was subsequently disbursed in four countries, Russia, Belarus, Kazakhstan and the Kyrgyz Republic.
8. I should not have been surprised: on December 1, in a referendum, 90% of Ukrainians had voted in support of independence from the Soviet Union.
9. I spent 1992 mostly on issues related to Ukraine and later Moldova. Starting in 1993 and until 1997, I worked on World Bank operations primarily in Russia, while researching policy issues of trade and payments in Russia and the so-called Commonwealth of Independent States (CIS).

10. The Ukrainian authorities told me early in 1992 that they were prepared to shoulder part of the debt burden as evidence of their sovereignty. Russia took over all the debt but also assets of the USSR abroad such as embassies.
11. The World Bank had actually prepared a program of privatization that it had submitted to the government in 1989, but implementation was delayed until 1993.
12. Ira Lieberman was the first adviser to the Russians on their privatization program from the World Bank. He managed the World Bank loan in support of privatization and provided to the Russian advisers a comparative analysis on the Polish and Czech programs based on work he had done for US AID. The Bank then hired a consulting consortium—lawyers, fund experts, voucher experts and consultants—with EU funds through EBRD, the partner in the design of the Mass Privatization Program.
13. There were in fact two privatization agencies—GKI run by Anatoly Chubais and another one, the State Property Fund reporting to the Parliament. Chubais worked out a compromise whereby the State Property Fund handled the auctions at the Oblast and municipal level and GKI designed the program and set the rules and policy governing the program. The State Property Fund later handled the cash sales from which the state received little to no money.
14. Uneximank bought 38% of Norilsk Nickel for a loan (unpaid) of $170 million. Norilsk was estimated to have had profits of 2 billion in 1999 (Nellis 2008, p. 112).
15. Bulgaria, Croatia, Czech Republic, Poland, Romania, Slovenia, Slovakia.

References

Ashlund, A. (2007) *Russia's Capitalist Revolution*, Peterson Institute for International Economics, Washington D.C.

Balcerowitz, L. and A. Gelb (1994) "Macro-policies in Transition to a Market Economy" *Proceedings*, Annual Conference on Development Economics (Washington, DC: World Bank).

Gaidar, Y. (1999) *Days of Defeat and Victory* (Seattle and London: University of Washington Press).

IMF, World Bank, OECD, EBRD (1991) *A Study of the Soviet Economy*, (Paris: IMF, World Bank, OECD, EBRD).

Kornai, J. (2002) "Discussion", in *Trade, Integration and Transition,* R. Grawe and A. Inotai, Eds. (Budapest: Institute for World Economics).

Lieberman, I. W and S. Rahuja, (1995) "An Overview of Privatization in Russia" In I.W. Lieberman and J. Nellis, *Russia, Creating Private Enterprises and Efficient Markets,* Studies of Economies in Transformation #15, (Washington, DC: World Bank).

Lieberman, I.W. and R. Veimetra (1996) 'The Rush for State Shares in the "klondyke' of Wild East Capitalism: Loans for shares transactions in Russia" *George Washington Journal of International Law and Economics,* 29(3).

Lieberman, I.W. (2008) "The Rise and Fall of Russian Privatization" in I.W. Leiberman and D. J. Kopf, Eds. *Privatization in Transition Economies: The Ongoing Story,* (Amsterdam: Elsevier).

Mako, W. P. and C. Zhang (2008) "Why is China so Different from other Transition Economies?" In I.W. Lieberman and Daniel Kopf Eds. *Privatization in Transition Economies: The Ongoing Story,* (Amsterdam: Elsevier).

Michalopoulos C. (1991a) "Economic Reforms in the USSR" Processed, March 11, (Washington, DC: World Bank).

Michalopoulos, C. (1991b) "Events in the Soviet Union and Implications for the Bank" memorandum to Wilfried Thalwitz, August 27.

Michalopoulos C. (1994) "Housing for Whom?" Memorandum to Adrianne Nassau., May 3.

Michalopoulos C. and D. G Tarr (1994) "Summary and Overview of Developments Since Independence" in C. Michalopoulos and D.G. Tarr Eds. *Trade in the New Independent States,* Studies of Economies in Transformation #13, (Washington, DC: World Bank).

Michalopoulos C. (1996) "Krasnodar" Memorandum to Jonathan Brown., April 10.

Michalopoulos C. and D. G. Tarr (1997) "The Economics of Customs Unions in the Commonwealth of Independent States" *Post-Soviet Geography and Economics,* 38, No. 3, March.

Nellis, J. (1995) "Introduction" in I.W. Lieberman and John Nellis, *Russia, Creating Private Enterprises and Efficient Markets,* Studies of Economies in Transformation #15, (Washington, DC: World Bank).

Nellis, J. (2008) "Leaps of Faith: Launching the Privatization Process in Transition" in I. W. Lieberman and Daniel J. Kopf, Eds. *Privatization in Transition Economies: The Ongoing Story,* (Amsterdam: Elsevier).

Tarr, D. G. (2016) "The Eurasian Economic Union: Can it Succeed Where its Predecessor Failed?" *Eastern European Economics* Volume 54 (1).

World Bank (1990a) "The World Bank Group and Eastern Europe: A Strategy Note" EMNVP, March 2, (processed) (Washington, DC: World Bank).

World Bank (1990b) "Aide Memoire: World Bank Mission to Bulgaria" June 27–July 13, 1990.

World Bank (1991) *Bulgaria: Crisis and Transition to a Market Economy,* (Washington, DC: World Bank).

World Bank (2000) *Making Transition Work for Everyone,* (Washington, DC: World Bank).

World Bank (2002) *Transition, The First Ten Years,* (Washington, DC: World Bank).

6

The Birth of the WTO

Introduction

In the aftermath of the fall of the Berlin Wall, and the breakup of the
Soviet Union, the OECD countries were able to turn their attention to
some unfinished business of the 1980s: the protracted and to that point
inconclusive multilateral trade negotiations of the Uruguay Round. The
Uruguay Round negotiations had been stuck for a number of years on an
old-fashioned EU-US disagreement over agricultural trade liberalization
resulting in a failed Ministerial meeting in Brussels in 1990. Finally, in
June 1993, the US Congress passed a 'fast track authority' giving the US
administration the ability to negotiate an agreement which could not be
subjected to Congressional amendments with a deadline of December
15, 1993, for the conclusion of the negotiations. The deadline was met,
and on April 15, 1994, the agreements setting up the WTO were signed
in Marrakesh by the countries that participated in the Uruguay Round of
trade negotiations.

The agreements would broaden the scope of international rules to
cover not only trade in goods, but also trade in services as well as intellectual property rights and trade-related investment. They also contained
a commitment by the developed countries to include liberalization of

© The Author(s) 2017
C. Michalopoulos, *Aid, Trade and Development*,
https://doi.org/10.1007/978-3-319-65861-2_6

trade in agriculture—which to that point they had excluded from the
GATT—as well as elimination of non-tariff barriers (NTBs) that controlled trade in textiles and clothing, a sector of great importance to
developing countries.

As discussed in Chap. 3, in the course of the 1980s, developing countries' attitudes toward trade policy started to change. There was waning
interest in preferences and commodity stabilization, and an emerging consensus promoted by the World Bank and the IMF that more open trade
policies were needed to implement programs of structural adjustment. At
the same time, developing countries started to recognize the usefulness of
mutual trade liberalization undertaken in a multilateral context as a means
for improving their access to developed country markets. As a result,
GATT's importance as an institution within which developing countries
wanted to pursue trade objectives started to rise. This was manifested in
the decision by a number of developing countries, especially in Latin
America (e.g., Mexico and Costa Rica) to join GATT in the late 1980s.

The Round reflected a recognition of the need to address issues resulting from the forces of globalization that would inexorably push for greater
integration of the world economies in the 1990s and beyond. The establishment of the WTO at the end of the Round brought about a fundamental restructuring of the rules guiding the international trading system
as well as a significant change in the role played by developing countries
within the system. This chapter summarizes the main aspects of the new
agreements as they affected developing countries and their policy commitments regarding trade in goods and services. These commitments are
important as they reflect, with very few exceptions, the actual situation at
present—more than 20 years later.

The Uruguay Round and the Development Dimension of the WTO

The WTO was established on January 1, 1995, to 'provide the common
institutional framework for the conduct of trade relations among its
members in matters related to the Agreements and associated legal
instruments' (Article 2) signed at the end of the Uruguay Round. This

included a total of 20 agreements, including a revision of the GATT and several new agreements. Beyond the new agreements on intellectual property rights and trade-related investment measures, there were new agreements on subsidies and countervailing, safeguards, anti-dumping and standards, many of which had previously existed as 'codes' not required for all members. In addition, the dispute settlement mechanism was strengthened and a totally new agreement establishing a Trade Policy Review Mechanism was introduced (WTO 1995).

Article III of the Marrakesh Agreement sets out the four main functions of the WTO as follows:

* Facilitate the implementation, administration and operation and further the objectives of these trade agreements
* Provide the forum for negotiations among members concerning multilateral relations
* Administer the Dispute Settlement Understanding
* Administer the Trade Policy Review Mechanism

The WTO agreements resulted in the strengthening and deepening of the multilateral trading system in ways that offered to developing countries the possibility of greater integration. One of the issues that emerged in the late 1990s, however, was precisely whether this potential was being realized.

Two aspects of the Uruguay Round Agreements were of great potential importance to developing countries. First, as noted earlier, the market access negotiations covered areas of interest not previously subject to GATT disciplines, such as agriculture and textiles and clothing. Moreover, the agreement on safeguards benefited developing members' market access through the elimination of voluntary export restraints, which had acted as significant barriers in developed country markets for products such as footwear and steel. And, of course, the negotiations on tariffs resulted in further reductions in tariffs on industrial imports with the average trade-weighted tariff rate on such imports from developing countries falling by 34%. Second, the strengthening of the dispute settlement mechanism by introducing greater certainty about the adoption of quasi-judicial decisions by dispute settlement panels was of great potential benefit to developing countries: it offered judicial protection against the larger and more powerful developed countries and a better chance of prevailing in a bilateral trade dispute with them than would be the case outside the WTO. Finally, the main objective of the new Trade Policy Review Mechanism was to 'contribute to improved adherence by all WTO Members to rules, disciplines and commitments under the Multilateral Trade Agreements by achieving greater transparency and understanding of the trade policies and practices of members' (WTO 1995, p. 434). The reviews, which were patterned after the OECD's DAC review of assistance programs, offered the opportunity to developing countries to assess and comment on developed country trade policies which had a bearing on their export prospects.

At the same time, by participating in the Uruguay Round Agreements in services, trade-related intellectual property rights (TRIPs) and trade-related investment measures (TRIMs), developing countries would have to conform to rules and policy disciplines in areas where they had previously enjoyed complete latitude. The same was true of the new agreements on subsidies, technical barriers to trade (TBT), customs valuation, sanitary and phytosanitary measures (SPS), all of which converted previous multilateral agreements, in which few developing countries participated, into general developing country commitments to abide with multilaterally agreed rules, albeit within a framework of certain special provisions. Tighter discipline was also introduced under Article XVIII (B)—which justified protection for balance of payments reasons—on actions that ran counter to trade liberalization. The agreed 'Understanding about the Article' encouraged the use of price-based measures, extended the documentation and notification requirements and provided procedures for the phasing out of restrictions. These modifications were at least partly informed by the developments in economic policy described earlier, most notably in respect of the greater effectiveness of fiscal and monetary instruments in meeting balance-of-payment shocks.

The Uruguay Round continued to be guided by the general principles on special and differential treatment agreed in previous negotiating Rounds, and these were even extended in a number of ways by providing transitional time frames and technical assistance in the implementation of the various agreements reached in the WTO. The basic reason for the extension of special treatment through these two new elements was simply that developing countries did not have the institutional capacity to implement the commitments demanded of them in some of the new areas covered by the WTO. They would not have signed the agreements had they not been promised both additional time and technical assistance to build the necessary capacity.[1]

Special and Differential Treatment for Developing Countries

The legal texts of the agreements embodied in the WTO contain a very large number of provisions on the differential and more favorable treatment of developing countries and the least developed countries (LDCs).

Three conceptual premises underlie the provision of special and differential treatment. The fundamental one is that developing countries are intrinsically disadvantaged when participating in international trade and therefore any multilateral agreement involving them and developed countries must take this weakness into account when specifying their rights and responsibilities. In this context one should recall that the definition of a developing country is based on self-selection. Except for the LDCs, which are accorded even more flexibility but which are determined based on objective criteria set by the UN, countries like El Salvador, Ghana or China are supposed to enjoy the same privileges and responsibilities. A related premise is that the trade policies aimed at maximizing sustainable development in developing countries necessarily differ from those of developed economies, and hence policy disciplines applying to the latter should not apply to the former. The final premise is that it is in the interest of developed countries to assist developing countries to integrate fully into the international trading system.

Based on these premises, the WTO provisions for special and differential treatment (SDT) agreements fall into three broad categories: (1) positive actions by developed country members or international institutions; (2) exceptions to the overall rules for developing countries and, sometimes, additional exceptions for the LDCs; and (3) time extensions for the implementation of the agreements.

Developed countries agreed to take three kinds of actions to support developing countries' participation in international trade:

a. *Preferential Market Access*

Developed countries agreed to continue to provide tariff preferences for manufactured exports from developing countries under the GSP and, within that context, for special treatment of the LDCs.

b. *Technical and other assistance to permit developing countries to meet their WTO obligations and enhance the benefits they derive from international trade*

Weaknesses in the human and physical infrastructure and the institutions that deal with international trade are key impediments in the capacity of developing countries to benefit from international trade institutional capacity constraints significantly impede the effective integration of poorer countries and LDCs into the multilateral trading system. Assistance was and is needed to strengthen their institutional capacity in a way that will enable them to meet their obligations under the agreements. While it may be relatively easy to promulgate policies to liberalize trade, it is far more difficult to develop the capacity to take advantage of the opportunities international trade provides that are critical for economic transformation. The main areas in which technical assistance was envisaged included TBT, SPS, customs valuation, pre-shipment inspection, dispute settlement and TRIPS.[2] Concern was also raised regarding the high costs and affordability of implementing the Uruguay Round Agreements (Finger and Schuler 2000) and whether technical assistance alone will be sufficient to provide the physical and human capital costs needed to build capacity in areas where developing countries have assumed WTO commitments.

c. *Implementation of the WTO provisions in a manner favorable to developing country members*

The WTO agreements contain many references in the preambles and in the substantive provisions of the various texts that commit members to implement the agreements in ways that take into account the interests of developing countries and LDCs. Some of these references are of a general nature and are expressed in broad 'best efforts' terms, but in a few cases there are more explicit provisions on how developing countries should be treated more favorably or in ways that will least damage their interests. None of these provisions appear to be legally enforceable (Kessie 2000).

There are two fundamental ways in which developing countries and LDCs have accepted differential obligations under the WTO agreements: (1) they enjoy the freedom to undertake policies that limit access to their markets or provide support to domestic producers or exporters in ways which are not allowed to other members, which can be viewed as exemptions from WTO disciplines so as to take into account particular developing country circumstances; and (2) they are provided with more time to meet their obligations or commitments under the agreements.

a. *Exemption from disciplines*

The most general and fundamental way in which developing countries continue to be exempted from WTO disciplines in respect of market access policies is through the principle of non-reciprocity in trade negotiations whereby developed countries reduce or remove tariffs and other barriers to trade. This principle is recognized in GATT Article XXXVI and in the 'Enabling Clause'. Consistent with these provisions, many developing countries have not bound tariffs on their industrial products to the same extent as developed countries or have agreed to bind at levels that are substantially higher than the applied levels. Similar provisions for non-reciprocity are included in GATS, Article XIX (2), which states that 'there shall be appropriate flexibility for individual developing countries Members for opening fewer sectors, liberalizing fewer types of transactions, progressively extending market access in line with their development situation.'

b. *Protection of domestic industry*

A second way in which developing countries have greater flexibility in providing protection to domestic industry is through the provisions of

GATT Article XVIII, which enables developing countries to (1) provide the tariff protection required to establish a particular industry and (2) apply quantitative restrictions for balance of payments purposes. Since the establishment of the WTO there have been very few instances of these provisions being invoked.

The Agreement on Agriculture contains a variety of measures that exempt developing countries and, to even a greater extent, LDCs from disciplines and obligations that apply generally, and it extends longer timetables or more modest reductions in government support and subsidies than are required from other members. For example, investment subsidies or input subsidies to low-income producers are exempted from the calculation of aggregate measures of support; reductions in export subsidies are either set lower or may take place over a longer period of time; and there are specific provisions for the operation of government stockholding programs aimed at enhancing food security as well as less-demanding minimum-access provisions for primary agricultural products that are the predominant staple in the traditional diet of the developing country in question. A number of developing countries have notified the WTO that they are implementing programs that take into account the specific exemptions contained in these provisions.

There are similar exemptions from disciplines in the Agreement on Subsidies and Countervailing Measures. This agreement permits LDCs and countries with a per capita income of less than $1,000 to retain certain kinds of export subsidy that are otherwise prohibited; and for other developing countries, it extends the period over which subsidies can be provided. Again, a number of developing countries have invoked these provisions by notifying the WTO that they are maintaining their export subsidy programs.

Flexibility has thus emerged as the most widespread instrument of special and differential treatment. While there is little reason to question the overall principle of policy space and flexibility, there is a question as to whether the magnitude of the latitude permitted, for example, in respect of tariff bindings, results in policies that are more suited to development.

The final way in which special and differential treatment is conferred on developing countries and LDCs in the WTO is the extension of the time in which certain obligations under the agreements must be implemented. Such flexibility is provided in practically all the WTO agreements, with the exception of the Agreements on Anti-Dumping Procedures and on Pre-shipment Inspection. For instance, the agreement on subsidies and countervailing duties permits a transition period of eight years, while the TRIPS agreement permits a transition period of five years. In the case of the Agreement on Textiles and Clothing, flexibility took the form of an accelerated phasing out of MFA quotas for developing countries.

Transition-time flexibility, like the other types of flexibility discussed earlier, is thus a mechanism for providing special and differential treatment in the context of reciprocal and multilateral commitments.[3] And a strong case can be made that the special provisions extended to the developing countries—unlike the provisions calling for developed country actions—are legally enforceable (Kessie 2000).

Special Measures for LDCs

The Enabling Clause of 1979 provided the basis for special treatment of LDCs 'in the context of any general or specific measures in favour of developing countries'. The Uruguay Round Agreements contain 17 provisions that apply specifically to LDC members, in addition to those applicable to all developing countries. These include a longer transition period than that granted to developing countries under the TRIPS, TRIMS and SPS agreements. In addition, the agreements on agriculture and subsidies exempt LDCs from all reduction commitments, with the subsidies agreement allowing for an extended phasing out of subsidies once export competitiveness is established.

The main issues that arise in connection with special and differential treatment for developing countries and LDCs have to do with the relevance of the provisions to address problems arising for very different countries, all of which are considered developing and some of which are considered LDCs. Does China or Singapore really need preferential treatment for their exports to penetrate developed country markets or more time to implement the agreement on TRIPS? There is no mechanism for graduation from preferential treatment when it is no longer needed.

On the other hand, are the time extensions laid down in the agreements adequate to build the institutional capacity needed for full implementation of the obligations by LDCs or other poor developing countries? The Uruguay Round negotiators do not appear to have consulted anybody involved in institution building in developing countries about the transition periods agreed upon. The extensions have already expired and there is little evidence that many countries have made sufficient progress with institution building to permit them to implement their obligations. Similarly, is the technical assistance needed to help build the institutional capacity forthcoming in sufficient amounts and appropriate terms? These would be questions that developing countries started to raise almost as soon as they signed the agreements.

Developing Country Trade Policies

The conclusion of the Uruguay Round brought about significant changes in developing country trade policies especially through the binding of tariffs, the commitments to liberalize trade in services and the adoption of a variety of rules affecting the use of safeguards, subsidies, antidumping and other measures that affect the flow of goods in international trade. These changes were made in the context of even greater liberalization of applied tariffs and rules affecting services on a unilateral basis. The analysis of developing country policies in this section documents the great progress made by many developing country WTO members in liberalizing their trade regimes since the early 1990s. It is based on information from 50 developing countries, which includes 15 economies in Latin America and the Caribbean, 17 in Asia, 13 in Sub-Saharan Africa and 5 in Europe, the Middle East and North Africa. They account for over 95% of the total trade of the developing members of the WTO and as such their policies and problems can be taken to represent the developing countries as a whole. Their formal commitments in the WTO today are as they were in 1995. Their actual trade policies are as of the latest year on which information is available (Michalopoulos 2014).

Tariffs

Developing countries bound some of their tariffs to specific levels as part of their obligations to the WTO in 1995. This means that if they were to impose tariffs *higher* than the bound levels, they would be in violation of their treaty commitments and other countries could seek legal redress including by demanding reductions of other tariffs, the imposition of penalties or retaliation. But their actual tariffs can and usually tend to be lower either because of unilateral reductions or because of the existence of preferential trade arrangements (PTA). The simple average applied MFN tariff level for the latest year available, as well as the average level of binding, the average difference between applied and Uruguay Round bound rates and the proportion of tariff lines unbound for the 50 developing countries in the sample, are presented in Table 6.1.

The average applied rates in the 50 countries range from zero in Hong Kong and Singapore to 5–10% in many countries in Latin America, to 10–20% in most of the rest of the countries except Tunisia, which has an average of over 20%. Perhaps the most interesting aspect of the table is the comparison of the applied rates over time. Only three countries (Benin, Brazil and Senegal) had a lower average applied rate in the 1990s than in the 2000s and that by a small margin. Hong Kong and Singapore, with zero rates, showed no change. The remaining 45 developing countries showed a decline in their average applied rates, frequently by more than half. The simple average applied tariff rate for the 50 countries was 17% in the 1990s and 9.1% in the 2000s.[4]

There are significant variations in the proportion of total tariff lines that developing countries have bound in the Uruguay Round: while all WTO members have bound all their agricultural tariff lines, many developing country members have bound only a small proportion of the lines in the rest of their tariff schedules. There is an apparent regional pattern. In Latin America all the countries have bound virtually all their tariff lines. But in Africa and Asia many countries have bound only a small proportion of tariffs outside agriculture. In Hong Kong and Singapore, which are committed to zero applied tariff rates, 54% and 30%, respectively, of the tariff schedule is unbound.

Table 6.1 Bound and applied tariffs in developing countries

	Latest year	Bound rate (%)	Applied rate (%)		% of unbound
			Mid-1990s	Latest year	
Argentina	2011	31.9	14.4	9.8	0.0
Bangladesh	2008	167.1	26.7	14.0	84.3
Benin	2011	28.3	12.3	13.3	60.9
Bolivia	2011	40.0	9.6	9.1	0.0
Brazil	2011	31.4	13.2	13.5	0.0
Cameroon	2011	79.9	21.0	18.9	86.7
Chile	2010	25.1	11.0	4.9	0.0
China	2011	9.9	22.0	7.8	0.0
Colombia	2011	42.8	12.2	6.8	0.0
Costa Rica	2009	43.0	9.7	4.7	0.0
Côte d'Ivoire	2011	11.1	21.0	12.9	66.6
Dominican Republic	2010	34.9	20.0	8.3	0.0
Egypt, Arab Rep.	2009	36.8	24.3	12.3	0.7
El Salvador	2010	36.7	10.0	5.0	0.0
Fiji	2011	40.1	12.4	11.8	48.9
Ghana	2009	92.5	17.5	13.0	85.6
Honduras	2009	32.4	9.6	6.4	0.0
Hong Kong, China	2011	0.0	0.0	0.0	53.6
India	2009	49.4	37.0	10.1	25.6
Indonesia	2011	37.2	10.8	5.0	3.4
Jamaica	2011	49.6	21.1	8.4	0.0
Kenya	2011	95.1	32.1	12.3	85.2
Korea, Rep.	2010	15.8	15.0	10.1	5.4
Kuwait	2009	100.0	6.0	4.1	0.1
Malawi	2011	74.7	25.5	12.3	68.0
Malaysia	2009	14.6	8.9	5.3	15.9
Mauritius	2011	94.4	32.7	1.2	82.2
Mexico	2010	35.0	12.6	7.3	0.0
Morocco	2009	41.3	23.5	9.1	0.0
Mozambique	2010	97.5	15.6	7.7	86.4
Nepal	2011	26.0	14.8	12.3	0.6
Nigeria	2010	118.3	23.0	10.9	80.8
Pakistan	2009	60.0	50.1	14.7	1.3
Paraguay	2011	33.4	11.7	8.4	0.0
Peru	2011	30.1	16.2	3.1	0.0
Philippines	2010	25.6	19.8	5.3	33.2
Saudi Arabia	2009	10.7	13.0	4.0	0.0
Senegal	2011	30.0	12.3	13.3	0.0
Singapore	2010	7.0	0.0	0.0	30.0

(continued)

Table 6.1 (continued)

	Latest year	Bound rate (%)	Applied rate (%)		% of unbound
			Mid-1990s	Latest year	
South Africa	2011	19.2	15.0	7.0	4.0
Sri Lanka	2011	29.9	20.0	9.0	61.6
Taiwan, China	2011	6.0	7.8	4.2	0.0
Thailand	2009	25.7	21.0	10.5	24.6
Tunisia	2008	57.2	29.7	21.8	41.6
Uganda	2011	73.0	16.8	12.1	84.2
Uruguay	2011	31.5	12.7	9.5	0.0
Venezuela	2011	36.5	12.8	11.8	0.0
Vietnam	2010	11.5	13.0	7.1	0.0
Zambia	2011	106.0	14.7	10.6	83.2
Zimbabwe	2007	89.8	17.2	14.7	77.6
Average		46.3	17.0	9.1	27.7

Source: UNCTAD TRAINS (applied tariffs) and WTO IDB (bound tariffs) databases.
Notes: Bound and applied tariffs are based on simple averages made in the mid-1990s and the latest year for which data are available.

The table also illustrates the large differences, on average, between Uruguay Round bound and applied rates in most developing countries. Developing countries have bound their tariffs at substantially higher rates than those they apply, if they have bound them at all. For example, Brazil has bound its whole tariff schedule but at ceiling rates of 31%. Sometimes (e.g., Nigeria) the differences are in excess of 100%. For countries which have bound the whole tariff schedule (Latin America, and a few others, e.g., Morocco), the average difference between applied and bound rates is 30 percentage points. In some cases, such as India, Nigeria and Pakistan, countries have bound a small portion of their tariff schedule and have used ceiling bindings with high average rates for that part which has been bound.

Ceiling bindings, just like unbound rates, allow flexibility in developing country policy when governments feel the need to increase protection. Domestically, they are an invitation to particular interest groups to exert pressure on governments to increase protection. For foreign suppliers they reduce predictability and increase uncertainty in terms of the market access barriers they will be facing. This in turn impedes the activity of private agents, especially where investments are marked by a degree of irreversibility, and could result in reduced inflows of foreign financing. At the same time, their widespread existence undermines developing countries' arguments that their development requires intrinsically higher levels of protection than those agreed in the WTO.

The amount of actual policy flexibility that ceiling bindings offer is much less than the formal difference between the MFN and the bound rates: some of the bound rates are so high as to be redundant and economically meaningless, in the sense that no imports would occur, even if the rates were substantially lower. Similarly, some of the applied rates are based on preferential agreements and thus cannot be increased without retaliation or other adverse trade repercussions. About a third of the difference between bound and MFN rates is thus not available as policy space for low- and middle-income developing countries (Folleti et al. 2009). Perhaps the greatest usefulness of ceiling bindings is as part of developing country bargaining in multilateral trade negotiations.

For most countries average applied tariffs on agricultural products are higher than tariffs for the rest of the product groups—which include raw materials, fuels and manufactures. But there are many exceptions, especially in Latin America (Argentina, Brazil, Chile) as well as in South Africa and Malaysia.

Tariff averages are higher for lower income countries and lower for middle and higher income developing countries. For many developing countries, tariff escalation, which results in higher protection for final goods, is also an issue, as other developing countries are becoming more important as markets.[5] By and large, and for most sectors, escalation again seems to be inversely related to per capita income. With few exceptions, low-income countries and Sub-Saharan Africa tend to have the highest degree of escalation and hence the highest protection for their final goods producers.

Non-tariff Measures

The evidence about developing country use of non-tariff measures (NTMs) to restrain imports has three main dimensions:

* The relative importance of the different policy measures employed by developing countries as measured by the frequency of their use,
* The main product categories whose importation is affected by NTMs,
* The overall use of NTMs by developing countries to control imports over the period 1990–2012, as measured by the overall frequency of application of such measures.

Frequency ratios are indicators of the extent to which countries resort to particular measures and the proportion of total products in terms of tariff lines or product groups that are affected by such measures, irrespective of the value of the products actually imported. They do not necessarily capture the protective effect of the measures taken.

The data reveal several policy tendencies (see Michalopoulos 2014, Table 4.6). First, non-automatic import licensing (including various forms of administrative approvals) continues to be the measure that affects by far the greatest number of products imported into these countries, with prohibitions of various kinds ranking second. Agricultural products were the most subject to overall controls especially in the early 1990s. The number of countries imposing these controls has substantially declined in the period 1995–1998, following the tariffication in agriculture under the Uruguay Round Agreements. In addition to agriculture, mineral products, in particular fuels, rubber products, machinery, especially electrical machinery and precious stones and metals continued to be subject to controls, especially through licensing in a significant number of countries.

The Uruguay Round Agreement subjected the agricultural sector for the first time to some of the same trade disciplines that apply to other sectors. However, it did not result in significant liberalization of developed country policies (see below). At the time the agreements were being negotiated, the main developing country concerns focused on the market access issues and the benefits that some of the key agricultural exporters would obtain, as well on the possible adverse impact that reduced export subsidies in developed countries would have on developing countries that were net food importers. Little attention was focused, until the decade of the 2000s, on the level of support and the kinds of measures appropriate for developing countries to implement in pursuit of their own agricultural development which is essential to the elimination of poverty, itself very often mainly a rural phenomenon.

The Uruguay Round Agreement on Agriculture contains provisions which permit developing countries to increase their support to agriculture (and of poor consumers) through means not available to developed countries. For example, direct and indirect investment and input subsidies to poor farmers are excluded from the calculation of aggregate measures of support (AMS); reduction of the support commitments by developing countries may take ten years to implement, while LDCs are totally exempt; and food subsidies to the urban and rural poor are excluded from the calculation of AMS. However, a number of critics have pointed to the 'unfairness' of the agriculture agreement as it still permits greater support levels for developed countries (which in the past have given a great deal of assistance to their agricultural sector) than developing countries which penalized agriculture in the base period (Das 1998).

Trade Remedies

Trade remedies include anti-dumping, countervailing and safeguard actions. In principle, such actions are consistent with WTO provisions. The legal basis and procedures for the imposition of trade remedies in each instance are as various as are the remedies, which usually do not involve quantitative restrictions but changes in duties and charges to address the problem appropriately in each case. In the case of anti-dumping and countervailing duties, these remedies are intended to correct for distortions that occur when exporters are obtaining subsidies and engaging in discriminatory pricing practices which result in injury to domestic producers. In the case of safeguards, the issue is simply injury to domestic producers, even if no unfair trade practices are involved.

There is strong evidence that the use of these measures has increased substantially over time by both developed and developing countries. Until 1986, no developing country had initiated an anti-dumping action, although they were subject to some anti-dumping actions by the developed countries. Over time the situation has been totally reversed: developing countries initiated the majority of the actions and were the subject of most of the anti-dumping actions, both by other developing countries and the developed countries. The peak year for anti-dumping investigations (206) by developing countries was 2002, while 2001 was the peak year for investigations against them (227). Since that time anti-dumping investigations appear to have declined both by developed and developing countries.

Anti-dumping is by far the most popular instrument, dwarfing countervailing or safeguard actions. Indeed, an earlier investigation showed that out of 50 countries, 24 initiated anti-dumping measures, 15 safeguards and only 9 took countervailing actions. As of mid-2011, 19 developing countries had trade remedy measures in place involving at least some anti-dumping, which accounted for over 90% of the remedial actions they took (Michalopoulos 2014).

Among developing countries, anti-dumping is, for the most part, a middle and higher income developing country practice. Argentina, Brazil, China, India, Korea, Mexico and South Africa account for the bulk of developing country actions. Pakistan is the country with the lowest per capita income that has initiated an anti-dumping action. India is the country that has taken the most measures over the period.

Services

There are no comparable international data that permit a systematic examination of the state of policies regarding restrictions on trade in services in developing or developed countries. The reasons are well known: because many of the modes of delivery of services are intangible, there are no barriers that take the form of tariffs. Barriers take the form of quantitative restrictions—sometimes involving complete bans, and often government regulation.

Some of the latter may be explicitly discriminatory against imports of services or foreign providers; others may be of a general regulatory nature that apply equally to national and foreign service providers. And to date no general description of the barriers to trade in services that cuts across all four modes of delivery (cross-border supply, consumption abroad, commercial presence and temporary entry) and all sectors has been attempted—and may not be feasible with the present state of data collection.

Some general impressions can be obtained as to what the actual policy situation tends to be by using a recently developed World Bank database (see Table 6.2). The first impression from the existing data is that developed countries have liberalized far more than developing countries, especially in the financial, telecommunication and retail service sectors. The differences are smaller in the transport sector and even less in professional services, which frequently requires the movement of natural persons.

Table 6.2 Sectoral Service Trade Restrictiveness Indices (STRI) in developing countries

Country	STRI (0 = open; 100 = close)					
	Overall	Financial	Telecom	Retail	Transport	Professional
Argentina	17	10	0	0	22	49
Bangladesh	44	46	63	25	63	35
Benin	–	–	–	–	–	–
Bolivia	14	19	25	0	10	21
Brazil	23	36	0	0	10	58
Cameroon	26	21	0	25	30	43
Chile	23	22	25	25	19	27
China	37	35	50	25	19	66
Colombia	18	25	50	0	4	34
Costa Rica	29	29	38	0	30	60
Cote d'Ivoire	26	14	25	0	31	68
Dominican Rep.	12	3	0	0	22	33
Egypt	52	43	25	50	50	82
El Salvador	–	–	–	–	–	–
Fiji	–	–	–	–	–	–
Ghana	18	25	25	0	6	44
Honduras	21	7	50	0	35	34
Hong Kong, China	–	–	–	–	–	–
India	66	48	50	75	62	88
Indonesia	50	23	25	50	66	76
Jamaica	–	–	–	–	–	–
Kenya	30	23	25	0	31	73
Korea, Rep.	23	2	50	0	21	66
Kuwait	52	42	75	50	50	57
Malawi	34	35	50	25	32	38
Malaysia	46	45	25	25	55	73

(continued)

Table 6.2 (continued)

Country	STRI (0 = open; 100 = close)					
	Overall	Financial	Telecom	Retail	Transport	Professional
Mauritius	17	9	0	0	31	42
Mexico	30	15	38	0	62	43
Morocco	21	14	25	0	28	46
Mozambique	19	17	75	0	6	30
Nepal	43	23	50	25	56	76
Nigeria	27	26	25	25	24	36
Pakistan	28	49	13	0	25	48
Paraguay	16	22	38	0	5	25
Peru	16	42	0	0	3	28
Philippines	54	45	50	50	44	80
Saudi Arabia	43	46	25	25	39	72
Senegal	19	16	25	0	25	37
Singapore	–	–	–	–	–	–
South Africa	35	20	25	25	41	62
Sri Lanka	38	24	50	25	46	57
Taiwan, China	–	–	–	–	–	–
Thailand	48	49	50	25	47	74
Tunisia	45	33	25	25	55	79
Uganda	35	28	25	50	21	38
Uruguay	28	45	63	0	41	11
Venezuela	35	23	25	25	32	69
Viet Nam	42	41	50	50	39	32
Zambia	21	8	75	0	10	44
Zimbabwe	64	56	63	75	68	60
Average	32	28	35	19	33	51
Memo Items						
EU-20	26	4	0	25	37	54
United States	18	21	0	0	8	54

Source: World Bank, DECTI Service Trade Restrictions database
Note: Data is based on the latest year available from 106 countries in the database

Service protection in developing countries can have serious implications on efficiency and growth: protection causes high-cost expensive service inputs, which results both in waste of resources and in adverse effects on export performance of both goods and other services. A protected and inefficient banking sector can be as damaging to profitability of exportables as the imposition of high tariffs on imported components used in the production of these same exportables.

Among developing countries, there is strong evidence that countries in Latin America and the Caribbean have liberalized far more than other developing country regions in all sectors. In retail and transport their liberalization is at least as great as that of developed countries. There are few differences in the degree of service liberalization by sector in other groups of developing countries classified by region or income level. Some low-income developing countries, such as Ghana and Nigeria, have relatively liberal regimes, while several economies in Asia with fast-growing export sectors, such as China, India, Indonesia, Malaysia and the Philippines, have restrictive service sectors.

As to the trend over time, it is clear that developing countries are moving, in general, toward more liberal regimes in services. A large number of developing countries made forward liberalization commitments in the Uruguay Round Agreements on Financial Services and Telecommunications with many of the commitments to start in 2000.

Following the Uruguay Round Agreements, the situation regarding the formal commitments of developing countries to maintain a liberal services trade regime parallels the situation with respect to tariffs: in both cases the actual policies are far short of the commitments. Except in the case of services, the difference is often greater. Actual policies in developing countries in all major regional groupings, restrictive as they may be, are still far more liberal than their commitments—just like applied tariffs are far lower than bindings.

Looking at the pattern of commitments in the Uruguay Round by the range of commitment and degree of development, a similar pattern develops to that observed in trade policy on goods: the degree of liberalization appears to increase with the level of income. Lower income countries appear to have committed to much less liberalization than higher income ones. The basic justification that low-income countries make for not liberalizing their service sector is the same infant industry argument used for so very long in the areas of merchandise trade. There are obvious dangers and limits to such a strategy as many developing countries have realized in the areas of goods. These dangers have to be seriously evaluated by low-income developing countries which continue to protect their service sectors. The service sector continues to offer opportunities for further liberalization as well as for action by developing countries to create more secure access to their markets, which in turn could have beneficial effects on their long-term development.

Preferential Trade Arrangements

In tandem with global integration, many developing countries have made intensive integration efforts at a regional level. Two types of measure can be distinguished in this regard: regional PTAs with other developing countries, and similar PTAs with developed countries. Examples of the former include the MERCOSUR customs union, which involves several countries in South America, and the South Africa Development Community (SADC), a free trade area among 14 developing countries in South and East Africa. Examples of North–South regional integration include the North America Free Trade Area (NAFTA) as well as the various regional agreements between the EU and the different groups of ACP countries (WTO 2011).

Although developing countries are involved in a lot of PTAs, the total trade involved is relatively small: almost 50% of all trade among PTA partners involves the EU and another 13% involves NAFTA. The bulk of the PTAs involve preferential tariffs on merchandise trade; but there are also a few involving only services; and a growing number involve both goods and services as well as other aspects of 'deeper integration' such as cooperation in competition policy, investment and protection of intellectual property rights.

The preferential margins on tariffs on average are small, only about 2%, as MFN tariffs have come down in many countries; and developing countries enjoy other unilateral preferences in developed country markets. Few tariff lines have preferential margins of more than five percentage points. However, for some countries, for example Mauritius, preferential margins in EU markets are high as a number of its products (e.g., textiles and sugar) are subject to substantial barriers.

The trend toward more PTAs by developing countries raises questions about the effects on the participants as well as third countries. There are also issues as to consistency with broader multilateral efforts to liberalize trade under the WTO.

First, regarding the effects on non-participants, there is some evidence that trade diversion effects in some cases, for example MERCOSUR, can be adverse and substantial (Chang and Winters 2002). The question of consistency with the multilateral trading system has two aspects: a narrow (and less interesting) one, which has to do with the consistency of the multitude of PTAs with Article 24 of GATT and the Enabling Clause Provisions; and the broader one of whether the spread of PTAs benefits or hurts global welfare and whether it undermines future efforts to liberalize trade on a multilateral basis.

The WTO established a committee to review the very large number of PTAs which had been notified to it in order to determine their consistency with WTO provisions. After several years of reviewing dozens of the more than 400 PTAs that had been notified, the WTO gave up. In 2006, the General Council decided that it would no longer attempt to determine consistency—rather it would opt for transparency, that is, information on what is happening. Any member who wished to challenge consistency would have to use the dispute settlement mechanism. Few of them have taken that route.

The problem derives from the fact that existing WTO provisions are broad enough to give considerable latitude of interpretation. The lack of consensus results primarily from the desire of many members, including developing countries, to have as much flexibility as possible in the conclusion of such agreements. One can take a relaxed attitude about the current situation. There has been a lot of MFN liberalization under the previous Rounds, thus reducing the chance of trade diversion. And many of these agreements contain provisions which have little to do with preferences. Still, there is a danger that the multiplicity of agreements will yield welfare-reducing results both for the participants and for the rest of the world (Panagariya 2000). Some of the non-trade-related provisions pose dangers for developing countries. And, there is also the danger that the existing preferential arrangements will result in a reluctance to engage in multilateral MFN reductions on account of many countries losing preferences.

Developed Country Policies

Since the 1980s, the role of developed country markets in determining demand for developing countries exports has shrunk as the role of the emerging economies increased, especially in the decade of the 2000s. On the other hand, the market access conditions for developing countries improved, partly as a result of standstills and subsequent liberalization linked to the Uruguay Round Agreements, the termination of the Agreement on Textiles and Clothing and as a result of numerous preferential arrangements concluded between developed and developing countries.

The implementation of the Uruguay Round Agreements took a number of years to complete and there was some retrogression following the severe economic crisis of 2008. But there is little doubt that access to developed country markets was much better at the end of the 1990s than at the beginning as a consequence of the Uruguay Round and the establishment of the WTO. Access continued to be impeded by high trade barriers in certain sectors, such as agriculture; and while progress was made on tariff escalation, the problem persisted in textiles and leather products. More barriers are also appearing connected to the implementation of the TBT and SPS agreements.

Broadly speaking, under the Uruguay Round Agreements, MFN tariffs on imports of manufactures into the major industrial countries' markets were reduced by an average of 40% from a trade-weighted average of 6.3% to 3.8% with the reductions to be phased in over five years and the first installment to be put in place on January 1, 1995.[6] Countries have reduced their tariff rates accordingly since then. Moreover, in 1997, following the Information Technology Agreement, the duty on a number of products in this sector was reduced to zero on an MFN basis (Finger and Schuknecht 1999). Applied rates are even lower, averaging 3.2%, reflecting various preferential arrangements (see Michalopoulos 2014, p. 139).

MFN tariffs on products other than agriculture range, for example, from an average of 0.8% in Japan to 3.7% in the US and 4.0% in the EU (UNCTAD 1997, Annex Table 1). But the rates are higher on products of interest to developing countries (Hertel and Martin 1999). At the same time, for the Quad countries (Canada, the EU, Japan, the US), one-third of all MFN tariff lines are duty free, involving a large range of products of export interest to the developing countries.

The tariffication of various measures of support and protection in the agricultural sector resulted in substantial increases in the initial tariffs on a wide range of agricultural products in some major markets. Thus, the average applied MFN rate for agricultural commodities (production weighted) in 1996 ranged from 7.9% in the US to 10.7% in the EU (OECD 1997, Table 3.1). Subsequently, developed countries were to reduce agricultural tariffs by 36% across the board, at the same time as access for agricultural products would be enhanced by reductions in domestic support measures.

The problem was that developed (and developing) countries chose to bind their tariffs at higher rates than the actual tariff equivalents during the years just before the conclusion of the Uruguay Round Agreements (1989–1993). For example, the final bindings for the EU were almost two-thirds higher than the tariff equivalents for 1989–1993 (Binswagner and Lutz 2000, p. 9) and for the US, they were more than three-quarters higher. Binding the tariffs at such high levels allowed countries to vary actual tariff rates according to the results they wished to achieve in protecting their domestic markets—much as the EU used to do with the variable levies, which have been prohibited since the Uruguay Round. The result of this so-called dirty tariffication has not been improved market access, merely that protection has become more transparent. Similarly, commitments to reduce export subsidies were made relative to a base period in the early 1990s when these subsidies were at very high levels.

The actual tariff rates applied to imports from individual developing countries tend to be even lower than the above MFN rates, however. There are two main reasons for this: (1) the GSP, which further reduces tariffs on selected commodities and countries; (2) the existence of preferential arrangements for particular countries in specific developed country markets, for example, the preferences afforded to the ACP countries in the EU market, the ones enjoyed by Mexico as part of NAFTA, and the Caribbean and Central American countries' preferential treatment in the US market as a consequence of the Caribbean Basin Initiative and the AGOA initiative affecting low-income countries in Africa. In addition, individual developed countries have granted even more preferential treatment to LDC imports following the WTO High Level Meeting on Trade-Related Measures for LDCs in 1997 (see below).

Despite the overall decline in the average applied MFN tariffs since the Uruguay Round, there are a number of sectors and product groups in various developed countries where tariffs are substantially higher, thus limiting market access. But in all countries there are many products and product groups in which the average MFN applied tariff level exceeds 12%, or roughly three times the overall average MFN applied tariff level of developed countries. These products and groups can be defined as having tariff 'peaks'. They exist in both agriculture and manufactures in a number of developed country markets. But the very high rates typically have been the consequence of tariffication in agriculture.[7]

Tariff escalation is a matter of concern for developing countries in the context of market access because it tends to increase the rate of effective protection at higher stages of processing, thereby making market access more difficult for finished manufactured products, which in turn can adversely affect developing countries' industrialization efforts. As a consequence of the Uruguay Round Agreements, the degree of overall escalation has decreased. But it continues to be a matter of concern for many developing countries and their exports of specific products, such as pro cessed foods (wheat flour, orange juice, vegetable oils, dairy products), clothing, leather and wood products (Lindbland 1997; UNCTAD 1997). These results should be interpreted with caution because data limitations as well as the continued existence of quantitative restrictions in some of these product chains make it difficult to calculate the effective rates of protection. But they do suggest that tariff escalation—as with tariff peaks—in certain products, though reduced by the Uruguay Round Agreements, continues to be an area of concern in respect to market access for developing country exports.

Non-tariff Measures

Since the Uruguay Round and until about 2009, the pervasiveness of core non-tariff measures in developed country trade regimes had fallen to its lowest point in more than 50 years. By core non-tariff barriers, I mean the use of non-automatic licensing, quotas and tariff quotas and voluntary export restraints as well as price control measures such as variable charges, minimum prices or voluntary export price restraints. Since 2009, there has been some resurgence of protectionism (see Chap. 10). The key issues for the future relate to the use of trade remedies, that is, anti-dumping, countervailing and safeguards, all of which are permitted under the WTO agreements, as well as the expanding use of SPS and TBT measures, which have an impact on trade.

Voluntary export restraints were phased out by the end of 1998—although there have been some reports of their 'informal' re-emergence in recent periods. Some remaining export restraints in developed countries appear to be directed in significant measure against non-WTO members. The termination of the Agreement on Textiles and Clothing in 2005 as well as the end in 2008 of the special quantitative restrictions applied to imports from China as part of its WTO accession ended the last vestiges of formal 'legal' quantitative restraints in manufactures.

The Uruguay Round resulted in the drastic reduction of non-tariff measures in agriculture, where only tariff quotas were permitted to exist in a number of products in some of the major developed markets. These range from a few tariff lines in the US and Australia up to 1.5% in Japan and 4.9% in the EU (see Michalopoulos 2014, Table 6.1). At the same time, the use of non-automatic licensing has been reduced in all major developed country markets and is now focusing primarily on restraints linked to the maintenance of sanitary, phytosanitary and technical standards or protection for the environment where concerns have been raised as to whether the implementation of WTO agreements in these areas has been motivated by protection of domestic industries.

The reduction of NTMs in agriculture after the conclusion of the Uruguay Round does not seem to have resulted in significant improvements in market access for developing countries for a variety of reasons. First, there were problems with the way tariffication was implemented, as discussed earlier. Second, the reductions of AMS have not affected the significant supports to products of interest to developing countries such as cotton, sugar and dairy products. Third, despite the commitments to reduce export subsidies, these have been maintained at such high levels as to continue to undermine incentives provided to developing country producers. Examples of the adverse effects of export subsidies on developing country producers abound: subsidies in dairy products have hurt production in a large range of countries, including Brazil, Jamaica and Tanzania; subsidies on tomato concentrate impact especially on West African countries like Burkina Faso, Mali and Senegal; support for beef has undermined efforts to raise livestock production in some of the same countries; and EU beef has come to dominate the markets of Benin and Ivory Coast for which Burkina Faso and Mali were once important suppliers. In effect, there was far less 'real' improvement in the agricultural sector than was anticipated.

Trade Remedies

Over the last 30 years, as the incidence of quotas and other explicitly protective quantitative controls has diminished, the importance of trade remedies—anti-dumping, countervailing and safeguards—has risen in both developed and developing countries. The establishment of WTO has resulted in more explicit rules and greater transparency in the application of these measures. In the US, which over the years has instigated the largest number of total anti-dumping investigations and still has some measures in place which were instituted more than 40 years ago, only 1.1% of total imports are affected by trade remedies (Michalopoulos 2014, Table 6.1). At the same time, as discussed earlier, the evidence is extremely clear that the share of developing countries in the total remedies has increased dramatically.

Most of the developed-country anti-dumping measures against developing countries have been directed at higher- and middle-income developing countries, often the same countries that have themselves made increasing use of anti-dumping measures themselves. Bangladesh is the only LDC to have been subjected to anti-dumping investigations and definitive measures on three occasions, in 1992 (see Miranda et al. 1998).

Developed countries, on the other hand, are the least targeted group both by other developed countries and developing countries. In particular, the share of anti-dumping actions in which developing countries are affected is much higher than the share of developing countries in world exports. So much for the WTO provision which calls for the developed countries 'to give special regard to the special situation of developing countries' in applying anti-dumping measures.

There is also evidence (Michalopoulos 2014, Table 6.3) that in the 1990s, the incidence of anti-dumping actions taken against China, Chinese Taipei and non-WTO members, especially so-called non-market economies, which consisted mostly of countries other than the Baltics that emerged from the former Soviet Union, in particular Russia, Ukraine, Belarus and Kazakhstan, was much greater than their share in world trade. Indeed, controlling for the value of total exports over the last three decades, anti-dumping measures were at least four times more likely to be directed against a product from a non-market economy which is not a WTO member than a product from a developed market economy. And with respect to so-called non-market economies, there is evidence indicating that the procedures used tend to be more opaque and may well lead to a greater incidence of definitive findings than those against other economies (Michalopoulos and Winters 1997).

SPS and TBT

The implementation of the SPS and TBT agreements has raised two sets of issues for developing countries. First, standards along with testing and certification represent between 2 and 10% of overall product costs. Thus, they impose a burden on developing country exports—even when the standards are used for legitimate reasons and the countries are able to meet them. Second, while the two agreements may make developed countries actions more transparent and force a degree of accountability, they may also serve to legitimize developed country NTMs that unnecessarily restrain developing countries' trade.

The pioneering work of Otsuki et al. (2001) estimated that a 1998 EC regulation that imposed more stringent controls on the maximum level for certain types of aflatoxin (a toxic substance) found in foodstuffs and animal feed, than those required by the Codex Alimentarius, would cost close to $700 million in lost revenue to African exporters of groundnuts. Wilson et al. (2003) found that the stringency of antibiotics regulation in developed countries significantly reduced bovine meat exports for Argentina, Brazil and South Africa. And several studies have concluded that SPS regulations inhibit developing country agriculture and food exports (Cadot and Malouche 2012, p. 6).

Early complaints by developing countries that developed countries may be using the SPS agreement as disguised protection had focused on meat (Burkina Faso), fresh fruits and vegetables (Kenya), canned tuna (Papua New Guinea) and fish (Uganda). In 2001–2012, more than 1,000 notifications of new SPS measures and a slightly larger number of TBT notifications were submitted to the WTO. About 60% of the SPS notifications and the bulk of the TBT notifications came from developing countries. As the overall developing country share of world trade as well of SPS and TBT notifications is increasing, it is clear that this may not be a North–South problem but a general NTM issue. But the establishment of the TBT and SPS agreements in 1995 and the increasing use of these measures as well as an increasing number of disputes arising from their use is posing a major challenge for the future of international trade in commodities.

Services

There are no systematic investigations of developed country policy regarding trade in services and the implications of restrictions they impose on potential exports from developing countries. Existing data suggest that their overall policies on service imports are more liberal than those of the developing countries and that the gap between actual policies and Uruguay Round commitments is smaller. But, there is one mode of delivery, the movement on natural persons, in which they tend to be more restrictive than developing countries, regardless of the sector. Liberalization in this area would be of considerable benefit to developing countries because of their comparative advantage of providing labor-intensive services across all modes of supply. In addition, there is one sector, maritime services, where international competition is extremely limited and there are serious constraints deriving from national legislation that actively discriminates against foreign suppliers.

While some progress has been made regarding the movement of qualified professionals to work abroad, developed country restrictions inhibit increased service earnings for developing countries through this mode of supply. The commitments on trade in services have tended to emphasize measures regulating commercial presence—which is important for foreign direct investment, rather than 'mode four' involving movement of natural persons.

There are various kinds of quantitative restrictions on the number of persons that are provided with visas annually. There are also restrictions deriving from the existence of qualification and licensing requirements of professional organizations that formally discriminate against foreign qualified professionals. Still other barriers involve wage-matching requirements such as those demanding wages paid to foreigners be the same as those to nationals or those demanding the provision of local training.

There are many sectors in which developing countries have a comparative advantage, usually based on labor costs, and which can benefit from developed country liberalization, in particular software development and construction services. The former is an area where developing country exports, for example from India, have been expanding very rapidly in recent periods. A lot of these exports involve on-shore delivery because of the importance of the need for continuous contact between client and programmer. While technological and managerial innovations may result in a decline of the share of on-shore delivery, and an increase to come mainly through cross-border trade, the increase in software demand from developing countries may be so high as to require continued liberalization of existing limitations in 'mode four' restrictions. Similarly, several developing countries, especially in Asia, have the capacity of exporting construction services based on their comparative advantage in labor-intensive activities which are constrained by developed country restrictions on 'movement of natural persons'.

In maritime services there are extensive government restrictions in cabotage and cargo handling. At the same time, oceans continue to be populated by cartels known as shipping conferences. These cartels set prices and pursue other collusive activities in the substantial portion of maritime services they control and are often exempted from anti-trust law in developed countries (Francois and Wooton 1999). Their impact in raising transport costs to poorer developing countries, especially to low-volume, high-distance destinations such as in Africa and poorer island economies, can be even more important than further tariff liberalization: shipping margins on merchandise trade in Sub-Saharan Africa exceed 6% compared with OECD tariffs (after preferences are taken into account) of less than 2%. Liberalization in this sector, which would lead to increased competition and reduced margins, may be of great importance to many of the small economy members of the WTO.

WTO's Early Years

The ink on the WTO agreements had not even dried before both developed and developing countries started pushing for their modification. The developed countries wanted to extend the WTO mandate to cover aspects of competition policy, environment issues, labor regulations, investment and trade facilitation. Their objective was to establish legally enforceable rules in these areas and use the enhanced WTO dispute settlement mechanism to protect their interests. The developing countries opposed further expansion of the WTO mandate and on their part started to complain that the developed countries were not meeting their commitments to 'implement' the Marrakesh agreements regarding special and differential treatment especially with respect to the provision of technical and financial assistance.

At WTO's first Ministerial Meeting in Singapore in 1996, a new agreement liberalizing trade in Information Technology was signed among 40 members. It was also agreed to establish working groups to study the issues of trade and competition, foreign investment, government procurement and trade facilitation. Finally, members decided to review aspects of the implementation of the agreements on services, TRIPS and agriculture as well as the provision of assistance to the LDCs.

In order to implement the latter agreement, a high-level meeting on LDCs was organized jointly by UNCTAD and the WTO in Geneva in October 1997. The meeting formalized a twin-track approach in respect of special and differential treatment of these countries in the WTO, with one track emphasizing their limited commitments to liberalization, and the other track emphasizing the increased commitment by developed countries in respect of market access and technical assistance. In that context, a number of WTO members announced measures for improved and preferential market access for LDCs. With regard to technical assistance, an 'Integrated Framework for Trade Related Technical Assistance to Support Least Developed Countries in their Trade Related Activities' was developed, involving the IMF, ITC, UNCTAD, the United Nations Development Program (UNDP), the World Bank and the WTO. This Integrated Framework seeks to address shortcomings in technical and institutional capacity, particularly in the areas of trade policy, human resources, export supply capability and regulatory regimes. After a lot of international discussion, a new WTO unit was established to implement the mandate of this program, a decade later in 2007.

I arrived in Geneva to start my two-year assignment as special advisor to the WTO secretariat on loan from the World Bank in late June 1997, just as the preparations for the high-level meeting on the LDCs were going into high gear. I quickly found out that nobody in the WTO hierarchy was interested in my advice about anything in particular, whether linked to the LDCs or otherwise. However, my contacts both with the developing country delegations and WTO Secretariat staff convinced me of the great weaknesses in the developing countries' institutional capacity to participate and represent their interests effectively in the new organization.

I heard many stories from delegates to the effect that they had been pressured to sign the Marrakesh agreements by the EU and the US or else—meaning lower bilateral aid levels; and that some had not even understood what they were signing. The facts were that many developing country delegations did not even have representation in Geneva but were trying to follow WTO activities through their representatives in Brussels—with pretty bad results (see Michalopoulos 2001). I devoted considerable time in the next two years analyzing the institutional constraints limiting these countries' participation in the WTO and developing recommendations as to how to address them.

Before the end of the century several new institutions were set up in Geneva to help developing country participate more effectively in the WTO. Most notable were the Advisory Centre on WTO Law, which was established in 1998, and it still provides assistance to developing countries in matters related to specific cases involving the DSM, be this as a complainant or plaintiff; and the Agency for International Trade Information and Co-operation (AITIC), which starting from 1998 and for a decade helped low-income developing country delegations participation in the WTO through seminars, information dissemination and training. UNCTAD also is playing a smaller role as a political forum than in the 1960s and 1970s, but is focusing more on analyses of developing country trade and foreign investment issues and perspectives. And the International Trade Centre, jointly sponsored by WTO and UNCTAD, provides technical assistance to developing countries for export development and promotion.[8]

In 1998, the WTO celebrated the 50-year anniversary of the GATT with a big ministerial-level meeting in Geneva. The meeting achieved nothing of substance, except to agree to a work program aimed at a ministerial meeting in Seattle that would launch a new round of multilateral negotiations. Probably the most important new element was the extreme security precautions that were taken in advance of the meeting to protect the participants from the expected massive demonstrations against the WTO, which in the very short period of its existence had managed to become the symbol of the all the ills of globalization. In the end, it was mostly a false alarm as not too many demonstrators showed up. But it was a warning of things to come, and a signal of the fundamental issues resulting from globalization that were just emerging at the time but which were to materialize with great force 20 years later.

The Debacle in Seattle

Developing countries were not very interested in a new Round of negotiations. They were very concerned that developed countries had not been implementing in good faith their commitments under the Uruguay Round Agreements. There was considerable evidence that the Agreement on Agriculture had made developed country support for their farmers more transparent but had not significantly reduced protection. Their so-called dirty tariffication and the continued, if somewhat reduced, export subsidies inflicted a considerable burden on developing countries agricultural exports. Thus, while the letter of the agreement may have been followed, in practice it had generated few benefits to the developing countries. Similarly, developed countries were back-loading the liberalization of textiles and clothing—as they were entitled to do under the agreement. On TRIPS, the EU and the US had aggressively pursued their rights and had successfully prosecuted complaints against India through the dispute settlement mechanism for its non-performance under the provisions of the agreement and were threatening similar action against South Africa. At the same time, the TRIPS provisions for technology transfer by developed countries were nothing but empty promises.

In this climate, it was extremely important that the Seattle ministerial be very carefully prepared to ensure that developing country concerns be addressed. This did not happen and the texts that went to Seattle in early December constituted a 'hodgepodge of issues that no one thought was adequate for a ministerial conference' (Hoekman and Kostecki 2001, p. 107). The US representative Charlene Barshevsky, who was to chair the conference, spent some of her time in advance of the meeting in China—which was not a WTO member yet and would not be for a few more years, instead of trying to help iron out differences among the participants, especially developing countries. The Seattle meeting itself turned out to be a disaster for a variety of reasons: Barshevsky was perceived to pursue the US agenda, including trying to respond to domestic concerns arising from the opposition of US labor unions, instead of trying to bridge differences among the various participants. Smaller developing countries felt they were being left out of the discussions partly because massive anti-WTO and anti-globalization demonstrations impeded access to the meeting venues. In the end, the conference ran out of time. Its venue had to be vacated as it had been previously booked by an optometrist convention. Its communiqué concluded without agreement except that the WTO would continue its work on its in-built agenda—services, agriculture and TRIPS.

By the time of the conference, I had returned from WTO to a position with the World Bank office in Brussels. Deeply disappointed by its outcome, I wrote a letter to the *Financial Times,* holding Barshevsky personally responsible for its failure and suggesting that she should resign.

I signed the letter in my personal capacity, gave my Brussels home address and did not indicate my World Bank affiliation. Its publication apparently caused some consternation to US trade officials who complained to my superiors at the World Bank. They in turn complained to me about this great misdeed. What a difference from the times when I was in USAID and I would publish long articles and letters incompatible with US policies and sign them with my name and formal US government affiliation. I believe the incident reflects only in small part the sensitivity of my Bank superiors to a demarche from the largest shareholder. It shows primarily how sensitive the US executive is on trade as opposed to aid policy issues.

The Seattle meeting was a sad end to a decade when a great deal of progress had been made in setting up a new trade institution that had the capacity to address the multiple challenges posed by globalization. It is an institution in which developing countries would play an increasing role after overcoming a great number of problems created by their own institutional weaknesses. But it is an institution which maintained the tradition of the GATT in reflecting primarily the commercial interests of its members. Whether the representatives are from developed or developing countries, they have little to say about the impact of the trade policies over which they argue in addressing the problem of global poverty. Progress in reducing the latter depends very much on a whole range of additional other supportive policies and institutions which will be discussed in Chaps. 7 and 8 below.

Notes

1. Participants in the final negotiations for establishing the WTO have indicated that there was a tacit understanding that transition periods in the implementation of some of these agreements were linked to transition periods in the implementation of the Agreement on Textiles and Clothing.
2. See inter alia SPS Article 9.1; TBT Articles 11, 12.7; Implementation of GATT Article VII–Article 20.3; The Agreement on Pre-shipment Inspection, Article 1.2; TRIPS Article 67; DSB Article 27.2; the Trade Policy Review Mechanism (TPRM).

3. However, developing countries seeking to accede to the WTO do not benefit automatically from transitional provisions (Drabek and Laird 1998).
4. The simple arithmetic average should be interpreted with care: the data refer to different years in each of the decades. Some rates may have also increased since the data were collected.
5. Escalation is measured by calculating the average tariff rates applied to three groups of products: raw materials, intermediate products and final goods.
6. The EU advanced from January 1, 1997, to January 1, 1996, its schedule of implementation of the third stage of tariff reductions for most non-agricultural products as part of its compensation for the EU enlargement through the accession of Austria, Finland and Sweden (WTO 1997, p. 15).
7. One can speak of 'mega-tariffs' for tariff lines in excess of 100%. According to one report, in agriculture alone the US has 24 mega-tariffs, the EU 141 and Japan 142.
8. A number of NGOs also devoted significant attention to the WTO and trade issues, in particular, the South Centre and the International Centre for Trade and Sustainable Development.

References

Binswagner, H. and E. Lutz (2000) *Agricultural Trade Barriers, Trade Negotiations and the Interests of Developing Countries*, UNCTAD X, TD(X)/RT.1/8.

Cadot, O. and M. Malouche (2012) 'Overview,' in O. Cadot and M. Malouche, (eds.) *Non-Tariff Measures: A Fresh Look at Trade Policy's New Frontier*, (Washington, DC: CEPR and World Bank).

Chang, W. and L. A. Winters (2002) "How Regional Blocks Affect Excluded Countries: the Price Effects of Mercosur" *American Economic Review*, 92(4): 889–904.

Das, J. (1998) *The WTO Agreements: Deficiencies, Imbalances and Required Changes,* (Penang: Third World Network).

Drabek, Z. and S. Laird. (1998) 'The New Liberalism: Trade Policy Developments in Emerging Markets,' *Journal of World Trade*, 5(3):241–269.

Finger, J. M. and P. Schuler (2000) 'The Implementation of Uruguay Round Commitments: The Development Challenge' *Policy Research Working Paper* No. 2215, (Washington, DC: World Bank).

Finger, J. M. and L. Schuknecht (1999) Market Access Advances and Retreats since the Uruguay Round, *Policy Research Working Paper*, No. 2232, (Washington, DC: World Bank).

Folleti, L. et al. (2009) 'Smoke in the Water' in S.J. Evenett, B.M. Hoekman and O. Cattaneo (Eds) *Effective Crisis Response and Openness* (Washington, DC: CEPR and World Bank).

Francois, J. and I. Wooton. (1999) 'Trade in International Transport Services: the Role of Competition,' mimeo, Erasmus University, Rotterdam, August.

Hertel, T. and W. Martin (1999) 'Developing Countries Interests in Liberalizing Manufactures Trade,' CEPR Workshop: London, 19–20 February.

Hoekman, B.M. and M.M. Kostecki (2001) *The Political Economy of the World Trading System*, (Oxford: Oxford University Press).

Kessie, E. (2000) 'Enforceability of the Legal Provisions Relating to Special and Differential Treatment under the WTO Agreements', paper presented at WTO Seminar on Special and Differential Treatment of Developing Countries, Geneva., 7 March.

Lindbland, J. (1997) The Impact of the Uruguay Round on Tariff Escalation in Agricultural Products, ESCP, No. 3, FAO: Rome.

Michalopoulos, C. (2001) *Developing Countries in the WTO*, (Houndmills: Palgrave).

———. (2014a) *Emerging Powers in the WTO*, (Houndmills: Palgrave Macmillan).

Michalopoulos, C. and L. A. Winters (1997) 'Summary and Overview,' in P. D. Ehrenhaft *et al, Policies on Imports from Economies in Transition,* Studies of Economies in Transformation, No. 22, (Washington, DC: World Bank).

Miranda, J., R. Torres and M. Ruiz (1998) 'The International Use of Antidumping: 1987–1997,' *Journal of World Trade*, 32(5): 5–71.

Otsuki, T., J. Wilson and M. Sewadah (2001) 'What Price Precaution? Europe's Harmonization of Aflatoxin Regulations and African Groundnut Exports,' *European Review of Agricultural Economics*, 28(3): 263–84.

Panagariya, A. (2000) 'Preferential Trade Liberalization: The Traditional Theory And New Developments', *Journal of Economic Literature* 38(2).

OECD (1997) *Indicators of Tariff and Non-Tariff Barrier,*(Paris: OECD).

UNCTAD (1997) "Post-Uruguay Round Tariff Environment for Developing Country Exports," UNCTAD/WTO Joint Study, TD/B/COM.1/14, October.

Wilson, J. et al. (2003) 'Balancing Food Safety and Risk' Journal of International Trade and Economic Development, (12) 4:377–402.

WTO (1995) *The Results of the Uruguay Round of Multilateral Trade Negotiations: The Legal Texts*, WTO, Geneva.

WTO (1997) *Trade Policy Review: European Union*, PRESs/TPRB/65.

WTO (2011) 'The WTO and Preferential Trade: from Co-existence to Coherence', *World Trade Report*, WTO: Geneva.

7

The Many Faces of Globalization

Introduction

Globalization is a process. It is difficult to pinpoint a particular event or year as a starting point. Various aspects of it affect countries and communities at different speeds and at different times. Earlier chapters have noted the increasing integration of developing countries in the world trading system and the large private and public capital flows that permitted financing of the huge deficits resulting from the first oil crisis in the 1970s.[1] Some writers make a case that the new wave of globalization started in the 1980s when a large group of developing countries broke into global markets (World Bank 2002b, p. 31). Chapter 5 highlighted the seminal events of 1989. Richard Baldwin in a recently published volume makes a case that 1990 is a good starting point for the latest globalization storm because it is the beginning of a 'most shocking share shift' involving a massive decline in the share of G-7 countries of world income. This decline was mirrored by an increase in the world share of just 11 countries which include the usual suspects, Brazil, China, India but also Indonesia, Korea and Nigeria[2] (Baldwin 2016, p. 2). It was precipitated by 'revolutionary advances in information and communication technol-

© The Author(s) 2017
C. Michalopoulos, *Aid, Trade and Development,*
https://doi.org/10.1007/978-3-319-65861-2_7

ogy (ICT) which made it possible to organize complex production processes even when they were separated internationally' (Baldwin 2016, p. 8).

Whatever we may think about Baldwin's hypothesis, it is clear that by 1990, globalization in various forms was happening and spreading across all regions. Its impact on various countries and groups was diverse. It was affected by policy decisions: trade policy liberalization either autonomous or in the context of multilateral negotiations affected trade in goods and services, one of the traditional dimensions of globalization. The opening up of the capital account of the balance of payments to flows of short-term capital by many developing countries was equally policy driven. The political decisions involved in the breakup of the Soviet Union, obviously, increased the openness of the new states and their involvement in the global economy. But in the short run, and for many of them for the whole decade, it involved such dislocations as to increase their poverty.

This chapter will review the experience with growth and poverty alleviation of the main regional groupings of developing countries during the 1990s. Then I will discuss the results of a number of studies which have attempted to link globalization with particular outcomes in terms of growth and poverty alleviation. The final two sections examine the impact of two key globalizing policies on developing countries poverty alleviation: the policies on international trade and capital flows, including both official assistance and private capital. The latter is important to review as it has undoubtedly played a far more greater role in development than aid in the 1990s and in the years thereafter.

Growth and Poverty in the 1990s

Developing country experience with growth and poverty alleviation in the 1990s was on the whole significantly better than during the debt-ridden 1980s. But it was extremely varied, with China and East Asia moving rapidly ahead leaving Sub-Saharan Africa far behind, with the rest of the developing world performance falling somewhere in between.

East Asia: Miracles and Controversies

The East Asian economies are quite diverse, ranging from very populous large countries like China to very small island-states like Singapore and countries with a large natural resource base like Indonesia and Malaysia and others with a very limited one like Korea and Taiwan. Yet, they share many similarities both in policies and in outcomes.

On the policy front, all the countries have given priority to the pursuit of policies to maintain macroeconomic stability. Over long periods, the budget and current account deficits of these countries were half the average for other developing countries (Leipziger 1997), partly because most had not borrowed as much as Latin America and partly because they pursued more outward-oriented trade policies sooner (see below); they weathered the 1980s storm better.

They also maintained high rates of savings and investment. From 1990 to 1997, their domestic savings rate was 36% of GDP compared to 20% in Latin America and the Caribbean and 17% in Sub-Saharan Africa. This was augmented by an open door policy to foreign direct investment. The combination of high domestic savings and large inflows of foreign private capital led to very high investment rates, which, moreover, were utilized productively, including high rates of investment in education, health and infrastructure.

Their trade policy involved a complex set of credit and other incentives to exports combined with domestic protection but with extensive rebates on imported inputs. They also maintained a relatively stable real exchange rate. These policies resulted in substantially neutral incentives for sales to the domestic and the foreign market and, most of the time, avoided the large inefficiencies associated in earlier periods with import substitution industrialization.[3] Some of them pursued active 'industrial' policies involving 'picking winners' for domestic production and export, but showed willingness to abandon supports when 'winners' turned out to be losers. This was facilitated by a relatively effective bureaucracy and a cooperative culture between the government and the private sector— with some unique features in China. The package of policies—with some exceptions involving a more extensive role for the public sector—had amazing similarities to the 'Washington Consensus'.

The results in terms of both growth and poverty reduction were so spectacular that in 1980s there was talk about the 'East Asian Tigers' and by the mid-1990s the whole world was talking about the 'East Asian Miracle' (World Bank 1993). It involved high GDP growth rates, roughly double of those achieved in the rest of the developing world. And it was labor-intensive growth with widespread benefits. Everybody was starting to ask why the East Asia achievements could not be replicated elsewhere in the developing world.

Then something happened: in July 1997, the Thai government abandoned the baht peg to the dollar, leading to its rapid depreciation, as foreign investors started to withdraw their money from Thai banks. The crisis jumped over to Indonesia with an attack on the rupiah and later to Korea. Other currencies in the region also came under attack as 'hot money' involving foreign investors attempted to get out of the rapidly depreciating currencies and leading to what is called the East Asia financial crisis.

The reasons for the crisis were many and controversial and different in each country: there was an asset bubble in Thailand; there was a lot of corruption and crony capitalism in Indonesia; there were a lot of weak bank portfolios in Korea. There was not much wrong in Malaysia and the Philippines but they both were adversely affected, if somewhat less severely, by contagion. All countries had used high real interest rates to attract capital inflows (as well as foreign direct investment) and had liberalized the capital account, thus permitting destabilizing short-term capital outflows which led to financial contagion.

The IMF and the World Bank came to the rescue with significant additional funding. The situation was brought under control in 1998—not before very large riots in Indonesia led to the fall of President Suharto. But there were recriminations: Stiglitz, the World Bank chief economist, openly accused the IMF for mishandling the situation, both for imposing too abrupt an adjustment leading to a large GDP contraction and increased unemployment and for having encouraged the liberalization of the countries' capital accounts without ensuring the adequacy of institutional safeguards and protection. Bhagwati, a strong defender of globalization, wrote: 'This crisis, precipitated by panic-fueled outflows of capital, was a product of hasty and imprudent financial liberalization, almost always under foreign pressure, allowing free international flows of short term capital without adequate attention to the potentially potent downside risks of such globalization' (Bhagwati 2007, pp. 199–200) and 'The reason why capital flows are tricky is simply because when confidence is shaken, the fact that the situation is inherently one of imperfect information, implies that the actions of a few can initiate herd action by others' (Bhagwati 2007, p. 202).

In the end, the countries affected started to recover in 1999 and at the end of decade, despite the crisis, were able to halve the number of poor living in absolute poverty between 1990 and 1999 (World Bank 2002a, p. 30). In 2003, the International Labor Organization (ILO) Commission on the Social Effects of Globalization conducted extensive dialogues on the impact of globalization throughout the world. Most participants in China and East Asia gave happy faces to globalization. But one respondent in the Philippines articulated the basic concern of all affected by trade liberalization: 'There is no point to a globalization that reduces the price of a child's shoes, but costs the father his job' (ILO 2004, p. 13).

This is nothing more than the old trade policy dilemma: each of the consumer benefits is small and spread out among thousands or millions of consumers. But the costs are individually large and concentrated to a few. The gains almost always outweigh the losses. The voices of the losers need to be heard and their needs addressed not through protection but through the establishment of effective safety nets, a difficult task in developed and even more so in developing countries.

Sub-Saharan Africa: Left Behind?

The faces of globalization in Sub-Saharan Africa were decidedly very worried. And with good reason: GDP growth in the 1990s recovered from the low 1980s level and the percent of people living in absolute poverty decreased slightly (see Table 7.1), but given the high rates of population growth, the number of absolutely poor grew by 25%. The absolute number of poor grew five times more than the figure for Latin America and twice that for South Asia in the period 1980–1997 (White and Killick 2001, p. xiii). Social indicators improved but much more slowly than in other regions.

Table 7.1 Poverty in developing countries 1990–1999

Region	Number of people living on less than $1 per day (millions)		Number of people living on less than $2 per day (millions)	
	1990	1999	1990	1999
East Asia & Pacific	452	260	1,084	849
(excluding China)	92	46	285	236
Europe & Central Asia	7	17	44	91
Latin America & Carib.	74	77	167	168
Middle East & N. Africa	6	7	59	87
South Asia	495	490	976	1,098
Sub-Sahara Africa	242	300	388	484
Total	1,276	1,151	2,718	2,777

Region	Head count index (percent)		Head count index (percent)	
	1990	1999	1990	1999
East Asia & Pacific	27.6	14.2	66.1	46.2
(excluding China)	18.5	7.9	57.3	40.4
Europe & Central Asia	1.6	3.6	9.6	19.3
Latin America & Carib.	16.8	15.1	38.1	33.1
Middle East & N. Africa	2.4	2.3	24.8	29.9
South Asia	44.0	36.9	86.8	82.6
Sub-Sahara Africa	29.0	22.7	76.4	75.3

Source: World Bank, *Global Economic Prospects, 2002*

Economic stagnation in many countries caused much poverty. A handful of countries achieved growth rates close to 5% per annum (e.g., Botswana, Cape Verde). In others, like Ghana and Uganda, earlier reforms started to yield results. And of course, South Africa witnessed the end of apartheid and its rise into regional leadership under Mandela. But overall per capita growth was negative. At the same time, the continent had high levels of inequality which apparently worsened in the 1990s. Gender inequality was especially grave with limited access for women to physical, social and human capital.

Both the state and markets failed the poor: Education, health, water and sanitation services were deemed inadequate, especially in rural areas which had the highest concentration of the poor. Employment opportunities were limited: Sub-Saharan Africa was far behind in participating in global value chains that had helped reduce poverty in other regions. Access to land and capital was limited and markets were frequently biased against the poor, in particular women. One hopeful sign was that the demographic transition was under way as by the end of the decade, mortality, fertility and population growth were all falling in many countries (White and Killick 2001, p. xxiii).

The participants in the dialogue about globalization essentially concluded that Africa had fared worse than other regions: 'at best Africa felt bypassed, at worse abused and humiliated' (ILO 2004, p. 15). In Mali, it was argued that there was no reason to respect trade rules when one of its few competitive exports, cotton, was being undercut by developed country subsidies (see below). Tariff escalation resulted in discrimination against local commodities such as coffee, making producers hostage to the declining price of raw materials. But African participants in the dialogue did not only blame others. They felt that their governments were equally responsible for failures to build trade, integrate effectively and benefit from the positive aspects of globalization (ILO 2004, p. 15).

Latin America on the Rebound

The reform programs undertaken by the Latin American countries in the 1980s yielded results in the 1990s. The strong economic performance of countries like Chile and Peru contributed to robust growth through the whole region with positive results on poverty. Although the absolute number of the very poor (less than $1 a day) or the poor (less than $2 a day) did not change very much over the decade, their share in the population fell to 15% and 33%, respectively (see Table 7.1).

Latin America has less poverty than Sub-Saharan Africa or South Asia. The most widespread poverty was in Central America where up to 60% of the population was poor. There was poverty in the cities and in the rural areas, with the latter having the largest proportion of the very poor. The rural poverty tends to be concentrated in remote areas especially among indigenous people.

The poverty problem was exacerbated by income inequality. Latin America had and still has the worse income distribution among all the developing regions. In a country like Peru with a large indigenous population, it was estimated that in the mid-1990s the income of the wealthiest 10% of the population could have been 80 times the income of the poorest 10% (World Bank 1996b, p. 6).

The reasons for the income inequality were many and varied. There was and still is substantial inequality in the access and quality of education. Secondary school education is primarily available only to middle- and high-income groups. Access to land has been severely constrained. There are too many large, inefficient estates and too many rural landless. Domestic industry continues to be substantially protected in countries like Brazil, resulting in huge profits for a small group of wealthy industrialists.

Attacking the problem of income inequality was seen as a major priority in the latter parts of the decade. The innovative programs of conditional cash transfers initiated by Brazilian President Cardoso started to have an impact on poverty at the end of the century and were to be greatly strengthened by President Lula in the 2000s. The success of these programs led to imitation in other parts of Latin America and the rest of the developing world.

The opening up of the Latin America to the rest of the world during the 1990s had less of an impact on poverty than in East Asia in part because it was not as focused on labor-intensive products and processes for export. Intra-Latin America trade was also less important than in East Asia, although there were some efforts at regional integration involving, for example, the MERCOSUR (Argentina, Brazil and Paraguay) and links to North America through NAFTA.

Attitudes toward globalization were on the whole more positive than elsewhere. People were talking about globalization's 'humane' face. 'It was associated with the spread of democracy in the region and with growing public awareness of issues such as gender inequality, human rights and sustainable development. The "smaller" world was making the cross fertilization and circulation of ideas easier ... it was helping to shape a new global ethic based on universal values and principles shared by people all over the world' (ILO 2004, p. 18).

Middle East: Treading Water

Poverty in the Middle East and North Africa has been the lowest in the developing world with only about 2.3% of the population very poor at the end of 1999. But there was a lot of shallow poverty, with almost 30%

of the population earning less than $2 a day (Table 7.1). What is more, it appeared that in the 1990s poverty increased both in absolute numbers and as a percent of the total population for this group of people. This occurred despite reasonable growth rates for most countries in the region.

The region consists of a varied group of countries. For many, the oil sector is critical to their growth performance. This includes the high-income countries of the Gulf and Saudi Arabia with very little poverty, but also Libya and Algeria. For these countries, the 1990s were significantly better than the 1980s (Table 7.2). Some of the countries, for example, Morocco and Tunisia, benefited from structural reforms and macroeconomic stability that resulted in significant increases in

Table 7.2 GDP annual growth (in % per annum)

Country groups	1965–1970 average	1971–1980 average	1981–1990 average	1991–2000 average	2001–2010 average	2011–2015 average
OECD members	5.27	3.52	3.19	2.67	1.60	1.62
Middle East and North Africa	9.90	6.87	1.98	3.84	4.76	3.13
Europe and Central Asia[a]	–	–	–	−2.21	1.95	2.35
Latin America and Caribbean	5.73	6.03	1.51	3.12	3.28	2.09
Brazil	7.01	8.51	1.77	2.60	3.73	1.02
East Asia and Pacific[a]	7.11	6.59	7.25	8.15	9.08	7.29
China	9.00	6.27	9.35	10.45	10.57	7.87
Sub-Saharan Africa	4.86	3.77	1.28	2.10	5.68	4.08
South Asia	3.74	3.09	5.48	5.31	6.89	6.43
India	3.37	3.08	5.57	5.60	7.42	6.74
Least developed countries[b]	–	–	–	3.26	6.71	4.65

Source: World Bank Development Indicators
[a]Excluding high-income countries
[b]UN classification

labor-intensive exports in textiles, leather and agro-industries. They seemed to have created a large number of low-skilled, low-paying temporary jobs in these export-oriented industries (World Bank 1996, p. 7).

The opening up of these countries to globalization was less affected by the greater economic interdependence. The main impact was cultural and in contrast to some of the views expressed in Latin America, globalization was perceived more as a threat than an opportunity. The pattern of integration involved a heavy dependence on oil exports and migration both from within and outside the Arab World. There were two kinds of fears of globalization: first, it threatened cultural identity and local traditions; and second, it encouraged the intrusion of foreign powers into the region's economic and political affairs, thus undermining their sovereignty (ILO 2004, p. 16).

Europe and Central Asia: Transition and Disruption

Except for the developed countries, this region had the smallest amount of poverty in the world in 1990. But the sharp and protracted declines in incomes following the transition from plan to market combined with increases in income inequality resulted in large increases in poverty for the decade. There were 10 more million very poor people in the region in 1999 than in 1990 and the number of people with less than $2 a day increased by 47 million over the same period.[4] As a consequence, the incidence of poverty more than doubled in the decade.

In most countries in the region, poverty was shallow with many households around the poverty line. However, there were some deep pockets of poverty in countries like the Kyrgyz Republic and Tajikistan. The new poor were largely working families with children, typically with low education levels which reduced their ability to find jobs. The transition was also associated with significant decreases in health status as the previous system which was based on the provision of health services through the enterprises disintegrated with the transition and new health systems were slow to be set up. In many countries, such as Russia and Georgia, this resulted in increasing mortality rates.

The transition process involved spectacular changes in the openness of these societies and economies from the previous system. This coincidence of globalization with increased poverty resulted in disappointment visible in the faces of most, especially the older generation. In some cases, there were also regrets over the abandonment of the secure cocoon offered by the previous regime and most commonly a sense that the new system yielded far less benefits than had been anticipated or promised.

South Asia: Steady Progress

Next to East Asia, South Asia was the developing country region that showed the greatest progress in reducing poverty during the 1990s. This region, which had traditionally been plagued with massive poverty, achieved substantial GNP growth during the decade (Table 7.2) and was able to reduce the absolute number of very poor people. This led to significant declines in the proportion of poor, both those living below the $1 and the $2 a day poverty lines (Table 7.1).

There were still very large numbers, almost half a billion, of very poor people in the region at the end of the twentieth century. A great number of these were in rural areas largely illiterate and depending on low-wage employment or subsistence farming for their livelihood. But the economies in the region were more open at the end of the decade than in the beginning and globalization resulted in a very large increase of new jobs in the information technology sector in countries like India. Bangladesh, a least developed country, showed a large increase in export-related employment in textiles.

As a consequence, the globalization faces were mixed: there were smiling ones among those with education whose lives were enriched by rewarding jobs in the new sectors. But the benefits had not reached the majority. And there were some who feared that globalization could erode values such as democracy and social justice, as Western perceptions encouraged consumption in the midst of extreme poverty (ILO 2004, p. 17).

Globalization, Growth and Poverty Alleviation

The events of the 1990s juxtaposed the increasing reach of globalization with continued stagnation in some parts of the world. The main region of the developing world being left behind was Sub-Saharan Africa. There were also serious problems in some parts of Europe and Central Asia on account of the disruption resulting from the transition from central planning. But many of these countries are essentially developed economies for which the disastrous decade was an aberration and they were soon able to recover to a significant extent their previous living standards and in many cases exceed them. For the rest of the developing world, the 1990s saw the beginning of sustained growth and poverty alleviation with major strides being made in East Asia but also in both South Asia and Latin America.

A number of studies have tried to link the outcomes regarding growth and poverty alleviation during this and subsequent decades to the degree to which particular developing countries or groups have globalized or not. A World Bank study in the early 2000s (World Bank 2002b) argued that more globalized developing countries had a better growth performance than less globalized ones. The definition of more or less globalized was arbitrary: The more globalized were defined as the top one third of a group of 72 developing countries ranked according to the change in the share of trade to GDP over the period 1977–1997. They included such obvious 'globalizers' as Brazil, China, India, Mexico and Thailand, but also countries like Haiti, Nepal and Zimbabwe.[5] Pakistan, Kenya, Honduras and Nigeria were among the less globalizing ones. The study suggests that globalization is good for poverty alleviation based on the following argument: it found little evidence of increased inequality within countries among the more globalizing ones—except for China. As they grew more rapidly and poverty is reduced when countries grow, then the conclusion must be that globalization was good for poverty alleviation.

The link between openness, however defined, and growth is an old story which was discussed in Chap. 3. There is an identification problem: countries with substantial openness also tend to have stronger institutional capacity, higher investment rates and sometimes higher education achievement (but certainly not in the case of Haiti, or Zimbabwe identified as 'globalizers' in this study). Still, the preponderance of evidence suggests that openness is good for growth. Certainly, there have been no studies worth the paper they were written on that have shown that *closing economies* through protection is good for long-term prosperity or poverty alleviation. But there are several caveats: while globalization may have been good on *average, there are obviously both winners and losers.* Also, there is evidence that in low-income countries (read here Sub-Saharan Africa), openness is associated with greater in-country inequality (World Bank 2002b, p. 49).

Baldwin's more recent study focused primarily on the impact of globalization on changes in income distribution not within but between countries. He argues that the ICT revolution starting around 1990 radically lowered the cost of moving ideas. This enabled multinationals to move their technical knowhow, including marketing and managerial expertise, to offshore production facilities that exploit the low-wage advantage of developing nations. The new phase of globalization involves different trade patterns than before: it is trade based on global value chains, where parts and components are an increasing share of the total. It also involves international movement of production facilities and knowhow as well as increased flow of services to support the dispersed production.

The study suggests that globalization resulted in a great convergence of incomes between developed and developing countries. Between 1990 and 2008 (the latter year chosen because of the onset of the financial crisis), the share of world GDP accounted by the G-7 fell by about 20%, which was gained by 11 countries: China, India, Brazil, Korea, Indonesia, Nigeria, Australia, Mexico, Venezuela, Poland and Turkey. The share of the world GDP for the remaining countries of the world stayed flat (Baldwin 2016, p. 93). Half of the gains were accounted by China's phenomenal increase in the share of world GDP, based on manufacturing production and exports. Some of the gains of the others such as Korea and Mexico were due to increases in manufacturing. For others (Australia, Indonesia, Venezuela), the increases were due to the rapid expansion of raw material exports in the 2000s (Baldwin 2016, pp. 93–94).

Baldwin's analysis offers some interesting insights, but is not conclusive about the impact of globalization on income distribution either in the North–South divide or within countries. To begin with, some of the 'winners' are developed countries like Australia and Poland. Moreover, the definition of winners focuses on countries which gained three-tenths of 1% of world GDP over the past 20 years. This definition required that only very large countries were included. Smaller countries which also did well over the period, including such 'globalizers' as Chile and Taiwan, were thrown together with the rest of the world which included low-income countries in Sub-Saharan Africa and Asia.

The analysis suggests (using World Bank data) that globalization has had a positive effect on poverty improving the lot of hundreds of millions of people primarily in lower middle-income and upper middle-income countries in the period 1980–2010 while noting that, over the same period, the number of people below the World Bank poverty line increased in low-income countries, most of whom are in Sub-Saharan Africa. The analysis on this point is not rigorous but rather impressionist as it simply notes that low-income countries have not taken advantage of the latest burst of globalization involving outsourcing and participation in global value chains.

Baldwin also refers to B. Milanovic's (2016) study which combines inter-country and intra-country income distribution estimates for the period 1988–2008. Milanovic shows that over this time period, for the world as a whole, income growth was greatest for the middle classes of global income as well as the very rich, while it was stagnant for the globally very poor and the lower income groups in developed countries.

Irrespective of the conclusions of the various studies about the impact globalization has had on average incomes, poverty or income distribution, it is clear that globalization has created anxiety as it plays into the universal human fear that we are imperiled by forces beyond our control. It has also become clear that globalization creates new winners and losers. And that it requires new thinking about trade policy as well as many aspects of labor policy, social safety nets, training, education, as well as the flow of resources from developed to developing countries.

Trade and Poverty[6]

Developing Country Policies

Despite the extreme polemic by globalization opponents about the deleterious effect of trade liberalization on poverty, there is simply no way to
generalize about the impact of a more liberal trade environment on poverty alleviation in developing countries. The general theoretical presumption is that more open trade would tend to help alleviate poverty because
of two factors: the often repeated finding that, for whatever reason, more
openness is associated with greater growth, which typically translates in
poverty alleviation; and because of the theoretical presumption that
increasing developing country exports would tend to increase returns to
unskilled labor, the relatively abundant factor of production in these
countries. But beyond these generalities, the actual situation is very complex and the link between trade, trade policies and poverty is complex,
often indirect and subject to a variety of other influences of policy and
institutions in both developed and developing countries.

Trade liberalization changes relative prices of tradeable goods (exports
and imports) versus non-tradeables (domestic goods). It may involve the
reduction in barriers to imports and/or exports or it may involve changes
in the form of protection (from NTBs to tariffs) or in the institutional
arrangements for international trade (e.g., the elimination of a state
monopoly for marketing and export). Typically, the benefits from the
reform are scattered among many and take time to materialize, whereas
the costs tend to be more short run and affect specific groups. How such
reforms would affect the poor would depend in the first instance on who
are the poor and what is the impact of the reforms on their incomes and
the prices and availability of the goods they consume. But the impacts
would also be significantly affected by other institutions and policies
which affect the poor.

Who the poor are varies from country to country, but they are not a
monolithic group anywhere. Until recently, in low-income countries,
most were typically rural and were either self-employed (small-scale
farmers, informal sector) or wage-earners (on other farms or small

enterprises). In the 1990s, the poorest and least vocal were probably small-scale farmers and rural laborers not connected to the main markets and trying to subsist on marginal lands where they have been pushed by population pressure and other reasons. Both poverty and employment in certain professions or in the production of specific crops is gender specific, with women frequently suffering from less labor mobility and greater poverty. More recently, the growth of mega-cities in the developing world has shifted a lot of the poverty to urban centers.

In the short run, when the levels and productivity of factors are fixed and factors are not mobile between sectors, part of the answer to the question of the impact of trade reform on the poor is obtained by determining the impact on their assets. The main asset of the poor is unskilled labor, though they may possess some skills, small amounts of capital and land in the case of small-scale farmers. Income from unskilled wages and income imputed from consumption of own production usually are the two largest sources of income for the poor frequently accounting for more than 80% of the income of the lower deciles in the income distribution.

The other side of the ledger involves the impact of trade reform on the cost of the consumption basket of the poor, that is, on the purchasing power of their earnings. A large portion of the consumption basket of the poor consists of food and shelter, usually more than 75% of the total.

The two effects may move in the opposite direction, with trade reform helping raise the incomes of the poor while raising the prices of some of the things they consume. Typically the income effect would be most important, as trade reform usually affects many prices of consumer products some of which may rise and some of which may fall, thus canceling their overall impact on the poor. At the same time, the poor typically devote a lot of their consumption on food which in subsistence economies is also their main source of imputed income. In some cases, changes of relative prices at the border may have little effect on rural low-income households because of their isolation from the cash economy. In others, the effect of such changes may not be felt or may be more than fully offset because of weaknesses in other policies and institutions.

The bulk of the analysis of the links between developing country trade policy and poverty has focused on the trade policy regarding manufactures. And it has emphasized the important contributions that increased exports of labor-intensive manufactures have made to alleviate poverty in China, and other countries elsewhere ranging from East Asia to Bangladesh, Lesotho, Haiti and Mauritius.

Much less analysis has been made of the effects of openness in agriculture, although this is the sector in which the bulk of the poor find employment and derive their incomes. The reason for this has been twofold. First, until recently when it became apparent that the way of the future involved participation in global value chains, there was a continuing fascination with the import substitution paradigm for industrialization and development. Second, border protection in agriculture accounts for a small proportion of the overall government interventions that affect incomes and output of the sector. Indeed, if one takes all these policies into account, and develops a measure of aggregate support to agriculture (AMS), there is substantial evidence that until recently many developing countries penalized rather than supported agriculture.

The driving force for such policies in agriculture has been the desire of governments to keep food prices low for urban consumers. At the same time, agricultural exports have been taxed as a means for generating revenue. The effect of both policies was to create adverse incentives for production and incomes to the farm sector.

On the other hand, it is fair to say that the Green Revolution, which had undeniably positive effects on increasing productivity and incomes to farmers, including the poor, could not have occurred without developing countries being open to the foreign technology and the inputs, frequently imported, that were necessary for the revolution to take hold. Notwithstanding this experience, the links between agricultural trade policy and poverty alleviation are complex and tend to be situation and country specific.

Even if increased trade enhances output growth, it is possible that opening up an economy to international trade increases the volatility of output, which in turn results in greater fluctuations of incomes and greater risks that individual households would fall below the poverty line. Large income fluctuations can have a devastating effect on poor households in developing countries where safety nets are seriously underdeveloped or completely lacking. However, a number of studies which have explored this issue have not found a significant correlation between openness and increased volatility of incomes and outputs. Indeed, one study (Lutz 1994) has found the opposite.

Another concern raised by the trade liberalization of the 1980s and 1990s relates to the implications of reduced protection on government revenue. As developing countries depend on trade taxes for a significant share of total revenue, the concern is that reductions in protection will result in reduced revenues which in turn will result in reduced expenditures, some of which would have been directed to social programs or other benefits for the poor (McCulloch et al. 2001). The evidence on this issue suggests that these fears are rather exaggerated. A good deal of trade liberalization can occur which is actually revenue enhancing. This will result from the substitution of tariffs for non-tariff barriers which are still present in many developing countries (see Chap. 6).[7] There is considerable evidence that reductions in government expenditures have often resulted in reductions of spending on the poor (Wodon et al. 2000). But there has been no evidence which links reductions of revenues due to trade reform to reductions in aggregate expenditures which have led to cuts in programs that affect the poor.

Some examples of the impact of increased openness on the poor illustrate the complexity of the issues involved:

* In Vietnam, liberalization of previously suppressed rice prices raised farm incomes through increased exports, while also increasing the cost of food to urban consumers. But because the bulk of the poor were farmers and the initial distribution of income was relatively equal, it can be concluded that price liberalization increased openness and reduced poverty.
* In Mauritius, trade liberalization in the 1980s did not result in the contraction of employment in import-competing industries, while leading to significant expansion of overall employment, especially of women in the production of textiles for export.
* Liberalization of trade in Zambia and Zimbabwe in the 1990s resulted in higher levels and lower prices for imports but also increased industrial unemployment; liberalization of farm trade, on the other hand, tended to substitute private monopolies for government-run marketing arrangements with no benefit to the poor (Oxfam 1999).

Trade policy reforms work through changing relative prices for products. If markets do not work well, for a variety of reasons—lack of information, monopolistic or monopsonistic structures, huge transport costs, then there is serious danger that trade policy reforms will not have the desired impact. When markets are not working well—which will often be the case in low-income countries, the question arises as to whether it is necessary to wait until they do before introducing trade reforms. There are no easy answers. International trade promotes competition and the operation of markets. Competition in small economies is more easy to introduce and monopolies easier to break if the economy is open to international trade than if it is not.

The success of any reform which depends on so many other complementary policies and institutions is bound to be uncertain, as will be its potential impact on the poor. One needs to be especially careful regarding the effects of any reform on the poor as they are least able to bear risks: they may be unwilling to take risks to increase their income, as by doing so, they also increase their chances to make losses, because the losses will have dire consequences for their existence—as they do not have the resources, for example, through savings, to permit them to ride over a bad spell.

Keeping this in mind, the best outcomes for the poor can be expected when, as a result of the overall reform process—of which trade reform is a part, growth accelerates in the economy as a whole.

A recent report jointly authored of by the WTO and the World Bank Group (World Bank Group and WTO 2015) reaches the same conclusion regarding the impact of trade on the extremely poor. It notes that over half of the extremely poor live in fragile and conflict-afflicted areas and are engaged in the informal sector requiring governments to make even greater efforts to ensure that trade costs are reduced for their benefit.

Last, governments should not refrain from liberalizing trade because somebody will lose in the short term; rather, if the losers are the poor, they should assist them—through the establishment of an appropriate safety net. Protecting the poor should be a general objective of public policy and not only associated with trade openness. Governments should implement programs to help the poor, whether trade reforms take place or not. Most analysts recommend the establishment of general safety nets, not specific ones linked to trade adjustment and globalization. Having said that, it is important to recognize that in low-income countries safety nets of any kind are often inadequate. Thus, establishing an effective safety net is a priority for all countries. Weakness in safety nets will undermine the success of many reforms, including those related to the opening up of trade.

Developed Country Trade Policies

Restrictions in the access of developing country exports to developed country markets and other distortions introduced by developed country policies, especially in agriculture, hinder development and undermine global efforts to reduce poverty. While developed country tariff protection of manufactures has declined to very low levels in general (1%–2%), there are still pockets of protection which affect adversely incomes and employment of the poor in developing countries as they are typically concentrated on labor-intensive products, in which developing countries tend to have a comparative advantage. In Canada and the US, tariff peaks are concentrated in agriculture, textiles and clothing; in the EU and Japan, they are concentrated in agriculture, food processing and footwear. The World Bank made some rough calculations of the effective tariffs faced by the poor globally. They showed that the very poor (less than $1/day) and the poor (less than $2/day) faced effective trade weighted tariffs on the goods their countries exported around 15% compared to 6% for the non-poor (World Bank 2002a, p. 57).

Preferential trading schemes such as the Generalized System of Preferences offer limited benefits. They typically exclude 'sensitive' products, which are often the very products of export interest to developing countries; and their utilization rates are low partly due to restrictive rules of origin or environmental or technical and phytosanitary standards. Other preferences, such as the EU 'Everything but Arms' (EBA) scheme that offers quota and tariff free market access to all LDCs imports, are more promising by providing greater product coverage.

Restrictions to developed country market access resulting from the imposition of a variety of new phytosanitary and technical barriers to trade are growing in importance. They have become a serious overall hindrance to developing country trade since many low-income developing countries do not have the institutional capacity or can shoulder the costs for meeting new and complex requirements.

In agriculture, where roughly three quarters of the poor live, the problems of market access are compounded by developed country support policies and export subsidies. The example of the impact of OECD policies on cotton presented in the box below is only one of many horror stories of the effects of OECD agriculture supports on the poor worldwide.

Cotton

In Benin, Burkina Faso, Chad, Mali and Togo, all of which are LDCs, cotton growing and trading is an important part of the economy, accounting on average for 10% of GDP and 30% of exports and involving 10 million people. Perhaps as many as 1 million of the farmers and the families they support are extremely poor, with land holdings of less than 5 acres and per capita income of less than $1 a day. Production of good quality cotton is relatively efficient, with costs frequently less than 50% of those in developed countries. The effect of US and EU domestic supports as well as export subsidies has been to reduce substantially the exports and incomes of the five LDCs, costing an estimated $1 billion in foregone income directly or indirectly. Most of these costs were borne by the very poor farmers engaged in cotton production in these countries. In the US, it is estimated that 50% of the benefits from cotton supports went to farmers holding 1,000 acres or more. And AGOA, the US program of support for Africa, excludes imports of cotton.

Globalization has created winners and losers in developed countries as well, through its impact on employment, wages and incomes. The degree and extent of this impact, in particular the importance of trade as opposed to general technological change, has been the subject of a very large, growing and controversial literature. The main points of contention have to do with the loss of jobs in the manufacturing sector of the OECD countries, in particular in the US and Europe, the stagnation of real wages at the lower end of the spectrum and the increasing wage differential between skilled and unskilled workers. Has the increased North–South trade been at fault?

A comprehensive review of the various issues and the many studies was done by William Cline in the late 1990s (Cline 1997). The main conclusions from his and other studies at the time can be summarized as follows: on the issue of job losses in manufacturing, the main culprit has been the broader shift in the overall composition of GDP from manufacturing to services. Trade as such has played a very small role, much less than changes in technology.

With respect to wages, the issue was more complex, but one thing seems to be abundantly clear. At least through the 1990s, 'there are substantial grounds for concluding that there was little reduction in the absolute level of US unskilled wages as a consequence of increased trade over the past two decades… Any absolute reduction imposed by liberalization of international trade (as opposed to the effect of falling transport and communication costs) was no more than 1 percent and more probably close to zero' (Cline 1997, p. 272).

At the same time inequality increased between real wages for unskilled workers, which had been falling, and wages for skilled workers, which had been increasing both in the US and in Europe. In Europe there had been less reductions in real wages and more increases in unemployment. Cline argues that the rising inequality was the result of two competing forces: on the one hand, trade theory suggests that increased trade will result in relative reductions in the returns of unskilled labor, the scarce factor of production for developed OECD countries; on the other hand, global increases in skilled labor hold promise that the rising supply of skilled relative to unskilled labor will tend to decrease the wage differential over time. He concludes in a hopeful tone that in the future, the unequalizing force of globalization will decline as trade barriers had already been reduced to very low levels; and the equalizing force of higher supply of skilled labor will continue thus leading to decreased wage inequality (Cline 1997, pp. 238–239).

His recommendations for the US included the traditional emphasis on adjustment assistance for workers affected by trade as well as an increased emphasis on broader skill training, in some ways emulating the pattern of active interventions in the labor market championed by the EU. Despite the anti-globalization fervor toward the end of the 1990s manifested in the Seattle demonstrations, the developed countries did not substantially increase their protection against developing country products. Indeed they proceeded to implement the liberalizing commitments they had undertaken under the Uruguay Round negotiations, although, as discussed in Chap. 6 they tended to drag their feet in implementing the liberalization of the textile trade, and to keep within the letter but not the spirit of their commitments in agriculture. Alas, as we shall see in later chapters, Cline's hopeful expectations about trade being so liberal that wages differentials would shrink did not materialize and increased protection in the North started to show its ugly face at the end of the first decade of the twenty-first century and even more later on.

Political Economy Issues

The main conclusions economists reach about the impact of liberalizing trade on poverty are relatively benign. Increased trade openness in the North appears to have contributed to a small but significant part of increased wage inequality in developed countries, while the impact of trade liberalization on poverty in developing countries tends to be country specific and affected by a variety of other policies and supporting institutions. The impact of foreign direct investment on the poor in developing countries appears to be highly positive even in the short run. Given these findings, why is it that there were so many demonstrators in the streets against globalization? There are two sets of issues: first, there are different perceptions of what the real effects are; second, redistributing benefits from trade to those that are adversely affected is extremely difficult.

Perceptions may be different than reality for various reasons: economists typically address average effects at the national or global level, while individuals and groups are more sensitive to local situations; there may be differences between short-term losses and longer term gains—in the case of the poor who have limited resources, short-term losses may be catastrophic; and finally, beyond a certain level of income—which varies by country, individuals respond to perceptions of relative gains or losses—individuals may have adverse views of globalization even if they have absolute gains but others in their reference group gain more (Verdier 2005). Moreover, a worker who gains from globalization, for example, in Mexico by finding a job of making crankshafts for a new General Motors automobile assembly plant in Thailand, is not likely to attribute his new job to the nebulous forces of globalization but rather to his own industriousness and skill.

Whatever the perceptions, the reality also is that it is extremely difficult to redistribute the gains from trade. In principle, a government can establish a system of lump sum taxes/transfers that compensate the losers. In practice, no such system has ever been devised. The reason partly has to do with the informational requirements for devising such a system, partly because of the grave difficulties of identifying and targeting the millions of different tax rates and transfers for the individuals affected. The only solution is to provide increased resources to obvious losers involving training or either means of increasing mobility and/or transfer payments for a certain period. And as noted above, it is probably more efficient to have a general safety net than to establish separate safety nets for trade and other causes for people losing jobs.

The poor in developing countries are typically politically weak and unable to represent their interests. There are very few demonstrations in developing countries by the poor against trade liberalization or globalization even if they have been hurt by it. The demonstrations that occur in developed countries are usually organized by developed country NGOs on behalf of developing countries' poor. Their focus most of the time are international organizations such as the WTO which are thought to somehow take action against the poor, notwithstanding the fact that these organizations can never do anything without the full agreement of all their members. The demonstrations rarely focus on developed country trade policies, such as on cotton, which cause grave damage to the poor in very poor developing countries.

Labor in developed countries is far stronger and able to defend the interests of those actually or potentially adversely affected by imports. In the US, labor unions have been traditionally protectionist and the US has often tried—without success—in the 1990s to introduce 'labor standards' as a means of domestic industry protection in the WTO. In the post-World War II period, global trade liberalization depended very much on US initiatives. These in turn depended on the domestic political balance of labor interests versus the interests of export industries wishing to break into protected foreign markets. Every five to ten years, the export interests would prevail, the US Executive would be granted by Congress 'fast track' authority to engage in multilateral trade negotiations whose results Congress could not modify and a new negotiating Round would occur.

Capital Flows

Private

The globalization wave of the 1990s was characterized by a massive increase in private capital flows to developing countries. Initially these flows went primarily to small group of countries, primarily in East and South East Asia and Latin America. In the following decade, they spread also to Sub-Saharan Africa. The increased private capital flows in the 1990s were of two kinds: foreign direct investment (FDI) and portfolio and bank lending (see Table 7.3). Each had different motivations and different outcomes.

FDI flows grew for three major reasons. First, there was a general improvement in the global attitude toward the role of private capital in growth and development, in part deriving from the demise of the system of central planning and the dissolution of the former Soviet Union. This carried over to attitudes in developing countries which appeared to be less concerned about the potential that multinationals had for exploiting the weaker economies of the South than they had been in previous decades when they had pushed for restrictive 'codes of conduct' for FDI in UNCTAD and other fora. Second, there was a genuine belief that FDI could be beneficial to developing countries by combining their cheap but productive labor with the superior technology brought in by the multi-nationals to produce for both the domestic and export markets as part of

Table 7.3 Total net flows from DAC countries by type of flow

	$million							Percent of total						
	1965	1970	1980	1990	2000	2010	2015	1965	1970	1980	1990	2000	2010	2015
I. Official development assistance	6,489	6,713	26,236	54,329	54,021	128,369	131,433	59	42	35	69	40	25	42
II. Other official flows	314	1,122	5,037	8,771	-5,088	6,035	5,308	3	7	7	11	-4	1	2
1. Bilateral	312	845	5,144	8,529	-4,995	5,550	5,199	3	5	7	11	-4	1	2
2. Multilateral	5	276	-107	242	-93	485	108	0	2	0	0	0	0	0
III. Private flows	4,143	7,018	40,316	10,024	78,331	344,386	142,862	38	44	54	13	58	67	45
1. Direct investment	2,459	3,690	10,127	26,505	71,932	179,317	156,313	22	23	14	34	54	35	50
2. Bilateral portfolio		716a	27,467b	—	9,583	172,512	-22,397		4	37	-24	7	34	-7
3. Multilateral portfolio			1,469	2,523	-3,369	-6,157	11,013			2	3	-3	-1	3
4. Export credits					1,402	16,507	9,123					1	3	3
IV. Grants by private voluntary agencies		860	2,386	5,077	6,964	33,887	35,388		5	3	6	5	7	11
Total net flows	10,947	15,948	73,976	78,201	134,228	512,678	314,991	100	100	100	100	100	100	100

Net disbursements at current prices and exchange rates
Source: OECD
Notes: *1971 **1981

the emerging global value chains. Third, multinationals started to exploit significant advantages to offshore production resulting from differential taxation of corporate profits in both the developed and developing world. The increased flow of loans and portfolio investment resulted primarily from developing country liberalization of capital controls and the financial sector.

By the end of the previous century, there was little concern about the impact of FDI—which was generally considered benign. On the contrary, the East and South East Asia financial crisis of 1997–1998 stimulated a huge amount of studies that resulted in a significant reevaluation of the benefits and costs of capital account liberalization.

It may be useful to recall in this connection the warnings that many, including myself, had made in the 1980s about not liberalizing before establishing effective regulation of the financial sector. It is unclear whether, as Bhagwati suggested (see above), countries liberalized under external pressure—presumably from the Bretton Woods institutions— although following the demise of central planning, championing private capital became universally more fashionable including among staff of these institutions. Whatever the reason, based on the studies following the 1997–1998 crisis, it has become clear that developing countries should not open their capital accounts unless they have established effective government regulation and supervision of the financial system. This is necessary in order to avoid large mismatches between foreign assets and liabilities or the abundance of short-term assets to finance long-term investments. Such regulation is needed, especially as international financial markets are prone to errors and herd behavior that can be detrimental to developing countries even when their fundamentals are sound. Moreover, it appears useful to institute some kind of controls, especially on short-term capital inflows as practiced by Chile and Malaysia which managed to cope more effectively with external financial shocks.

Aid in the 1990s

Reducing global poverty became the clarion call of aid institutions all over the world during the 1990s. In 1990, the United Nations launched its first annual *Human Development Report* highlighting different dimensions of poverty and human deprivation. The World Bank's 1990 *World Development Report* (World Bank 1990) with its striking black cover was symbolic of the growing emphasis placed on poverty reduction by both multilateral and bilateral aid agencies. In the World Bank, this was followed by the publication of the *Poverty Handbook* (1992), the initiation of country poverty assessments and by the introduction in FY 1992–1993 of a program of targeted interventions (PTI). This included projects which either had a specific mechanism for targeting the poor or if the proportion of poor people among the beneficiaries was higher than in the population as a whole. Over the next several years, projects in the World Bank's PTI were to rise to about a third of total bank lending, but around 50% in its lending to poor countries and even more in Sub-Saharan Africa, except, as noted earlier, much less in Eastern Europe and the former Soviet Union (World Bank 1996).

The assistance programs also had a different slant: recipient government ownership was being emphasized. The World Bank was encouraged to persuade governments to undertake reforms rather than prescribe conditions. There was the beginning of understanding the fundamental fact that if policymakers in developing countries themselves want the reforms or are persuaded of their usefulness, conditionality is not needed; and if they are not, it will not work. Therefore, there was a shift of emphasis in providing assistance on the basis of *reforms already completed.*

Of course, governments are not monolithic. All too often in the past the World Bank (and the IMF) would persuade Ministries of Finance, who needed the external financing on committing to reforms, which did not have the support of the line Ministries that were supposed to implement them (see Chap. 4). The World Bank started to develop so-called policy framework papers (PFP) and, later in the decade, Poverty Reduction Strategy Papers (PRSP), which were supposed to reflect overall agreed government policies. In the case of the PRSP, the documents were reviewed and agreed upon by the Boards of Executive Directors of the IMF and the World Bank and provided the framework for future assistance by the two institutions. In the beginning, there were problems: recipient governments did not have the institutional capacity to draft the PFP and PRSP and had to rely on the staff of the Bretton Woods institutions for their preparation—which of course did little to improve ownership (Chibber et al. 2006, pp. 146–147; 162–163). However, over time these problems were overcome and the PRSPs would prove to be worthwhile innovations, useful in shaping both bilateral and multilateral assistance programs in the next decade.

The emphasis on poverty reduction by the World Bank in the early 1990s was accompanied by a curious reduction in emphasis on international trade policy at the very time that the WTO was being established and globalization was spreading. The World Bank symbolically shut down its Geneva office. In addition, both analytical work and loans linked to trade reform were reduced. A later evaluation report would speculate that perhaps this was because the World Bank felt that there was less need to concern itself with trade reform as developing countries had liberalized their trade sufficiently (World Bank 2006).[8] Following the Seattle debacle, the situation changed and the World Bank renewed its involvement in trade issues at the end of the decade and later with the establishment for the first time of a Trade Directorate in 2002.

The reduction in global political tensions following the breakup of the Soviet Union contributed to the convening of several UN sponsored conferences that resulted in recommendations on specific targets for improving various dimensions of poverty as well as what the international community should be doing to help developing countries achieve them. There were conferences on children (New York, 1990), the environment (Rio, 1992), population (Cairo, 1994), social development (Copenhagen, 1995) and the status of women (Beijing, 1995).

The DAC, under the leadership of its Chairman, J. Michel, picked up and consolidated the conclusions and recommendations from the various conferences and prepared a report whose first part presented a set of 'international development targets' (IDTs) that were intended to guide bilateral donors in the provision of economic assistance which by that time all had agreed, at least in principle, should be focusing on poverty reduction (OECD 1996). The second part recommended a partnership approach to development cooperation that was to form the basis of future donor-recipient relations. A key objective of the initiative was to generate support for reversing the downward trend in bilateral ODA. While the IDTs were essentially agreed by the global community in UN conferences which were in practically all cases influenced by the very large number of participating developing countries, the adoption of the IDTs by the DAC gave them an unwelcome imprimatur—as if they were being pushed by the donor community, at a time when there was a strong consensus that development priorities should be determined by the recipients—not the donors.[9]

Total ODA flows declined over the decade and bilateral ODA declined even further (Table 2.1). In particular, US aid programs in the 1990s declined substantially pari passu with the termination of the Cold War. US ODA fell by 30% from $18.5 billion in 1990 to $13.2 billion in 2000. As noted earlier, there was an increase in programs to the countries of the former Soviet Union and Eastern Europe but large decreases elsewhere. The USAID programs focused on population/health, the environment and the spread of democracy. There was a focus on 'broad-based' economic growth, with major emphasis on policies and institutions and without a huge emphasis on poverty reduction. Poverty was on the screen, but certainly not front and center.[10]

Bilateral ODA from other donors increased somewhat but not enough to make up for the US decline. The appointment of Clare Short as UK Development Minister in 1997 'marked the beginning of an era when the UK would become a major player in international development, would focus sharply on poverty reduction, would pursue a strategy of influencing the big players (World Bank, IMF, UN, US, Japan and EU) and would as it were "punch above its weight"' (Hulme 2009, p. 21). Short was looking for a device to focus Department for International Development (DFID), mobilize support in the UK and drive the international system forward. She found it in the IDGs…. 'It is probably accurate to say that Short did more than any other individual and more than many DAC member governments to promote the IDGs as a central component of the fight against poverty' (Hulme 2009, pp. 23–24).

> It was Richard Jolly who pointed me to the report of development committee of the OECD entitled *Shaping the 21st Century*. It drew together the recommendations of the great UN conferences of the 1990s and suggested that great advance was possible if we focused on a systematic reduction of poverty (Short 2004, pp. 53–54).

In this atmosphere of the late 1990s characterized by an emerging global consensus about the objective of eradicating poverty but reduced aid levels especially in the US and continued suspicion about donor motives by many in the South, a quartet of development Ministers from four European countries—Germany, the Netherlands, Norway and the UK—(Heidemarie Wieczorek-Zeul, Eveline Herfkens, Hilde F. Johnson and Clare Short, respectively) took a set of coordinated initiatives that helped move forward both the global agenda and the effectiveness of economic assistance. The fact that in 2000 their countries together accounted for more than 50% of bilateral ODA obviously helped make their voices heard.[11] Moreover, these development ministers were in charge of all the ODA their countries provided while most donor country ODA is fragmented and managed by various ministries and agencies.

The four Ministers recognized that their intended aid policies were very similar: they focused assistance on projects and programs aimed at addressing poverty; they were committed to a mode of operation in which the recipient took the lead in setting priorities; they were keen in coordinating their assistance to avoid duplication and ensure that the donor with the greatest expertise took the lead in particular sector(s) or countries as well as in adopting common positions on issues in international bodies where they were represented. Finally, they also wanted to enhance policy coherence not only among themselves but also between foreign policy/security and development objectives as well as between aid and trade policy of their governments and other global policies affecting the developing country prospects and poverty reduction.

I saw the possibility of a progressive team of female ministers making a difference in international development and invited them all to Utstein Monastery (Abbey) an island in my constituency, off the coast of Stavanger, for a couple of days. Our strategy was to pursue reform in development policies and practice on the basis of a global partnership with mutual accountability—"we do our bit, you do yours" a line of thought later codified as Millennium Goal 8 (Johnson, p. 26).

In pursuit of these objectives, they organized meetings among their staff and Ministerial level gatherings to coordinate policies and agendas.

Following their first major meeting at Utstein Abbey on July 26, 1999, they were called the *Utstein Group*. Subsequent meetings were organized in different countries on a rotating basis. At these meetings, detailed positions were developed on particular issues as well as coordination of interventions in particular meetings, for example, at the twice-a-year World Bank/IMF Development Committee meetings and the annual DAC High Level meetings in which they all had seats representing their governments or their constituencies.

They also took trips together to visit countries in which they all had programs:

> The four of us visited Tanzania, acknowledging what a headache each individual donor was, pledging we would merge our efforts into ONE headache instead of four, prompting an incredible successful endeavor among all donors in Dar es Salaam to harmonize, which experience touched off the global agreement that culminated and later was codified in the Paris Declaration... Together with the then Executive Secretary of UN ECA K. Y. Amoako, we created this platform called the "Big Table" of Ministers in which African Finance Ministers felt less inhibited to tell the truth on the African side... Also, we developed this concept of "mutual accountability" and recipients should not only be accountable to donors, but donors should be accountable to partner countries for their pledges and efforts, including the importance of multiyear predictability of aid (Herfkens 2008, p. 10).

They identified recipient countries in which each had particular interests or expertise and designated lead donors as appropriate. 'As part of the division of labor in our group, I took on more of the Sudan portfolio and Eveline Herfkens instructed her officials in the Netherlands Ministry of Foreign Affairs to take their cues from Norway' (Johnson 2011, p. 26).

Their Utstein press statement is worth noting as it reflects the thinking of the most progressive and forward looking bilateral aid agencies at the time. They followed the press statement with a long Op-Ed in the international edition of *The New York Times*, with the title 'If We Are Serious, We Do Something About Poverty' in which they stated that 'The great moral problem of our time is poverty' and they proceeded to outline a series of steps to fight poverty based on their press statement and ranging from debt relief to strengthening the multilateral system to efforts to draw private investment to the most needy countries (Herfkens et al. 1999).

Press Statement—Utstein Abbey, Norway, 26 July 1999 (Excerpts)
Four Development Ministers on a Common Course

Donors must coordinate better, put more resources into development assistance and strengthen the multilateral system in order to help developing countries eradicate poverty and support global sustainable development. This was the message of the four development Ministers, Ms. Clare Short (United Kingdom), Ms Eveline Herfkens (the Netherlands), Ms Heidemarie Wieczorek-Zeul (Germany) and Ms Hilde F. Johnson (Norway) gathered at the Utstein Abbey in Western Norway. On the 25–26 of July they met to discuss future strategies for cooperation on a number of development issues.

Making a difference in development is the ambition of the network of these four Ministers. They identified eleven key issues that need to be addressed jointly with other countries and international organizations:

In four important areas the donors in particular need to get their act together

- *Increased coordination.* All donors must be prepared to adjust their programmes to achieve better coordination and thereby more effective assistance. The recipient country must be in the driver's seat.
- *Untying of aid:* further untying of development assistance will imply increased efficiency, improved quality and more development.
- *Institutional and financial gap:* Closing the gap between humanitarian assistance and long-term development cooperation is vital.
- *Greater coherence of all policies affecting developing countries:* Better aid practices are not enough. Donor countries need to be equally concerned to put in place coherent policies on matters such as trade, investment and environment which support sustainable development.

We need to see provision of more resources and the setting of new priorities

- *The debt initiative:* Implementing the debt relief measures by the recent Cologne Summit will enable poor countries to allocate more funds for poverty reduction.
- *The multilateral system:* It is vital to support the United Nations and the development banks both through fulfillment of the financial obligations, international coordination effort and through policy priorities.

(continued)

(continued)

- *Financing development:* Fighting the global poverty menace requires imaginative thinking and action to reinvigorate development financing... We will work together to reverse the decline in ODA. We call for a renewed commitment by all partners concerned to the international development targets, including halving the proportion of people living in absolute poverty by 2015...

  The developing countries need to put their act together:
- *Combating corruption:* Corruption is stealing from the poor, it is a major obstacle to development...
- *Strengthening democracy and good governance:* Democracy and competent and strong public authorities are the best guarantees for sustainable development.
- *Preventing conflicts:* Peace is a fundamental prerequisite for development.
- *Implementing poverty reducing policies:* Developing countries themselves have to create an enabling environment to stimulate private sector investment, ensure an equitable distribution and make public expenditure more efficient and transparent.

  The Utstein Meeting is only the beginning

  The four Ministers will continue their collaboration on these eleven key development issues. Ms Eveline Herfkens, Development Minister from the Netherlands, will host the next meeting in the summer of 2000. In the meantime the four Ministers will work jointly and separately to carry the Utstein agenda forward.

We four established a real offensive and defensive alliance at our first Utstein meeting. We considered: how do we do this now? How do we integrate the Cologne Decision (about debt forgiveness for HIPC) within the World Bank and the IMF? Which conditions do we combine with the forgiveness? How do we secure that the freed money will actually go to fighting poverty? How do we prove that the money reaches the poor and how do we strengthen, at the same time, the characteristic of individual responsibility in developing countries? What has to be done so that each country includes civil society in the development of its poverty fighting strategy? (Wieczorek-Zeul 2007, p. 37).

Their forceful and coordinated interventions were not always welcome by their colleagues at these meetings. 'We made quite an impact on the Development Committee, traditionally dominated by male-only Central

Bank Governors and Finance Ministers. But with Clare, Heidemarie, Hilde and me, during a few years 4 out of 24 Members were women. And we organized ourselves well: coordinating our interventions, agreeing in advance on points to push, speaking order and division of labor. We were so effective that the Brazilian Finance Minister, while walking out of the meeting, sighed: "I am all for gender equality, but this is too much..." Well—we were 4 out of 24' (Herfkens 2017 note).

'How often did Clare end up in conflict with the then US Treasury Secretary Larry Summers. It was about steps in the debt forgiveness: not all countries received that at the same time. In the end, a process with clearly defined conditions was negotiated. In the disagreement over specific points in the Communique, Clare wanted to see her and our position, anchored, which Larry Summers had contradicted often enough. Since the Communiques need to be accepted by consensus, some stubbornness can go a long way. And Clare could be stubborn. Normally the Communiques would be adopted in the morning sessions at the end of the World Bank Meeting, after which there was a luncheon hosted by the Governors. Clare sometimes extended the disagreement so long that the point in question could only be decided upon at the luncheon. That was the point at which Larry Summers finally gave up' (Wieczorek-Zeul 2007, p. 38).

Herfkens recalls that on one occasion Summers was so upset that walking out of the meeting he told Hilde Johnson that we were mistaken if we thought the Development Committee was the Socialist International. At which point Johnson clarified that she was actually a Christian Democrat (Herfkens, note 2017).

'In so far as we, as a Power-Troop, were feared, it affected even James Wolfensohn, the President of the World Bank. I recall a meeting just prior to the fall Washington meetings, at which we still had quite opposing opinions. Wolfensohn did not want to give in, and neither did I. I became quite sharp at this discussion, I got up, thanked for the coffee, and left. His team stared. That was not the norm. With "Jim" one did not carry conflicts outside' (Wieczorek-Zeul 2007, p. 38).

Their coordination extended beyond the issues of aid and finance to include questions of climate change, fragile states, and other issues impacting development such as corruption which are not the focus of this volume. For example, one of their legacies was the U-4 Anti-Corruption Resource Center still functioning in Bergen, Norway. The group's influence was felt most forcefully starting with 2000 and will be discussed in the next chapter.

Approaching the Millennium

Despite concerns surrounding the impact of globalization, as the world was approaching the millennium, global prospects were on the upswing. China was continuing its spectacular growth performance. Prospects were improving in both Latin America and Asia and there were some hesitant beginnings in Sub-Saharan Africa. Similarly, Russia and many countries in Eastern Europe were recovering their dynamism. A number of CEE countries were looking forward to becoming members of the EU, which itself was evolving with several countries forming a currency union and introducing the euro, a new convertible currency. There were problems in some selected areas and country groups: for example, the Balkans had not fully recovered from the breakup of the former Yugoslavia and in Africa there were several local conflicts ranging from Sudan to Somalia.

But internationally there was also a general feeling of cooperation as the cold war confrontation was receding in memory. Private capital flows were growing spectacularly, and while there was some migration from South to North, and from the former Soviet Union and CEE countries to the rest of Europe, the flows appeared manageable.

Trade was also growing rapidly, and despite the setback in Seattle, there was a feeling that international cooperation will succeed in the end: after all, previous efforts to launch multilateral trade negotiations had been aborted only to succeed after a number of false starts; and both China and Russia which had hitherto been excluded were on a path to becoming WTO members.

On the other hand, efforts to introduce coherence in global policies toward developing countries continued to fail spectacularly. Following the agreement reached in the IMF/World Bank meetings in the autumn of 1999 to increase the international effort in support of debt relief for the HIPC, and in advance of the Seattle WTO Ministerial, the Managing

Director of the IMF and the President of the World Bank proposed that market access preferences provided to LDCs should be extended to HIPC. This proposal was an extension of earlier proposals by the Director General of the WTO which had been supported by many countries to extend duty and quota free treatment for all LDC exports.

The BWIs argued that as export growth in the HIPC was an important determinant of their capacity to service debt, it would make sense that the HIPC got as good access as any country, and that quota and duty free treatment be extended to them as well. The two lists coincided to a large extent, as 30 LDCs also appeared on the HIPC list of 40. The difference was 10 lower income countries: Bolivia, Honduras and Nicaragua in Latin America; Cameroon, Congo, Ghana, Ivory Coast, Kenya and Senegal in Africa; and Vietnam in Asia—with total exports of $25 billion or 0.47% of world exports in 1999. Even with the two lists together, the countries involved accounted for less than 1% of world exports.

Both the EU and the US signaled non-support for the proposal, in the EU case by referring to concerns that such preferential treatment would have adverse implications for other low-income countries—alluding to the ACP countries which may have wished to be included in any such extension of preferences—but most probably because the extension of any such duty and quota free treatment would not have been acceptable to EU farmers.

The BWIs attempted to formalize this proposal as part of the joint declaration of the heads of the three institutions in advance of the Seattle Ministerial. The WTO Director General balked and the proposal was dropped.

There is little reason to believe that the problems faced by LDCs were significantly different from those of other low-income countries. The measures which the international community takes should address both. In this case, the international community and the BWIs had exhaustively analyzed the problems of the HIPC. But the trade ministers of the same governments could not be convinced that it would be useful to reduce trade barriers to them. Continuation of trade restraints on HIPC exports meant that the consumer in developed countries was hurt twice: first by having to pay higher prices on imports from these countries and second by having to pay more in aid and debt relief to assist them to recover. The effect that such preferences would have had on exports of other low-income developing countries appears to have been no more than a convenient excuse for doing nothing in an area where all logic suggests that concerted international action was urgently needed.

Besides the lack of policy coherence, a problem that would continue to be a major challenge, there was of course this vague uncertainty about what would happen to all computers at the turn of midnight; but, as we now know, that turned out to be the least of the problems that would have to be addressed in the twenty-first century.

Notes

1. Mundell (2000) argues that the 1970s saw the beginning of a new international financial system resulting from the need to finance the oil price-driven deficits.
2. The full list includes Mexico, Venezuela, Turkey, Poland and Australia—the latter three of which can hardly be called 'developing' or part of the 'South'.
3. China has often maintained an exchange rate policy which many observers have felt resulted in significant undervaluation in order to maintain export competitiveness.
4. The countries in this region for which these data are reported included several countries, such as Russia and Ukraine which in this volume have been included in the 'developed country' grouping.
5. Chile, Hong Kong, Korea, Singapore and Taiwan were excluded from the 'globalizing' group for unstated reasons. One wonders whether their inclusion in the analysis would have changed the results.
6. This section draws from C. Michalopoulos (2004).
7. In a number of World Bank-supported trade reforms, experience with revenue generation was mixed. In three of five countries examined, the reforms resulted in increased revenues. In the two cases where they did not, the main reason appears to have been that tariffs were lowered; but when NTBs were also removed, there was no compensatory increase in tariffs, nor an enhanced effort of tariff collection (Greenway and Milner 1991).
8. At about the same time, the foreign exchange gap rationale for World Bank financing had come under internal questioning. Latin American experience in the 1980s and more recent experience in the former Soviet

Union countries suggested that the problems developing countries were facing stemmed primarily from budget deficits reflecting a domestic savings constraint. This resulted in a long but unresolved debate over how to justify adjustment lending which did not materially affect the lending program (World Bank 1996a).

9. The IDTs were also referred by some as the International Development Goals (IDGs), see McArthur (2014).

10. Communication from Michael Crosswell, former Chief Economist of USAID/PPC.

11. Herfkens, Short and Johnson knew each other already, but the addition of Wieczorek-Zeul doubled their leverage. Herfkens knew Wieczorek-Zeul from the 1980s when they both were parliamentarians. When she heard of the new German Minister's appointment, she cleared her schedule, contacted Wieczorek-Zeul and went to Bonn to brief her and discuss how they could work together.

References

Baldwin, R. (2016) *The Great Convergence* (Cambridge, Mass: Belknap Press).

Bhagwati, J. (2007) *In Defense of Globalization* (New York: Oxford University Press).

Chibber, A.J., R. K. Peters, and B. J. Yale (2006) *Reform and Growth* (Washington, DC: World Bank).

Cline, W.R. (1997) *Trade and Income Distribution* (Washington, DC: Institute for International Economics).

Greenway, D. and C. Milner (1991) "Fiscal Dependence on Trade Taxes and Trade Policy Reform", *Journal of Development Studies* 27 (April) pp. 95–132.

Herfkens, E. (2017) Note on the Utstein Group (mimeo).

Herfkens, E., Johnson, H., Short, C. and Wieczorek-Zeul, H. (1999) "If We are Serious, We do Something About Poverty" NY Times/IHT., August 10.

Herfkens, E. (2008) *Africa and Development Cooperation* (Zimbabwe: ACBF Development Memoirs Series).

Hulme, D. (2009) "The Millennium Development Goals (MDGs): A short History of the World's Biggest Promise", Brook World Poverty Institute, BWPI Working Paper 100, University of Manchester.

ILO (2004) *A Fair Globalization: Creating Opportunities for All* World Commission on the Social Dimension of Globalization (Geneva: ILO) Geneva.

Johnson, H. F. (2011) *Waging Peace in Sudan* (Eastbourne: Sussex Academic Press).

Leipziger, D. (1997) *Lessons from East Asia*, D. Leipziger Ed., (Ann Arbor: Michigan University Press).

Lutz, M. (1994) "The Effects of Volatility in the Terms of Trade on Output Growth: New Evidence" *World Development 22*, 1959–75.

McArthur, J. (2014) "The Origins of the Millennium Development Goals" *SAIS Review* XXXIV, (2), Summer-Fall, pp. 1–24.

McCulloch, N., L.A. Winters and X. Cirera, (2001) *Trade Liberalization and Poverty: A Handbook* (London: Centre for Economic Policy Research and Department for International Development).

Michalopoulos, C. (2004) *Trade and Poverty*, SIDA Brief No. 1, (Stockholm: SIDA).

Milanovic, B. (2016) *Global Inequality: A New Approach for the Age of Globalization*, (Cambridge Mass: Harvard University Press).

Mundell, R. (2000) "A Reconsideration of the twentieth Century" *American Economic Review* (90)3, pp. 327–340.

OECD (1996) *Shaping the 21st Century*. https://www.oecd.org/dac/2508761.pdf.

Oxfam, -IDS (1999) *Liberalization and Poverty*, Final Report to DFID.

Short, C. (2004) *An Honorable Deception?* (London: Free Press).

Verdier, T. (2005), "Socially Responsible Trade Integration: A Political Economy Perspective" in F. Bourgignon, B. Pleskovic and A. Sapir Eds. *"Are We on Track to Achieve the Millennium Development Goals?"* ABDCE Conference, (Washington, DC and New York: World Bank and Oxford University Press).

White, H. and Killick, T. (2001) *African Poverty at the Millennium*, (Washington, DC: World Bank).

Wieczorek-Zeul, Heidemarie (2007) *Welt Bewegen*, (BerliN: vorwarts buch).

Wodon, Q, R. Ayres et al. (2000) *Poverty and Policy in Latin America and the Caribbean*, (Washington, DC: World Bank).

World Bank (1990) *World Development Report 1990*, (Oxford: Oxford University Press).

World Bank (1992) *Poverty Reduction Handbook*, (Washington, DC: World Bank).

World Bank (1993) *The East Asian Miracle*, (New York: Oxford University Press).

World Bank (1996a) "Issues in Adjustment Lending" (mimeo) Development Economics., January 10.

World Bank (1996b) *Poverty Reduction and The World Bank,* (Washington, DC: World Bank).

World Bank (2002a) *Global Economic Prospects,* (Washington, DC: World Bank).

World Bank (2002b) *Globalization, Growth and Poverty* (New York: Oxford University Press).

World Bank, (2006) *Assessing World Bank Support for Trade,* IEG Evaluation, (Washington, DC: World Bank).

World Bank Group and WTO (2015) *The Role of Trade in Ending Poverty* (Geneva: WTO).

8

Millennium Aid, Trade and Development

Introduction

The Millennium found me in Brussels, as Senior Advisor to the Director of the World Bank office in that city—an office primarily performing liaison functions with the European Commission. I had moved there in June 1999 at the end of my WTO appointment in Geneva. This was to be my last assignment with the World Bank, an easy assignment with few responsibilities. I was mainly involved in the World Bank's work in the Balkans, in particular, the efforts of these countries to forge a regional free trade agreement, while at the same time some of them were preparing to become full members of the EU. I also started to write a book based on my WTO experience about developing country participation in that institution. The assignment meant that I was not involved in any way with policy or program development or implementation. I had the time and inclination to follow aid and trade policy issues; and after my retirement in June 2001 to serve as a consultant to the Bank, the IMF and various other aid agencies on specific issues of interest.

This chapter will summarize the main developments in aid and trade in the period 2000–2008, a period during which developing countries made

© The Author(s) 2017
C. Michalopoulos, *Aid, Trade and Development*,
https://doi.org/10.1007/978-3-319-65861-2_8

tremendous progress but at the end were buffeted by a major financial crisis in the developed world. The first few years of the Millennium were characterized by a flurry of international agreements with three different objectives that aimed to: (a) strengthen the commitment of the international community to help developing countries reduce poverty and improve the well-being of their people; (b) shape the rules of international trade in ways that would be more supportive of development; and (c) increase the level as well as the effectiveness of economic assistance.

The first of the agreements, perhaps the one with the greatest global reach, was the UN Millennium Declaration, which contained what later became the Millennium Development Goals, signed by all heads of state and governments in late summer of 2000. Then there was the WTO agreement in the fall of 2001 to launch the Doha Round of multilateral trade negotiations, the International Conference of Financing for Development in Monterrey in March 2002, the Paris Agreements on Aid Effectiveness 2005, the UN Summit in the fall of 2005 and several others in between. It has been argued (Herman 2006) that to some extent the spirit of international cooperation embodied in these agreements was a global reaction to the events of 9/11. One can never know for sure. But the fact is that following 9/11, the US played a constructive role in forging global agreements and raised significantly its own level of economic assistance.

The Millennium Development Goals (MDGs)

The first year of the new century witnessed a major achievement in international cooperation: in September 2000, 189 counties signed at the UN the Millennium Declaration. The actual MDGs took a little while longer to settle. In June 2000, the IMF, the OECD, the UN and the World Bank launched a common document *2000. A Better World for All*, containing essentially the targets as they had evolved within the OECD (IMF et al. 2000). These, while similar, contained a number of differences from the UN list, and contained few commitments by the OECD countries. The MDGs set specific quantitative targets for eradicating poverty and reducing other forms of human deprivation as well as promoting sustainable development by 2015 (see Box).

It was not the first time that the UN passed resolutions embodying lofty objectives as well as commitments by the international community to do great things in support of development only to have these objectives and commitments forgotten the moment the delegates left New York. This time it was different in several ways. First, many of the goals were time bound and specific; second, they had been elaborated and discussed in previous UN conferences and there was already a significant international consensus about the desirability of their achievement; third, a number of developed countries took them very seriously and tried to focus their aid programs to achieve them; and finally, the UN itself established a new program, the MDG Campaign, to promote them.

The Millennium Development Goals and Targets

Goal 1—Eradicate extreme poverty and hunger

Target 1—Halve between 1990 and 2015 the proportion of people whose income is less than $1/day.
Target 2—Halve between 1990 and 2015 the proportion of people of people who suffer from hunger.

Goal 2—Achieve universal primary education

Target 3—Ensure that children everywhere, boys and girls alike, will be able to complete a full course of primary education.

Goal 3—Promote gender equality and empower women

Target 4—Eliminate gender disparity in primary and secondary education, preferably by 2005 and at all levels of education by 2015.

Goal 4—Reduce child mortality

Target 5—Reduce by two-thirds between 1990 and 2015 the under-five mortality rate.

Goal 5—Improve maternal health

Target 6—Reduce by three-quarters between 1990 and 2015 the maternal mortality rate.

Goal 6—Combat HIV/AIDS, malaria and other diseases

Target 7—Have halted by 2015 and begun to reverse the spread of HIV/AIDS.
Target 8—Have halted by 2015 and begun to reverse the incidence of malaria and other major diseases.

Goal 7—Ensure environmental sustainability

Target 9—Integrate the principles of sustainable development into country policies and programs and reverse the loss of environmental resources.
Target 10—Halve by 2015 the proportion of people without sustainable access to safe drinking water and basic sanitation.
Target 11—By 2020 achieve a significant improvement in the lives of at least 100 million slum dwellers.

Goal 8—Develop a global partnership for development

Target 12—Develop further an open, rule-based, predictable, nondiscriminatory trade and financial system (includes a commitment to good governance, development and poverty reduction, nationally and internationally).
Target 13—Address the special needs of the least-developed countries (includes tariff- and quota-free access for exports of the least-developed countries, enhanced debt relief for least-developed countries and cancellation of official bilateral debt, and more generous official development assistance for countries committed to reducing poverty).
Target 14—Address the special needs of landlocked countries and small island developing states (through the program of action for the sustainable development of small island developing states and the outcome of the 22nd Special Session of the General Assembly).
Target 15—Deal comprehensibly with the debt problems of developing countries through national and international measures to make debt sustainable in the long term.

Target 16—In cooperation with developing countries develop and imple ment strategies for decent and productive work for youth.
Target 17—In cooperation with pharmaceutical companies provide access to affordable, essential drugs in developing countries.
Target 18—In cooperation with the private sector, make available the benefits of new technologies, especially information and communication.

The MDGs brought together for the first time a shared vision on development, representing a global partnership based on a shared responsibility by all countries. Developing countries have the primary responsibility for achieving these goals. But rich countries acknowledged, in MDG 8—to develop a global partnership for development, that poor countries cannot achieve the goals unless rich countries increase and improve the effectiveness of their aid, and change the rules of trade to foster development (Herfkens 2007a, p. 1).

The Utstein Group played a significant role in their adoption. Short writes (Short 2004, p. 89), 'We joined with others to try to get the targets agreed by all international institutions. The group of women ministers-known as the Utstein Group from the place of our first meeting led the campaign. Gradually the targets were adopted by the World Bank, the IMF and EU and then, as the agreed objective of the Millennium Conference of the UN General Assembly were renamed the Millennium Development Goals.'

The MDGs had their limitations. They did not capture other commitments made in the 2000 Millennium Declaration on governance, transparency, participation and human rights, which are not simple to measure. Moreover, there was a very big difference between the first seven MDGs for which the developing countries had the main responsibility and Goal 8, which entailed the responsibilities of the developed countries: the first seven included concrete quantifiable targets, whereas Goal 8 contained a large number of non-quantifiable targets involving general and vague commitments without a target date.

Despite these shortcomings, the MDGs caught on. 'The MDGs have become the dominant framework for discussing development—a marker for what has been achieved and what still has to be done... That they did catch on was the result in part because the so-called "Utstein Group" of development ministers from four European countries pushed hard for the goals in forums like the G8 and the UN' (OECD 2011a, p. 31).

The Monterrey Consensus

The Utstein Group and other similarly motivated governments in Europe, such as Sweden, wanted to use the MDGs to promote more concrete and detailed understandings regarding financing for development as well as to push laggards in the EU to raise their level of assistance. This fit in well with developing country demands to strengthen the development community's commitments on trade and finance in Goal 8. The question was what forum could be used to achieve this.

Earlier discussions had demonstrated the unwillingness of developed country governments to negotiate meaningful financial and aid commitments in the UN. This was due to the lack of policy coherence at the national level: representation at the UN was by Foreign Affairs ministries, whereas Ministers of Finance or Development Cooperation represented governments in the IMF and the World Bank (the Bretton Woods institutions—BWI), where the real commitments on finance, debt relief and aid were being made. The position of these ministries on substantive issues was frequently different. And then there was international trade, where trade ministers held sway and who had typically stayed completely away from UN fora and were only partially and superficially involved in the deliberations of the Washington institutions.

It is not entirely clear whose idea was to have a separate non-UN finance for development (FfD) initiative. According to one source (Herman 2006), the genesis was a UN Economic and Social Council (ECOSOC) resolution in 1997 calling for 'consideration be given to modalities for the conducting of an intergovernmental dialogue on financing for development' (UN 1997). This was confirmed with a similar wording in UN General Assembly resolution 52/179 later that year. In April 1998, there were meetings between country representatives at UN ECOSOC and representatives of the Boards of the World Bank and the IMF. In the next two years, these evolved into what was called the 'Philadelphia Group', comprising of half a dozen developed country representatives from the UN and the BWI, including the four Utstein countries and the Nordics—Philadelphia being halfway between New York and Washington, but not necessarily meeting there. The Utstein countries supported the 'Philadelphia Group' and instructed their representatives at the various international organizations to participate in the FfD initiative.

Ruth Jacoby, Sweden's ambassador to the ECOSOC played a leading role in bridging the gap between the UN representatives—many committed to doctrinaire G-77 positions, and the BWI. She was eminently positioned to play that role as she had earlier been Executive Director at the World Bank where she had been close to Herfkens, then also an Executive Director at that institution.

Jacoby writes, 'When I came to our mission in New York in 1999, not even two years after having left the Board of the World Bank, I was shocked to find I was in a completely different universe. In the Second Committee of the UN General Assembly we spent weeks negotiating a resolution on "Debt of Developing Countries" but to my knowledge not a single delegation got instructions or even consulted their respective Ministries of Finance. The same went for trade. Paris Club negotiations were completely unknown in the drafting groups in New York as were the latest WTO— negotiations. UN matters were the unique playground of our Ministries of Foreign Affairs; those in our capitals who were responsible for economic issues in the real world (outside the UN) were at best uninterested, at worse contemptuous.

'To try and bring the worlds of Washington and New York together, to start a dialogue between them, the Philadelphia Group was founded by some like-minded countries with the Utstein Group as the core. Eveline

Herfkens championed and supported the concept. The idea was to meet with our own colleagues in the other institutions, to compare notes, exchange information and discuss our differing approaches to a common agenda. It was great fun and extremely useful. In practice, we never actually met in Philadelphia, but were hosted alternatively by colleagues in Washington or New York' (Jacoby 2017).

The work of Philadelphia group and other informal meetings between UN and BWI representatives contributed to the development of an understanding of what would be possible to reach agreement on a variety of finance and development topics. In late 1999, Jacoby went to Washington DC and met first with Managing Director Horst Kohler of the IMF, who was supportive as was World Bank President James Wolfensohn. She wanted them to be fully on-board the initiative and not simply attend the meeting as guests. Finally, in early 2000, a preparatory committee was set to prepare for the 'event'. This included a bureau of 15 UN members chaired by Jacoby and the Pakistan ambassador to the UN, Shamshad Ahmad, with Secretariat support from the UN, the World Bank, the IMF and the WTO. At this point it was not clear at what level or where the 'event' would take place. It was clear that it would not be a typical UN conference where developing countries could pass resolutions with no effect as developed countries which did not like them could simply note their reservations.

And there were other political considerations: the US had decided to engage politically with the developing countries in the aftermath of 9/11. When it was decided to hold the conference in Mexico, 'President Bush could not avoid attending this conference since his friend and neighbor President Vincente Fox of Mexico was hosting it' (Lancaster 2008, p. 16). This meant that other governments would be prepared to be represented at the highest level. It also meant that 'Having decided to attend, the President had to have a "deliverable"—something important and attractive to announce, and the only thing that made sense was an increase in US aid, the more so because European leaders were already planning on announcing significant increases in their own aid budgets' (Lancaster 2008, p. 16).

In this connection, in the fall of 2001, the EU Development Council (composed of Development Ministers, and later abolished) met on sev-

eral occasions to develop a common EU position in anticipation of the
Monterrey meeting. Belgium's Minister Eddie Boutmans, whose government held the EU Presidency, wanted an ambitious commitment in
order to take advantage of an international climate favorable to development in the aftermath of the 9/11 attacks. This was supported by the
Netherlands, Sweden and a few other governments who were already
meeting the 0.7 ODA/GNI target. Several, including Spain and Italy,
were opposed. The UK favored countries setting individual targets.
Germany could not make a commitment at that time. The November
Development Council looked like it was going to end in disarray without a recommendation. Under pressure from the Dutch delegation and
supported by the UK and Germany, it was agreed to keep the issue open
and that Koos Richelle, the EU Commission's Director General for
Development (and formerly Director General under Herfkens in The
Hague) would canvass the EU capitals and prepare a report for a consideration by the EU at a heads of government meeting in advance of the
Monterrey meeting. This was done at the EU Summit in Barcelona
(Spain having succeeded Belgium in the EU Presidency) where the heads
of government formally agreed that EU countries should increase their
ODA commitments so that by 2006 the overall EU average will reach
the target 0.39% ODA/GNI and no government will give less than
0.31%.[1]

As a consequence, in Monterrey the US and the EU engaged in a
beauty contest of who was going to be more generous, resulting in
significant actual increases in ODA over the next decade. The Monterrey
conference also adopted an impressive consensus document 23 pages
long with no reservations in six chapters on topics ranging from the usual
'Mobilizing Domestic Resources for Development', which in UN speak
relates to the things developing countries should do to the equally traditional 'Increasing International Financial and Technical Cooperation'
which refers to the commitments of developed countries to give more aid
for development. Perhaps the most interesting chapter had to do with
measures 'Enhancing the coherence and consistency of the international
monetary, financial, and trading system for development.' It was probably the most coherent and comprehensive internationally agreed document on finance, trade and development.

Some of the specifics were:

* Para 13 'Corruption is a serious barrier to effective resource mobilization and diverts resources from activities that are vital to poverty eradication.'
* Para 14 'Governments should attach priority to avoiding inflationary pressures and abrupt economic fluctuations that negatively affect income distribution and resource allocation.'
* Para 43 'Donors should harmonize their operational procedures so as to reduce transaction costs.'
* Para 52 'Efforts should be strengthened at the national level to enhance co-ordination between all relevant ministries and institutions.'
* Para 62 'We stress the need to broaden and strengthen the participation of developing countries in international decision making and norm setting.' (UN 2003).

On the question of the level of assistance, unlike the MDGs, the consensus para 42 is very concrete, stating that 'developed countries who have not done so to make concrete efforts towards the target of 0.7 of GNI as ODA to developing countries'. This famous 0.7ODA/GNI target had been put in literally hundreds of UN resolutions to which the US either abstained or entered a formal reservation as not accepting it. This is the first and only time that the US did not object to it. In practice, the US government promised a 50% increase in American foreign aid over three years, for which it created a new multibillion 'Millennium Challenge Account' that was to provide generous financing including budget support for developing countries that were found to support human rights, endorse democratic principles and coherent strategies to eradicate poverty. By creating the Millennium Challenge Corporation to channel these funds, the US was able to implement some of the agreements on aid effectiveness, as this new outfit, as opposed to USAID, was not restricted by all kinds of congressional mandates. In addition, the US launched a generous new program, the President's Emergency Plan for AIDS Relief (PEPFAR), to combat HIV/AIDS.

Some of the issues that were addressed such as the participation of developing countries in the decision making of international institutions were to be picked up again in discussions on the voting rights of rising powers such as China on the Boards of the IMF and the World Bank.

The other major accomplishment of the Monterrey meeting was the extensive reference to the need for greater coherence in government policies for development both at the national and international levels. This was the first and probably the last occasion in which world leaders agreed to take steps to improve policy coherence. What actually happened on this score as well as other aspects of the follow up to the Monterrey meeting will be discussed in Chap. 10.

'A Coherence Deficit

Our policies—national and global—should be coherent. We have to stop giving with one hand and taking with the other. If we underscore the importance of a sound enabling environment in developing countries, we should also enable these countries to export to our markets. The new WTO round should become a real development contributing to the achievement of the MDGs. The Doha agenda is a positive first step but the proof of the pudding is in the eating. The wealthy nations still put roadblock after roadblock on the way to development. The clearest example is agriculture policy.

The lack of coherence between multilateral organizations is primarily due to incoherence and compartmentalization of our own governments in the national capitals. The health ministry deals with the World Health Organization (WHO), the central bank with the IMF, the finance ministry with the multilateral banks, the trade ministry with the WTO and the social affairs ministry with the ILO. When two or more national actors disagree, they simply export their conflicting points of view to the international level; the ILO, WHO and WTO headquarters in Geneva become the battlefield. The same goes for the IFIs (finance ministries) on the one hand and the UN (foreign affairs ministries) on the other. Ensuring coherent policies is a primary task of ministers for development cooperation.' (Herfkens 2002).
Excerpts from E. Herfkens speech, Monterrey, March 22, 2002.

The Monterrey meeting marked the beginning of the end of the formal coordinated intervention of the Utstein countries in major international meetings on finance and development.[2] The coalition government in the Netherlands lost the elections in June 2002 as a result of a populist uprising and Herfkens lost her job. Her replacement, from the Christian Democratic Party, had different priorities for the aid program, promoting change for change's sake. At the July 2002 Utstein meeting, Sweden was formally added to the group, and later Canada also joined. In the following year, Clare Short resigned over the UK involvement in the Iraq War. Johnson and Wieczorek-Zeul continued as ministers but following Herfkens' and Short's departure and despite the addition of other countries, the Utstein group no longer functioned as effectively as the chemistry among the principals was not the same. Still, at lower levels, the ministries continued to coordinate positions. In 2003, the original four ministers received the first annual Commitment to Development Award by the Center Global Development, the preeminent US think tank/lobbying group for development. The award cited them for their 'dedication, vision, and leadership in reducing global poverty and inequality in developing countries, challenging the norms of the development establishment and highlighting the importance of policy coherence' (CGD 2003).

Aid Effectiveness

The question of how to make aid more effective has been the subject of a huge number of studies, discussions and meetings over the last half century, some of which have been referred to in earlier chapters. It is clear that effectiveness depends on actions both by the donor and the recipient. Bringing the two points of view together in a meaningful international agreement had proved very difficult. The Monterrey consensus was a first step in that direction with some of its chapters dealing with effectiveness issues (see above). The next step was the Rome Declaration on Harmonization.

Meeting in Rome in February 2003, ministers, heads of aid agencies and senior officials representing 28 aid-recipient countries and more than 40 multilateral and bilateral development institutions endorsed a declaration aimed at harmonizing practices in ways that would produce improvements in development effectiveness. The three-page document contained a number of specifics, as for example:

* Ensuring that development assistance is delivered in accordance with partner country priorities, including poverty reduction strategies... and that harmonization efforts are adapted to country circumstances.

* …We will work to reduce donor mission, reviews, and reporting, stream-line conditionalities and simplify and harmonize documentation.
* Providing budget, sector or balance of payments support where it is consistent with the mandate of the donor and when appropriate policy and fiduciary arrangements are in place.

Two years later in Paris, international cooperation on aid effectiveness reached a different level in terms of the countries participating, the range of commitments, the degree of specificity and the establishment of a fol-low up to monitor progress. The so-called Second High-Level Forum on Joint Progress toward Enhanced Aid Effectiveness was attended by 138 countries, 28 bilateral and multilateral donors and numerous NGOs, all of whom agreed to series of steps to increase aid effectiveness under five major principles:

1. *Ownership:* Developing countries set their own strategies for poverty reduction, improve the institutions and tackle corruption.
2. *Alignment:* Donor countries align behind these objectives and use local systems.
3. *Harmonization:* Donor countries coordinate, simplify procedures and share information to avoid duplication.
4. *Results:* Developing countries and donors shift focus to development results and results get measured.
5. *Mutual Accountability:* Donors and partners are accountable for devel-opment results (OECD 2011a).

The various commitments under the five general chapters involved spe-cific quantitative targets that were supposed to be achieved by 2010. For example, under 'Ownership' the specific target was that at least 75% of partner countries have operational development strategies. Under 'Alignment', donors committed that by 2010 at least 90% of them will use country public financial systems and country public procurement for their assistance. Under 'Harmonization' by 2010, 40–66% of donor missions to the field should be joint with the host country. Finally, it was agreed to monitor progress by the joint group of donors and recipients of the DAC Working Party on Aid Effectiveness organized under OECD auspices. The results of the Paris agreement were subsequently communicated to the UN Summit on the MDGs that was convened at New York in September 2005 (see below).

A third high-level forum on aid effectiveness was held in Accra during September 2–4, 2008, with the participation of a very large group of developed and developing countries, multilateral institutions, global funds and civil society organizations broadening the range of stakeholders involved in the discussions and the setting of the aid effectiveness agenda. The forum took stock of the progress made in the implementation of the goals set in Paris and proposed a large number of improvements in three aspects of implementation: developing country ownership, aspects of partnership and delivering results.

One of the important features of the forum was the participation of private global funds, such as the Gates Foundation, which had become substantial players in global aid giving. Between 2000 and 2010, disbursements by these funds rose almost fivefold from about $7 billion to $34 billion.

A fourth forum was projected to take place in 2011 to review the extent to which the quantitative targets set in 2005 were met. In the meantime, it was obvious that while some progress had been made, for example, by aid being more sensitive to supporting aid policy reform of developing countries, narrow political motives still played a role in deciding aid allocation and there was still little attention paid to issues of governance and corruption, including issues of state capture (Kauffman 2009).

Despite the flurry of international agreements aimed to improve aid effectiveness, there were still critics, both in the developed and developing world. Easterly (2007) was and continues to be a persistent critic. His main arguments at the time were that while agencies had been improving in some respects—allocating more aid to poorer countries, reducing the proportion of tied aid and the amount of food aid which undermines domestic food production in developing countries—there were still serious problems: they had learned little from the failures of structural adjustment lending, there was too much aid going to corrupt regimes and there was too much supply-driven technical assistance. He offered no solutions, other than the aid agencies should learn from their mistakes.

Some of the same criticisms were made by Moyo (2009). In a blistering critique of aid to Sub-Saharan Africa, devoted fittingly to Peter Bauer (see Chap. 2), she argued that the majority of these countries 'flounder in a seemingly non-ending cycle of corruption, disease, poverty and aid-dependency' *because* receiving $300 billion of aid since has encouraged corruption and conflict while discouraging free enterprise. Her answer is to increase foreign direct investment and exports, just like China did, and terminate aid in five years.

It is interesting to record the response to these criticisms by Herfkens, whose views I share.

In a speech in Berlin in August 30, 2007, she said:

'I wholeheartedly agree with Easterly's criticisms of certain aid practices:

* too much goes to countries that do not need external concessional resources—because of geopolitical and foreign policy reasons;
* tied aid, motivated by donor economic or export promotion reasons;
* donor tendencies to "plant their flags" in all countries and every sector, leading to inefficiencies, fragmentation, and, may I add, huge transaction costs for recipients.

I also agree with Easterly that there is very little point in increasing aid unless it is made more effective. In the past, the typical model of aid was a plethora of donor-driven isolated projects. At best, these projects were islands of perfection in the midst of seas of despair. And even these projects usually fell rapidly into decay once the donor left, as governments could not afford to continue to pay doctors or teachers, or even the electricity bills. Moreover, each project—of which there might be thousands—burdened the government with a host of rules and reporting requirements, draining weak local capacity, leaving governments unable to run their own countries. Worse still, governments felt accountable to donors and not to their own citizens, undermining governance. This aid did not work because it was based on the assumption that donors develop poor countries. They do not. Aid by itself cannot "buy" the MDG's. Particularly "one project (or village) at a time" will not make a dent, as it bypasses and ignores government policies and responsibilities.

I strongly disagree with Easterly's conclusion that if aid does not work, we should quit the aid business. We need to condemn where aid failed. But—while aid is not the miracle answer, we should not dismiss it, but should draw the lessons from where it succeeded, and build them into the aid programs of all needy countries.

Aid works, when it backs serious home grown social and economic reforms. Mozambique, one of the poorest countries in the world, has made giant steps in development—more than 7%, uninterrupted growth per year for more than 20 years, and on track for most MDGs—while heavily depending on aid.[3] But the aid it received was increasingly aligned with its development priorities; and donors minimized the burden they imposed on the government by harmonizing their procedures; over the last few years most aid was given in the form of budget support.

Easterly is out of touch with what is happening in the aid business. Now, seriously, for the first time in aid history we do have a broad-ranging agenda of measures to ensure that future aid genuinely contributes to development. This agenda is outlined in the 2005 Paris Declaration on Aid Effectiveness to which almost all donor countries and many developing countries are signed up (Herfkens 2007b).

In an Op-Ed in 2009, Herfkens says Moyo's point that 'without aid, it would be easier for citizens to hold governments accountable' should not be dismissed. Indeed, the attitude of 'we' (standing for foreign experts/money) will save Africa or 'we' will end poverty, lead to undermining incentives for poor people to demand action from their own government to improve governance, fight corruption and ensure that resources—not just aid, but also the far larger domestic resources—are spent transparently and well. This implies donors have to deliver aid in a fashion that does not allow developing country governments to shirk that responsibility, nor shift their citizens' expectations away from their own governments to those of the donors. Indeed, the type of aid that removes the link of accountability between political leaders and their electorate ultimately perpetuated poor governance and poverty. Aid must be channeled through recipient budgets to allow domestic accountability.

I also agree with Moyo's observation that too much aid has been driven by donors' own economic and geopolitical interests. Where 'aid' is given for geopolitical or export promotion objectives, it was never intended to reduce poverty; thus we should not be surprised if it docs not.

But I disagree with Moyo's conclusion that if aid does not work, we should quit the aid business. We should not throw out the baby with the bathwater, but should draw the lessons from its failures and successes. And that is exactly what we have been doing since the last decade. Now, seriously, for the first time in aid history we do have an agreed upon broad-ranging agenda of measures to ensure that aid genuinely contributes to development. The Paris-Accra agreements are not just slogans or buzzwords—each is backed up by a series of practical reforms, deeply grounded in reality, and responding to past failures, including many ills Moyo points out.

What worries me most about Moyo is that she does not say much new: it has all been said before by Peter Bauer in the 1960s and 1970s. By now it is not good enough for us in the aid business to just say we heard it and debate the finer points.

It is time to *implement* Paris-Accra, so aid responds to genuine local needs, builds local capacity to manage development and makes governments responsible and accountable. But implementation has been lagging as it demands political leadership and understanding of the rationale for the Paris/Accra reforms by public opinion in general and 'parliamentarians in particular' (Herfkens 2009).

The Millennium Development Goals Campaign

The active promotion of the MDGs in both the North and the South by the UN Millennium Campaign was intended to encourage citizens to hold their governments to account in developing countries for the commitments they made to achieve the goals, and in OECD countries for their commitments regarding aid levels, aid effectiveness and trade, as agreed at Monterrey. The Campaign was established in 2002 by UN Secretary General Kofi Anan for the purpose of raising awareness of the goals and promoting citizen advocacy to remind governments of their promises, reaching out beyond the usual suspects involved in the UN and the international NGOs accredited to the UN. The Campaign focused on action at country level, as it is at national level actions that policies and action have to take place to achieve the goals. It was the first time that the UN initiated an effort to build awareness of internationally agreed objectives and to inspire and mobilize citizens to hold their governments accountable for their achievement.

Kofi Annan appointed Herfkens to create and lead the Campaign, as Executive Coordinator. Under her leadership, the Campaign focused on developing countries, helping to strengthen constituencies for pro-poor inclusive and transparent policies and advocacy for the implementation of promises already made, to achieve Goals 1 to 7. In rich countries, the focus was on more pro-development policies, as committed to in MDG 8, and elaborated in Monterrey, such as increased and more effective aid, debt relief and trade opportunities. The Campaign partnered with local civil society, often already engaged in development, and reached out to other actors, parliamentarians, local authorities, faith-based organizations, youth networks, unions and popular media like MTV, fostering the use of the MDGs as a common rallying framework aimed at legislators and governments to encourage to implement policies aimed at achieving the MDGs.

The campaign was present in many countries. In developed countries, the focus was on encouraging civil society to promote government support for achievement of Goal 8 as well as the developed country commitments at Monterrey. In developing countries, the focus was on getting governments to be accountable to their commitments by implementing policies aimed at achieving the MDGs. It was active in countries as disparate as Brazil, Indonesia and Mozambique. It was not active in countries like China and others where prospects for government policy change based on advocacy by civil society did not appear especially promising. In Europe, there were large campaigns in countries like Italy and Spain whose ODA performance was lagging as well as in Germany. The campaign was not always welcomed: the US and India governments discouraged campaign activities in their territory, although in the end the campaign was active in both countries through partnerships with local NGOs and parliamentarians.

It is difficult to assess the campaign's impact in achieving the MDG objectives. It was clearly a loud voice among many pushing for the achievement of the goals. And it did achieve that, as opposed to earlier goals and targets formulated at the UN over the decades, the MDG's became wildly known worldwide, and were discussed in many national parliaments. During October 15–16, 2006, the campaign mobilized a record 23 million people worldwide to stand up for the MDGs. The record reached 173 million in 2009. In many developing countries it played a role in moving governments to articulate policies and programs and align budgets aimed at achieving the MDGs (Herfkens 2007a). In Europe, it is credited by Wieczorek-Zeul with promoting support for increasing ODA levels and the EU commitment in advance of the UN 2005 Summit to achieve the 0.7 ODA/GNP target by 2015.

In 2005, the UN Summit took stock of progress in achieving the MDGs and reiterated everybody's commitments to their achievement. At the time prospects looked pretty good for achieving the poverty objective especially because of rapid growth in China and India. Prospects in achieving the other goals appeared mixed (World Bank 2005). But there were encouraging signs, especially as Sub-Saharan African countries had started to grow very rapidly since the beginning of the century.[4]

The Doha Round

While all these agreements on aid were being concluded, the WTO Doha Round of multilateral trade negotiations was also launched in December 2001. The Round was supposed to focus heavily on issues of importance to developing countries (WTO 2001a). But despite some early successes, progress turned out to be very slow.

The so-called Doha Development Agenda had several important implications for TRIPS, a crucial developing countries' concern (Michalopoulos 2014, Chapter 7). By far, the most important of these provisions was the 'Declaration on Health', in which it was agreed that, under the compulsory licensing provisions of TRIPS, each WTO member has the right to determine what constitutes a national emergency and that public health crises relating to HIV/AIDS, TB, malaria and other epidemics can represent a national emergency. As it was apparent that provisions for compulsory licensing may not be very meaningful for developing countries that do not have the capacity to produce the drugs domestically, the 'Declaration' also instructed the Council of TRIPS to find a solution to this problem and report to the WTO General Council by the end of 2002 (WTO 2001b). An agreement was reached at the end of August 2003, under heavy political pressure to settle the issue before the Fifth WTO Ministerial meeting which was to occur in Cancun, Mexico in September 2003. This introduced various reporting requirements for countries that go beyond those in TRIPS, but permit developing countries to import pharmaceuticals cheaply in case of national emergencies. Initially this was a waiver until the TRIPS Agreement could be amended once two-thirds of the membership agreed, which finally happened in late 2016.

The 'Doha Development Agenda' also stressed that the concept of special and differential treatment (SDT) and policy flexibility should imbue all discussions and be imbedded in all agreed texts. In that connection, it was agreed early on that LDCs would not be asked to liberalize any of their trade restrictions in either manufactures or agriculture. On the part of the developed countries this was not done because they believed that this was good for development. Rather it was because the LDC markets are so small that they do not matter to developed country exporters, either of goods or services. On the part of the LDCs, this was done primarily because it gave them more 'policy space' to pursue whatever trade policy they believed would be helpful to their development unconstrained by international commitments. Moreover, Geneva developing country representatives tend to be more enamored with the traditional infant industry arguments for protection—irrespective of their validity or the policies actually pursued back home. As a consequence of excluding LDCs from liberalizing commitments, the potential benefits these countries would have obtained from liberalizing their own policies—which could have been quite substantial—were lost, with significant adverse effects on the potential overall balance of gains and losses of these countries from the Round.

On the other hand, neither the developed countries nor the more advanced developing countries provided substantial SDT to LDCs in the area they should have—market access. There was an early proposal to provide Duty Free and Quota Free (DFQF) access to LDCs agreed by a number of countries (e.g., the EU and Canada). But the US would only agree to provide DFQF access to 97% of the tariff lines of imports from LDCs. Several studies showed that the remaining 3% could include so many products that the market access improvement would be miniscule (Laborde 2008).

Perhaps the most important event of the Doha meeting was the accession of China to the WTO. China was soon to become the largest trading nation in the world and it was very important that it would conduct its trade in conformity with the rules that governed international trade worldwide. It was also thought that China's accession would result in providing additional incentives to strengthen the market orientation of its economic policies. But the developed countries wanted to take no chances: under the terms of its accession agreement, China was to be considered a 'non-market economy' for 15 years, which permitted WTO members to use somewhat arbitrary measures in determining whether China was 'dumping' products in their markets.[5]

The negotiations proceeded slowly over the next two years. Besides the agreement on TRIPS, little was achieved. At the Cancun Ministerial meeting it was agreed at the insistence of the developing countries that the negotiations would exclude three of the so-called Singapore Issues (foreign investment, competition and government procurement). But developing countries were prepared to consider an agreement on the fourth, trade facilitation (Michalopoulos 2014). Subsequently, the negotiations focused on two sets of issues: non-agriculture market access (NAMA) and agriculture. There were negotiations on other issues as well: services, TRIPS, trade facilitation and rules, especially as they relate to anti-dumping and preferential trade agreements—all these received differing degrees of attention. But the negotiating dynamic which developed required that fundamental agreement be reached in NAMA and agriculture before tackling seriously the other issues.

Aid for Trade

No agreement was reached on NAMA and agriculture in the next two years. In order to energize the process, developed countries decided to sweeten the deal by offering developing countries more aid—this time related to trade. Thus, at the Sixth WTO Ministerial in Hong Kong in 2005, there was a major new initiative on aid for trade. This was not totally new. Weaknesses in the very wide range of institutions, infrastructure and skills that are needed for effective integration in international trade define the very essence of underdevelopment and exist to some or other degree in practically all developing countries. They are obviously most pronounced in LDCs. It was because of the recognition of widespread weaknesses in a number of these new areas that the WTO agreements included extensive transition periods and developed country commitments to provide technical assistance to developing country members, as noted in Chap. 6.

The Integrated Framework

Based on the conclusions reached at the First WTO Ministerial meeting in Singapore, the high-level meeting on trade-related technical assistance to the LDCs was held in Geneva under the WTO's auspices in October 1997 to develop an assistance program (as well as to discuss improved market access) for LDCs. An important conclusion of the meeting was that it was not the lack of assistance per se that was the problem, but that it had been supply-driven, not effectively coordinated, and that the reforms supported were not 'owned' by the recipient countries. These issues were not new. Indeed, they were very similar to the issues on which the 'Philadelphia Group' was going to focus on, including lack of coherent advice, including on trade policy and reluctance by the BWI and the WTO to coordinate with the UN.[6]

The meeting adopted an Integrated Framework for trade-related technical assistance to LDCs. The framework envisaged that LDCs would conduct their own needs assessments, which would then be discussed at roundtables with the six agencies involved in the effort (the IMF, the ITC, the UN Development Program, UNCTAD, the World Bank and the WTO) plus other interested donors in order to develop an integrated program of technical assistance activities aimed primarily at institution building.[7]

Progress in meeting these needs by means of coordinated assistance programs was slow, for a variety of reasons. According to one report

(WTO 2000), developing countries expected the process to result in both improved delivery of assistance and increased amounts of funding, while the donors originally focused on the efficiency gains and synergies resulting from better coordination. Difficulties with coordination by the recipients and among the agencies emerged; and the very problems of institutional weaknesses in LDCs that the initiative was designed to address appear to have contributed to implementation delays.

A review of the Integrated Framework by the six international agencies concerned under the leadership of the World Bank was undertaken by independent consultants in mid-2000. The review recognized many of the difficulties noted above and recommended that

* the Integrated Framework should focus solely on technical assistance activities, and not on overall policy and the development of human resources and infrastructure;
* trade-related technical assistance in the World Bank's operations should be 'mainstreamed' (i.e., it should actively incorporate trade concerns in the project and program design at the country level) and coordinated through the Poverty Reduction Strategy Papers (PRSPs) prepared by low-income countries for consideration by the IMF and the World Bank;
* LDCs should have greater ownership and more oversight of the framework activities;
* the procedures and coordination mechanisms of the six agencies should be simplified and strengthened.

In late 2001, the Doha Declaration endorsed the Integrated Framework 'as a viable model for LDCs' trade development' and urged the six agencies to explore its enhancement. However, experience in the implementation of the Integrated Framework identified a number of problems highlighted in various evaluations (Liebrechts and Wimenga 2004; USAID 2005; World Bank 2004; WTO 2003). While there were some success stories (e.g., Cambodia), in many others the Integrated Framework had not been effective.

The three years following the Doha Declaration saw little progress in the trade negotiations and a great number of international meetings inside the WTO and in other forums—for example, the World Bank/ IMF Development Committee—to discuss ways in which to enhance the Integrated Framework. These meetings were helpful in clarifying two issues: first, institutional weaknesses constrained the capacity to trade, not only of LDCs but of many other lower income developing countries as well; and second, that feasibility studies and technical assistance alone were not sufficient to address supply side constraints in developing countries.

Partly in recognition of these realities and partly as an inducement to continued developing country participation in the Doha Round negotiations, in 2005 the WTO Ministerial in Hong Kong agreed to establish two task forces: one to develop proposals for the establishment of an Enhanced Integrated Framework (EIF) for helping LDCs; and another to develop proposals for increased Aid for Trade (AFT) more generally. Consistent with the lack of policy coherence between trade and aid institutions that has characterized international cooperation, governments pursued these proposals outside the actual WTO trade negotiations. This may have been a good thing, as the WTO trade negotiations stalled and the aid-related initiatives may have been one of the few tangible and lasting results of the Doha Round.

The task force on LDCs produced a set of proposals which were approved by the WTO in 2007. It took another two years for the EIF to become fully operational in mid-2009: more than a decade after the WTO first focused on LDC aid needs. It was and still is a modest operation with an annual budget of a few million dollars (Michalopoulos 2014).

Aid for Trade for Other Developing Countries

Since the establishment of WTO, a number of institutions and funds had provided trade-related assistance to developing countries. The WTO itself had a modest technical assistance program, as did UNCTAD and the International Trade Center—a joint WTO/UNCTAD institution based in Geneva that provides technical assistance for export promotion. In 2001, the Advisory Centre on WTO Law (ACWL) was established to provide assistance to developing countries in matters related to specific cases involving the WTO DSM, either as complaints or plaintiffs. The Standards and Trade Development Facility was set up in 2004 to improve developing countries' capacity to implement international sanitary and phytosanitary standards. The Facility, with an annual budget of about $5 million, represents a joint effort by five institutions (the Food and Agriculture Organization (FAO), the WHO, the World Bank, the WTO and the World Organization for Animal Health) using partly trust funds donated by bilateral donors and partly their own funding to provide technical assistance on SPS.

The resources needed for trade-related capacity building are so large that none of the above efforts will go very far without the support of the World Bank and other regional development banks and the main bilateral donors. The commitments in the WTO agreements made by the trade negotiators, mostly at the last moment in order to obtain developing country consent, were not coordinated with the rest of their governments, either in developed or developing countries. Thus, there was no serious link between the commitments made and the agenda of the national or international institutions which would be implementing them.

In the aftermath of the Hong Kong meeting, there was a lot of international soul searching as to how to mobilize additional resources for aid for trade. A number of proposals were made for setting up special funds for this purpose (Stiglitz and Charlton 2006), including one by me (Michalopoulos 2005). In the end, the WTO Aid for Trade Task Force did not set up a new fund except for LDCs, but concluded that 'additional, predictable, sustainable and effective financing is fundamental to fulfilling the Aid-for-Trade mandate' (WTO 2006, p. 1) and recommended 'additional targeted resources for trade related programs' as well as a series of procedural steps for donor coordination, country-level implementation, reporting and evaluation. The IMF/World Bank staff study in 2007 concluded that 'non-LDC low income countries have been overlooked in the effort by the trade community to mobilize aid for trade … The countries could use aid for trade for technical assistance projects, funding preparation of projects and funding legal and other reforms in implementing WTO obligations, notably for an agreement on trade facilitation' (IMF/World Bank 2007, p. 17). However, it did not recommend a new fund for this purpose.

One of the fundamental questions that had to be decided early on was what constituted 'Aid for Trade'. This was especially important because the major donors engaged in a beauty contest in Hong Kong promising vast amounts of assistance: Japan talked about $10 billion over three years, the US and the EU $2.7 and $2.0 billion, respectively, by 2010.

As the main source of information for aid flows had been the OECD, the WTO agreed to partner with the OECD in developing information on AFT flows. This resulted in the development of a joint WTO/OECD database, whose main source, however, was the OECD database on resource flows by the major bilateral and multilateral donors, a database that had been in existence for several decades and was adapted to address the information requirements on AFT. Since the main donors in OECD had a strong interest in showing that they were doing a lot to help developing countries strengthen their capacity to trade, the OECD/WTO secretariats were under strong pressure by the developed countries to adopt a very wide definition of AFT, which included not only aid activities that were directly linked to strengthening trade-related institutions, but also all aid to economic infrastructure (except water and sanitation) and building productive capacity.

The resulting totals showed that very large amounts of aid are 'trade related' and rising. According to OECD estimates (OECD 2013), total AFT commitments in 2010 amounted to $45 billion or 35% of total ODA commitments, compared to $25 billion or 22% of the total in 2002–2005. Total AFT disbursements were $29 billion in 2009, or 21% of total ODA, compared to $21 billion or 12% in 2006 (OECD/WTO 2011b).

The problems with this very wide definition of AFT flows are obvious: while it is clear that productive supply constraints inhibit developing country exports, not all assistance which aims at helping developing countries increase their productive capacity is 'trade related'. To address this issue, the OECD at the beginning in 2007 started including a slightly narrower concept of aid whose 'principal' or 'significant' objective was trade related. The resulting estimates showed that only 15–20% of AFT that built productive capacity was trade related. To give an idea of how little meaning the OECD definition of AFT had, consider the following: in 2009, using this definition, more than 60% of all 'other official flows'—primarily loans from the World Bank and other regional development banks which do a lot of infrastructure financing—would have been trade related (Michalopoulos 2014).

None of these issues troubled the beauty contest in Hong Kong. Unfortunately, the AFT initiative failed to do much to generate progress in the WTO negotiations. These continued to languish despite continued proclamations by both developed and developing countries about the importance of reaching an agreement. But in the end, people were not too worried. After all, trade negotiations always seemed to take forever. And besides, trade flows continued to grow spectacularly, despite the lack of agreement in Geneva, until of course 2008.

And What About Globalization?

During the first few years of the Millennium, the world witnessed impressive growth in output and trade. Both China and India grew very rapidly, lifting hundreds of millions of people out of poverty. Many countries in Sub-Saharan Africa also joined the parade of fast-growing economies. Brazil also grew impressively, and moreover did so while decreasing income inequality.

The growth in trade reflected two main factors: increased demand and rising prices of raw materials led to a very rapid (13.8% per annum for the period 2000–2010) increase in developing country non-manufacturing trade. Sub-Saharan Africa's was only slightly slower (12.3% per annum).

The growth of manufactured exports in the developing world was prompted by the expansion of global value chains. Developing countries benefited from large investments by both multinationals and local entrepreneurs in assembly or production of final consumer goods based on the importation of intermediates. This resulted in an annual rate of growth of manufacturing exports of 11.1%, per annum for the period 2000–2010. Sub-Saharan Africa's growth was even higher at 13.0% per annum. Growth was most impressive in the emerging markets, specifically five countries, Brazil, Russia, India, China and South Africa—the so-called BRICS.

This impressive growth was accompanied by a somewhat disturbing trend of increasing income inequality in many countries, including China and India. Only some countries in Latin America were showing increasing equality—albeit starting from significant inequality levels. The learned studies of the relationship between globalization and poverty continued to accumulate evidence that the links are complex and country specific. Ann Harrison's comprehensive review (2007) contained reaffirmation of earlier impressions based on many new cross-country and country-specific analyses.

* The poor in countries with abundant unskilled labor do not always gain from trade reforms.
* The poor are more likely to share in the gains from globalization when there are complementary policies in place, such as policies that increase labor mobility or provide farmers with credit, technical know-how and other inputs.
* Export growth and foreign direct investment reduce poverty.
* Globalization produces both winners and losers among the poor but is also associated with greater inequality.

The recommendations as to what to do are familiar: target very carefully the poor who lose from globalization, help increase their mobility and equip them with complementary inputs to help them take advantage of export opportunities (Harrison 2007, pp. 2–4; 27–28).

Notwithstanding the mixed picture, critics of globalization tended to focus more on short-run effects, while supporters look at the longer term; also, critics focused on effects on individual sub-groups of the poor, even when the poor as a whole benefit. Whatever the facts and ambiguous conclusions of two-fisted economists, by 2008, public opinion on globalization was turning decidedly negative. The report of the Commission on Growth and Development cites the Pew October 2007 Survey of Global Attitudes, which indicated that 'enthusiasm for further opening of the global economy is flagging in many advanced economies and some developing countries as well. Only countries in east Asia buck the trend' (World Bank 2008, p. 91). The report in a prescient manner goes on to argue that, to the extent that globalization leads to greater income inequality, it will create problems for maintaining openness and concluding the WTO Doha Round.

While most of the discussion of the impact of globalization on poverty focused on the problems of the South, there were some rumblings in the North: the Dutch election in 2002 reflected increased anxiety about immigrants whose conservative culture resulted in intolerant attitudes within the tolerant Dutch society. The concerns of parts of the British public about the impact of the 'Polish plumber' were voiced as early as 2003 when Poland's entry into the EU opened up immigration to other EU countries. And, of course, 9/11 itself could be attributed in part to aspects of globalization.

But none of these voices were loud enough to stymie the globalization onslaught. In retrospect, the turning point was the financial crisis that hit the developed world in 2008. The deep recession that followed, the worse since the Great Depression, laid the ground for increased protectionism and the rise of the anti-globalization forces in recent years. And it was not the charitable concern about globalization's impact on the poor in developing countries that started to turn the tide, but its impact on a relatively small but vocal group of lower middle class losers in the North.

Notes

1. Since 1993, the commitment of ODA was linked to Gross National Income (GNI) rather than GNP. GNI is typically somewhat smaller than GNP.
2. There was substantial coordination at the Johannesburg meeting on climate change in 2003.
3. Unfortunately, progress was not sustained in recent periods.
4. Herfkens left the campaign in 2008 and was not replaced. The campaign continued with a much lower profile under direction from the UNDP.
5. The 15 years ended in late 2016, but the EU and the US objected to changing China's designation, leading to a continued controversy on the issue.
6. There was a further complication indicative of the challenges of international coordination: as Taiwan was a member of the WTO but not of the UN, neither the UN nor UNCTAD nor the WTO could host the meeting. So the organizing institutions had to rent a separate building for this purpose.

7. See Chap. 6. Not surprisingly, Herfkens, who was the Netherlands' Ambassador to the United Nations and the WTO in Geneva at the time, used her World Bank experience and contacts to help produce a successful result.

References

CGD (2003) www.cgdev.org/commitment-development-award.

Easterly, W. (2007) 'Are Aid Agencies Improving' *Economic Policy*, 22 (52).

Harrison, A. (2007) *Globalization and Poverty*, (Chicago: University of Chicago Press).

Herfkens, E. (2002) Speech at Finance and Development Conference, Monterrey., March 22.

Herfkens, E. (2007a) 'The Successes and Challenges in Mobilizing Support for the Millennium Development Goals', *UN Chronicle* XLV (1).

Herfkens, E. (2007b) Speech, August 30, Berlin.

Herfkens, E. (2009) 'Dead Aid or Recovering Patient?' Op-ed on websites of *DAC News, World Economy and Development*; and *ICTSD Brides* 13(2).

Herman, B. (2006) 'The Politics of Inclusion in the Monterrey Process' DESA Working Paper #23, ST/ESA/2006/WP/23, (New York. UN).

Jacoby, R. (2017) Letter to C. Michalopoulos, January 30.

IMF/World Bank (2007) ' Aid for Trade-Harnessing Globalization for Economic Development', staff study prepared for Development Committee meeting (Washington, DC:IMF/World Bank).

IMF, OECD, United Nations, World Bank (2000) *2000 A Better World for All* (New York, UN).

Kauffman, D. (2009) *Aid Effectiveness and Governance, The Good, the Bad and the Ugly*, Special Report, (Washington, DC: World Bank).

Laborde, D. (2008) 'Looking for a Meaningful Duty Free Quota Free Market Access Initiative in the Doha Development Agenda' ICTSD, Issue Paper 4 (Geneva: ICTSD).

Lancaster, C. (2008) *George Bush's Foreign Aid: Transformation or Chaos?* (Washington, DC: Center for Global Development).

Liebrechts R. and P. Wimenga (2004) 'The IF for Trade Related Technical Assistance to LDCs' Country Reports of Ethiopia and Yemen (Rotterdam: ECORY/NEI).

Michalopoulos, C. (2005) 'Enhancing the Integrated Framework: A New Approach', mimeo, prepared for the UK Department for International Development.

Michalopoulos, C. (2014) *Emerging Powers in the WTO,* (Houndsmills: Palgrave).

Moyo, D. (2009) *Dead Aid,* (New York: Farrar, Straus and Giroux).

OECD (2011a) *The OECD at 50: Development Co-operation Past, Present and Future,* (Paris: OECD).

OECD (2011b) *Aid for Trade at a Glance 2011: Showing Results* (Paris: OECD).

OECD (2013) *Aid for Trade in 2010: Continued Growth, Modest Outlook* (Paris: OECD).

Short, C. (2004) *An Honorable Deception?* (London: Free Press).

Stiglitz, J. and A. Charlton (2006) 'Aid for Trade', *International Journal of Development Issues* 5(2): 1–41.

UN (1997) *Agenda for Development* General Assembly Resolution 51/240, Annex sales no. E98.1.3, (New York: UN).

UN (2003) *Financing for Development, Monterrey Consensus of the International Conference on Financing for Development,* (New York: UN).

USAID (2005) 'Integrated Framework Simulation' Geneva, October.

World Bank (2004) *Integrated Framework for Trade-related Technical Assistance: An Independent Evaluation of the World Bank's Approach to Global Programs OED* (Washington, DC: World Bank).

World Bank (2005) *Are We on Track to Achieve the Millennium Development Goals?* ABCDE Conference, F. Bourgignon, B. Pleskovic and A. Sapir Eds. (Washington, DC and New York: World Bank and Oxford University Press).

World Bank (2008) *The Growth Report,* (Washington DC: World Bank).

WTO (2000) 'Integrated Framework for Trade-Related Assistance to LDCs: The Process to Date, Concerns and Suggested Improvements', WT/COMTD/LDC/W/18, (Geneva: WTO).

WTO (2001a) 'Doha WTO Ministerial 'Ministerial Declaration', WT/MIN(01)DEC/1., November.

——— (2001b) Doha WTO Ministerial 'Declaration on the TRIPS Agreement and Public Health', WT/MIN (01) DEC/2.

——— (2003) 'Final Report of the Evaluation of the Integrated Framework: Summary' WT/IFSC/6/Rev2/Add.1, December.

——— (2006) 'Recommendations of the Aid for Trade Task Force' WT/AFT/1., July.

9

The Greek Crisis: Muddling Through Revisited

Introduction

Greek city states were the first true globalizers in the western world of the sixth and fifth centuries BC. They were the dominant traders, establishing trading posts and colonies throughout the Mediterranean and Black Sea and spreading at the same time Greek culture and religion throughout the area.[1] The Greek trading and sea-faring traditions continued through the Byzantine period and the Ottoman occupation to the modern era, when almost 15% of global shipping tonnage is owned by Greek interests and there are Greek traders in places as far apart as Accra Ghana, Perth, Australia and Oshkosh, Wisconsin, the result of Greek migration in the nineteenth and twentieth centuries.[2]

The track record of the Greek state in honoring its international commitments is not as glowing: there are reports that 13 Greek city states, including many of the globalizing/colonizing ones, defaulted on loans from the sanctuary of Delos in the fifth century BC; and more recently the modern Greek state defaulted on international loans on five occasions, in 1824, 1825, 1832, 1893 and most recently in 1932. In 1908, Greece

© The Author(s) 2017
C. Michalopoulos, *Aid, Trade and Development*,
https://doi.org/10.1007/978-3-319-65861-2_9

was also expelled from the Latin Monetary Union, which it had joined in 1877, for not fulfilling its obligations, only to be readmitted in 1910.

Greece was not able to borrow from private markets between 1932 and 1964. But after World War II it was able to obtain significant capital inflows through economic assistance, primarily from the US, and war reparations from Germany. The financial flows from the US started in 1947, pursuant to the announcement of the Truman doctrine in March of that year and later on under the Marshall Plan. When I started to look at the Greek economy in the mid-1960s, it was clear that the external accounts presented significant challenges. Exports of goods were about half of imports, creating a huge trade balance deficit which was only in part covered by a significant surplus on services, primarily shipping, tourism and private remittances. The resulting current account deficit was covered by official aid flows. According to my estimates, aid contributed a significant amount—slightly less than a third—to the robust 6.1% annual growth of the Greek economy over the decade 1952–1962, whether relieving a foreign exchange or a savings constraint on growth (Michalopoulos 1968). Subsequently, Greek GDP growth was quite respectable for several decades (see Table 9.1).

Roughly 40 years later, in 2005, the balance of payments had changed little: the composition of exports was somewhat different but the trade balance continued to have a large deficit which was not fully covered by a significant surplus on services, mainly shipping and tourism. The resulting current account deficit was financed by borrowing in the private capital markets, which supported a robust GDP growth of close to 4.0% per year between 1995 and 2005. This level of debt issuance at spreads that

Table 9.1 Greek annual GDP growth rate, 1965–2015

In percent	%
1965–1975	6.5
1976–1985	2.2
1986–1995	1.3
1996–2000	3.6
2001–2005	3.9
2006–2010	−0.2
2011–2015	−3.9

Source: World Bank

were only slightly higher than the German benchmark was only possible because creditors viewed Greek debt as Eurozone debt, and this complacency by the markets encouraged the Greeks to overborrow. Then came a period of massive current account deficits in 2005–2008, further borrowing, and the roof caved in during 2009 (Table 9.2). Since then GDP growth has been negative with a total decline of more than 25% over eight years, probably the largest decline for a non-conflict-ridden economy in recent history with more difficult years ahead.[3] The international accounts have become an albatross on Greek growth once again, 50 years later.

A great deal has been written about the mistakes made by the three protagonists in the modern Greek drama, the Greek government itself, the governments of its main creditors in Western Europe including the European Central Bank and the IMF. With a disaster of this magnitude, there is plenty of blame to spread around and I will not try to apportion it. In what follows, I will summarize the main elements of the rescue efforts and the reasons for their failure. It should not have taken that long to fix the significant problems that led to the disastrous performance of the Greek economy which has led to immense hardship for the Greek people, especially the poor. All three protagonists neglected to heed the lessons of recent history in dealing with debt and adjustment which ultimately succeeded in coping with similar problems of heavily indebted countries in the 1980s and 1990s. Muddling through has prevailed again, just as it did in the 1980s and its costs continue to pile up.

Re Various Sins

There is an immense literature about the euro and the Greek crisis which will not be discussed in detail here. The literature contains a number of different original sins according to the writer's, sometimes politically colored, perspective. First, there is the view shared by many economists that the original sin is the establishment of the euro, which is doomed to fail sooner or later (Friedman 1997) for a variety of reasons, including an unwillingness of the more productive and better governed group of countries in the North, to make transfers to the South. Or that a fiscal union

Table 9.2 Greece: current account for selected years (million US$, current prices and percent)

Items	1965	1970	1976	1980	1985	1990	1995	2000	2005	2009	2010	2012	2014	2015
Goods imports	914	1,509	4,997	9,717	9,370	16,564	20,343	30,322	51,705	63,833	59,801	53,176	65,108	46,608
Goods exports	331	612	2,258	4,175	4,357	6,458	5,918	10,120	17,469	20,976	22,249	27,895	35,568	27,489
Trade balance	−583	−897	−2,739	−5,542	−5,013	−10,106	−14,425	−20,201	−34,236	−42,857	−37,552	−25,281	−29,541	−19,119
Service imports	–	–	677	1,428	1,401	3,000	4,368	11,370	14,913	20,245	20,375	16,059	16,966	12,198
Service exports	–	–	1,808	3,947	2,600	6,560	9,605	19,285	34,053	38,047	37,667	35,344	41,259	30,975
Net services	303	491	1,131	2,519	1,199	3,560	5,237	7,915	19,140	17,802	17,292	19,285	24,293	18,777
CA balance	−280	−406	−929	−2,209	−3,276	−3,537	−2,864	−9,820	−18,233	−35,913	−30,275	−6,172	−3,736	218
CA balance/ GDP (%)	−5.31	−4.72	−2.98	−3.89	−6.85	−3.61	−2.09	−7.55	−7.36	−10.88	−10.11	−2.51	−1.58	0.11

Data Source: World Bank—World Development Indicators

should have preceded the monetary union. Dornbush (1996) concluded, 'If there was ever a bad idea, a European Monetary Union is it.' A variation on this is that the Eurozone, as currently structured, cannot accommodate members with significantly different cultures, economic policies and productivity levels—and that this should have been understood before permitting Greece to join.

Some argue that this is not a sin at all: the European 'project' is incomplete and it is still possible to a have a viable Eurozone with Greece in it, if only certain additional measures are taken (Pisani-Ferry 2014). Others simply believe that Greece should never have been permitted to join the euro as it cheated by producing fake statistics that enabled it to meet Eurozone criteria at entry. Another perspective lays the blame on the private capital markets which exhibit herd behavior based on incomplete information. And some lump all sins on the conservative Greek government that ruled during 2004–2008 which accumulated huge budget and current account deficits that precipitated the crisis. There is some justification for all of the above, but in my view the modalities of the first bailout negotiated in 2010 also contained sins committed by the Greek government, the Eurozone governments and the IMF that have played a big role in shaping the future course of events.[4]

Fake Statistics?

The fake statistics issue received prominence in 2010 when it became apparent that the previous Greek government had substantially underreported the 2009 budget deficit. Eurostat was brought in to assess the Greek budget and debt statistics. It found a very large underreporting of the budget deficit and, inter alia, that the government had not reported a series of foreign exchange swaps it had undertaken in 2001 with Goldman Sachs as well as a number of related interest rate swaps it had concluded with the same company which were later recapitalized. This resulted in the underreporting of outstanding debt by about 5.4 billion euros or 2.2% of GNP in 2010. However, at the time the original arrangements were made, in 2001, the Eurostat rules defining government debt specifically excluded swaps—as well as other forms of financial derivatives. The rules were subsequently changed in 2008 and the Greek government failed to report the debt at the time as it should have (Eurostat 2010). But the critical point is different: the swaps were undertaken in 2001. By that time, Greece had already been admitted to the euro based on a decision of the EU Summit of 2000 using statistics for 1999 (Sardelis 2013).

The details of the onset of the 2009 crisis are well known. As soon as the Papandreou (PASOK) government came to power following the October 2009 parliamentary election, it became clear that the budget deficit, which had been thought to be near 6% of GDP, was likely to be around 12% (Papaconstantinou, p. 32). Later, the estimate was increased to 13.6% with the final number reaching 15.4%. This was the culmination of a series of deficits run by the previous two governments but the Karamanlis (New Democracy, ND) government that ran the country since 2004 definitely produced the largest ones. In all cases the programmed deficits were supposed to be less than 3% of GDP, consistent with the Maastricht guidelines. In all cases they exceeded the target: they rose from 3.2% in 2000 to 7.2% in 2004 (the year of the Athens Olympics) and were in excess of 5% in 2005–2007 and more than 9% in 2008. Some of this spending could be attributed to large expenditures on pensions, where the replacement rate[5] was much higher than in other Eurozone countries. Another part had to do with increased government payrolls.

It was clear to the founders of the Eurozone that some coordination on fiscal policy was essential for its survival and that is why they set up the 3% budget deficit rule. When both Germany and France sinned by violating the rule with impunity early on, they jeopardized the credibility of the rules—as unobserved rules are no rules at all and rules enforced only on the weak members lead to resentment and non-observance. But despite the deficits and as a consequence of the rapid GDP growth, the 113% ratio of public debt to GDP in 2008 was only marginally higher than the 111% debt/GDP in 1996.

There was also massive private credit expansion after 2000, as the Eurozone real interest rates were much lower than what had prevailed in Greece for decades. There was finally a mortgage market to help satisfy the Greek desire for second homes. But the building bubble was nowhere near the levels reached in Ireland and Spain. Credit cards became common where none had existed before and the economy as a whole was booming until 2008. The ratio of private sector loans to GDP stood at 34% in 1998 before entry to the Eurozone and at the time it was about half of what it was in Italy, and slightly more than a third of Portugal and Ireland. As of 2008, they had more than tripled to 103% and were higher than Italy's, although still lower than Ireland and Portugal. Typically, when credit expansion is so much faster than GDP growth, trouble looms ahead.

The current account has been in deficit consistently for more than 50 years—until 2015. But it has always been managed effectively and rarely exceeded 5% of GDP, primarily because the Bank of Greece has typically had good and steady leadership. However, during 2001–2005, the current account deficit grew in parallel with the budget deficit: from 6–7% of GDP in 2001–2005, it exploded to 14% in 2007–2008.

In January 2010, the Greek government floated five-year bonds for 5 billion euros at 6.2%. The offering was oversubscribed and resulted in borrowing of 8 billion euros. But this would not be enough. In the next two months, the markets started to focus on the financing needs of the Greek economy resulting in credit rating downgrades and increases in borrowing costs. A serious problem was emerging as without help, Greece would have had to default on existing obligations (see also Gibson et al. 2014).

The debt problem was not without precedent. As discussed in Chap. 4, in the 1980s and 1990s, many developing countries, some with very large economies—albeit with slightly lower per capita incomes—had faced similar problems and had sought assistance from the IFIs. The international community had taken a long time, at considerable cost to the economies concerned, to come up with a solution. 'By 1986 informed opinion understood that Third World Debt would have to be reduced, written off, defaulted' (Galbraith, p. 52) But it took the international community three more years to launch the Brady Bond schemes which helped bail out more than a dozen middle-income countries (and more than a decade later for official debts of poor countries). Successful programs had several common characteristics:

* There was invariably an IMF program to restore macroeconomic balances, usually involving tight monetary policy, a reduction in budget deficits and overall absorption which resulted in temporary contraction of output and reduced employment.
* There was a program of structural adjustment, usually involving a number of measures that would reorient production toward exportables, through a real exchange rate depreciation (often a substantial

nominal devaluation combined with trade policy reforms), and a number of other structural reforms usually monitored by the World Bank—which would also provide additional longer term financial support.

* The conditions attached to the programs were expected to be few, measurable and focused on important aspects of reforms.

* Government ownership of the reform program was critical to its success as was its ability to convince public opinion about the necessity of the proposed reforms

* Foreign Private Debt was reduced: outstanding debt obligations to foreign private bond holders would be reduced through the exchange of the maturing debt with new debt of lower nominal value resulting in losses to private sector bond holders; the latter were forced to accept such losses in exchange for the greater certainty of the reforming countries servicing the new debt. The debt reduction was supposed to be of such magnitude as to restore the capacity of the reforming country to service it over time, that is, it was to meet the debt sustainability test.

In early 2010 the Greek government engaged in a series of tortuous negotiations with its Eurozone partners who initially were not keen in having the IMF participate in a rescue of a Eurozone country. Later, following a shift in the German position, the IMF was brought in resulting in another set of negotiations with the Troika (i.e., the European Commission, the European Central Bank and the IMF). Following a final set of discussions with the IMF, which had problems in participating in the rescue for a variety of reasons, including the projected debt profile for the Greek debt and the size of the borrowing from the IMF, agreement was reached in May on a two-year program of support involving credits of 110 billion euros (80 million euros from bilateral loans by Eurozone governments and 30 million euros from the IMF). The terms of the loans were onerous: three years at around 5% for the European government loans with a half point additional for the 'service' provided, and slightly lower interest rates for the IMF. 'It was decided to set punitively high interest rates in order to reassure those who considered that financial assistance was a dangerous encouragement of lax policies' (Pisani-Ferry 2014, p. 9). There was a memorandum of understanding containing the agreed reforms, including prior conditions and bench-marks. Crucially, however, there was no reduction of private sector debt, a fateful omission that doomed the program.

It was agreed that the Greek government would implement a very large upfront reduction of the budget deficit from what was originally thought to be 13.6% of GDP to 9%. It was also projected that GDP would decline for a year or two, but growth would be restored in 2012 as would access to the private markets, enabling Greece to repay the official credits and the IMF in short order as well as restore long-term debt sustainability. The IMF credit at 3,200% of Greece's IMF quota was the largest ever provided relative to the member's quota. The credit was provided despite staff misgivings about the projected debt sustainability. The very large IMF credit 'required a modification of the Fund's exceptional access policy framework, but the need for a policy change was not disclosed to the (IMF) Board until the staff report had been circulated. The policy change was embedded in the report requesting the Greek Stand-By Arrangement, and therefore was to be implicitly approved along with the formal and explicit request for Fund resources' (IMF 2017, p. vii; Wyplosz and Sgherri 2016). The justification for the policy change was that in the absence of the credit, there was 'systemic' risk, resulting from the possibil ity that the Greek problems would result in 'contagion' for other Eurozone countries which would face difficulties in rolling over their large private market borrowings (IMF 2017; IEO 2016).

The program was 'on track' from May to October 2010. In the fall of 2010, it became apparent that the very large upfront reduction in the Greek budget deficit of 5.5% would not be enough to produce the desired target deficit of less than 3% by 2014 as the actual 2009 deficit turned out to be even larger by an additional 1.8% of GDP. This would necessitate even greater austerity in the second year of the program. The Merkel-Sarkozy Deauville agreement in late 2010 to modify the Eurozone understanding in ways that could result in significant losses to private sector holders of official debt in case of a Eurozone country default led to further weakening of the prospects of Greece's returning to the markets in the near future. It also precipitated new IMF support programs in Portugal and Ireland and the establishment of the European Support Mechanism (ESM) in 2012.

In the meantime, the actual decline in Greek GDP and the increase in unemployment were much greater than projected by the IMF. This resulted in upward revisions of the projected debt/GDP ratio making the future debt profile unsustainable. The original standby was eventually abandoned in early 2012 and was substituted by an IMF Extended Fund Facility program on softer terms, including additional assistance from the newly established ESM as well as a significant 'haircut' of private sector debt. That program also eventually failed to produce the expected results for a variety of reasons, including issues that were not addressed by the first program as well as an unwillingness of the participants to learn the lessons from the first program's failure. Currently, Greece is on a third bailout. This time the IMF is participating in the monitoring of the program without participating in its funding. Meanwhile, GDP is stagnant and investment is 75% less than ten years ago. The problems created by the first ill-designed bailout saddled the Greeks with unsustainable debts and continue to hamper prospects for the Greek economy for many decades ahead.

Similarities and Differences: Sovereign Debt Crises and Greece

There were significant similarities and differences between debt crises in the 1980s and 1990s and the Greek bailouts:

First, debt levels in Greece were twice than the average of a sample of 57 economies that experienced some kind of debt crisis in the period 1980–2014, but not significantly different than Ireland, Italy, Portugal and Spain or for that matter some of the larger earlier defaults (Gournichas et al. 2016, p. 3).

Second, the crisis in Greece involved a combination of sovereign debt default, a boom/bust cycle in foreign borrowing and a sudden stop in such borrowing in 2010. This combination had only been present on nine other occasions in emerging markets (Gournichas et al. 2016, p. 64).

Third, of these ten most difficult cases, only in one other occasion (Argentina, 2001) did the country attempt for a limited period of time to undertake an adjustment through internal devaluation. Internal devaluation meant that competitiveness was expected to be restored and the current account improved, not through exchange rate adjustment but through relative declines in costs and prices of exportables. Unlike the other debt relief programs in developing countries, Greece was not a master of its own monetary, exchange rate and trade policies. Monetary policy was determined by the ECB which alone could decide the amounts of credit it would make available to Greek banks. And, as a member of the EU customs union and the Eurozone, Greece did not have the option of fixing or not fixing its exchange rate or change its trade policies in order to effect a real exchange rate depreciation; it had to rely on internal devaluation through changes in the domestic level of prices and wages.[6]

Fourth, the original Greek bailout did not involve a PSI (Private Sector Involvement), which would have reduced outstanding debt. There was a PSI in the second bailout, but in the meantime the private sector, mainly commercial banks in Germany and France, were able to unload about 40 billion euros of Greek debt and another 10 billion euros while the second bailout was being negotiated, thus forcing a greater burden of the haircut on domestic banks that had to be recapitalized as a result as well as Greek pension funds.

Fifth, unlike most emerging countries benefiting from the Brady schemes, who were only able to obtain support from the IFIs, Greece, as a member of the Eurozone, could ask and did obtain substantial financial assistance from its Eurozone partners.[7] On the other hand, Greece's participation in the Eurozone increased the politicization of both the reform package and the bailouts as well as increased the complexity of reaching agreement between the Troika and Greece.[8]

Finally, although Greece's per capita income was higher than the typical Brady country, Greece's governance, business practices, regulations, judicial system and many of its institutions were not significantly different from those of higher middle-income developing countries (IMF 2017).

Failures to Heed Lessons of the Past

The Eurozone

The governments of the Eurozone countries and the ECB were dead set against a PSI and debt reduction from the outset of the negotiations. They were in part concerned about the impact of a PSI on the health of the banking system, especially in France and Germany which had just started to emerge from the problems of the financial meltdown of late 2008. It has been argued that their main concern was not with the impact of a PSI in a Greek rescue as such but the precedent it would set for other Eurozone countries, in particular Italy and Spain where European banks had even larger portfolios. They agreed to a PSI in Greece later on, by which time their banking system had shed the bulk of the Greek debt and they had had time to put together a more formal defense mechanism for Eurozone countries needing assistance. Greece thus became the 'perfect culprit' in Pisani-Ferry's term (Pisani-Ferry 2014) or 'sacrificial lamb' (Stiglitz 2015) to maintain Eurozone cohesion and avoid problems with bigger countries.

It is also claimed that a PSI was only made possible after Jean-Paul Trichet left as President of the ECB (Papaconstantinou 2016, p. 254). This is quite plausible given his previous career: recall that in the period 1982–1985 as Deputy Chair of the Paris Club, he presided over dozens of official debt reschedulings, often on hard terms and no debt reductions; and of course he was President of the Bank of France between 1993 and 2003.

Finally, it is alleged that Eurozone members gave private assurances to other members of the IMF governing board at its crucial meeting in April 2010 deciding the IMF support of the Greek bailout that they would urge their private banks to maintain their exposure in Greece (Orphanides 2015). It is not known whether they did or not. But, even if they did, the lesson of the 1980s was clear: government entreaties to the private sector banks to maintain or increase exposure to highly indebted countries fall on deaf ears. Only debt reduction packages do. This did not materialize in the first bailout, as it should have. Greece was saddled with a very large official debt on onerous terms which has become a major constraint to its future growth. Reductions in its nominal value or its terms would entail formal budgetary losses to European governments which are always politically difficult and even more so today.

The IMF

A lot has been made about the way the IMF decided to participate in the first bailout: that proper procedure for such a size drawing was not followed, that warnings about debt sustainability were not heeded and that the Eurozone IMF Board members pressured others in light of their own participation in the aid package (Wyplosz and Sgherri 2016). It can also be argued that Dominique Strauss-Kahn, IMF Managing Director at the time, wanted Greece to get an IMF standby because he wanted to show the IMF relevance in resolving a systemic crisis only a year after the IMF had undergone a substantial downsizing because many of its important members no longer thought it useful.[9]

My concerns are more technical: the IMF staff projections under the first bailout (as well as the second) did not take into account the known and knowable facts about the Greek situation in making the projections of recovery and debt sustainability. There were problems with at least three aspects of the program: the multiplier used to estimate the real impact of the proposed reduction in the budget deficit; the implications of an internal devaluation for output and employment; the nature and impact of the structural adjustment conditions attached to the program. To its credit, the IMF has recognized some of these weaknesses recently (IMF 2017; IEO 2016). Unfortunately, they were not taken into consideration in the second IMF program in 2012.

Regarding the multiplier used, it was clearly too low as it did not take into account the fact that Greece's tradeables sector is a relatively small part of the economy (Bowerm et al. 2014). This meant that the projected impact of the deficit reduction on GDP was much smaller than the one actually observed.

Moreover, the impact of the internal devaluation on real output was equally underestimated. The IMF staff had at its disposal the extensive experience of West Africa where internal devaluation efforts led to massive GDP reductions over several years (see Chap. 4). Was it because the West African countries were poorer and smaller economies and hence were not considered relevant? Was it because the French government and the ECB did not want to focus attention on the experience in West Africa where Trichet as head of the French Treasury opposed the devaluation of the West African Franc for many years to the detriment of the countries concerned?[10] In Greece, the actual real exchange rate depreciation was only 4.5% between 2008 and 2014, compared with 10% for the average country facing a sudden stop in its lending and 35% for countries experiencing the massive problems of Greece (Gournichas et al. 2016). Given the low price elasticity for Greek exports (see below), it is not at all surprising that the adjustment of the current account resulted almost exclusively from contraction in imports which was related to the overall contraction of demand and GDP.

In any case, as the recent IMF assessment admits, had these factors been taken into account, it would have required a more gradual deficit reduction, which would have required more financial assistance to make the program workable. This would have required either more money from the Eurozone members or significantly softer terms which would have undercut their efforts to show that 'profligate' countries like Greece should expect to be punished not rewarded for their bad policies.

The conditionality on the structural side contained more conditions than usual because it was judged, correctly, that Greece had a weak institutional capacity. The program initially contained a smaller number of benchmarks than Latvia but more than Bulgaria, Hungary and Romania. As the program progressed however, and partly because passage of broad legislation did not necessarily result in actual system reform, confidence declined and the number of conditions mushroomed. As noted in the IMF's staff assessment (IMF 2013, p. 41): 'The blanket legislation to liberalize closed professions was succeeded under the EFF supported program by detailed legislative and regulatory changes on a profession by profession basis.' This did not succeed either, as will be discussed below. The point is that the lessons of experience were not followed from the beginning: there should have been fewer conditions and better focused (Tsoukalis 2016).

The conditionality attached to the program was focused wrongly if the objective was to shift resources to the tradeables sector—especially more exports. Following the 'Washington Consensus' which suggests that factor market imperfections should be addressed before market distortions, several adjustment measures were designed to lower wage costs, in order to help restore competitiveness. It turns out that wage costs were lowered but prices did not fall as much as expected. Or the overall price level would actually fall but exports would not rise. As Chap. 4 concluded, not all countries are the same. Greater efforts probably should have been made earlier on to address product rather than factor market imperfections. However, in my view the problem was deeper: very little attention was paid to the export sector and what it would take to expand Greek exports.

The only serious recent study on the composition of Greek exports confirms the apparent loss of competitiveness identified by many. It shows that in the period 1996–2006, growth of Greek exports was less than could be expected by the growth world trade: Greek exports consisted of commodities with less than average growth in world demand and within the group of commodities exported, Greece's share declined (Athanasoglou et al. 2010, p. 19). The study also shows that the long-run elasticity of price competitiveness of Greek exports is relatively low 'which means that the improvement in export performance through changing export prices requires a rather strong effort' (Athanasoglou et al. 2010, p. 49). Clearly the internal devaluation was not enough. There was no way that wage and price reductions could make up for the fact that Greece had a fixed exchange rate.[11]

A simple look at the performance of Greek exports over the period 2008–2015 will show why. The top five of these exports consisted of capital-intensive products in which labor costs turned out to be a very small component: Table 9.3 shows the ten largest Greek exports at the HS2 level for the period 2000–2015. The top five are petroleum products, aluminum, pharmaceuticals, plastics and machinery of various kinds. Greece is not a petroleum producer. The large exports reflect the production of several refineries which import crude oil and export refined products. Aluminum exports reflect production of a smelter using bauxite ores and the rest are capital-intensive products: it is not that Greece is not involved in global value chains (see Maisonneuve de la 2016). It is, but it is mostly focused

Table 9.3 Greece: top 10 exported commodities, selected years (million US$ and percent of exports)

Code	Commodity	2000 Rank	2000 Trade value	2000 % of Exp.	2005 Rank	2005 Trade value	2005 % of exp.	2009 Rank	2009 Trade value	2009 % of exp.	2010 Rank	2010 Trade value	2010 % of exp.	2012 Rank	2012 Trade value	2012 % of exp.	2015 Rank	2015 Trade value	2015 % of exp.
3	Fish	–	–	–	–	–	–	10	663	2.7	–	–	–	10	768	2.2	10	647	2.3
8	Edible fruit	8	434	4.0	10	571	3.3	8	858	3.5	8	955	3.5	8	978	2.8	8	884	3.1
15	Animal or vegetable fats and oils	–	–	–	–	–	–	–	–	–	–	–	–	–	–	–	9	829	2.9
20	Preparations of vegetables, fruit, nuts	6	472	4.4	8	651	3.7	7	941	3.9	7	993	3.6	6	1,128	3.2	7	1,037	3.7
24	Tobacco	9	389	3.6	–	–	–	–	–	–	–	–	–	–	–	–	–	–	–
–27	Mineral fuels, oils and products	1	1,593	14.7	1	1,642	9.4	1	4,924	20.3	1	7,193	26.1	1	13,691	38.9	1	8,431	29.8
30	Pharmaceutical	–	–	–	2	1,169	6.7	2	1,311	5.4	2	1,371	5.0	4	1,237	3.5	4	1,126	4.0
39	Plastics	–	–	–	7	796	4.6	6	998	4.1	5	1,126	4.1	5	1,154	3.3	5	1,103	3.9
52	Cotton	7	465	4.3	9	586	3.4	–	–	–	–	–	–	–	–	–	–	–	–
61	Apparel and clothing	2	991	9.1	3	1,092	6.3	9	693	2.9	–	–	–	–	–	–	–	–	–
72	Iron and steel	–	–	–	–	–	–	–	–	–	10	702	2.5	9	816	2.3	–	–	–
76	Aluminum	4	506	4.7	5	926	5.3	4	1,025	4.2	3	1,348	4.9	2	1,539	4.4	2	1,560	5.5
84	Machinery	5	483	4.5	6	856	4.9	3	1,048	4.3	6	1,013	3.7	7	981	2.8	3	1,395	4.9
85	Electrical machinery	3	633	5.8	4	950	5.4	5	1,021	4.2	4	1,157	4.2	3	1,375	3.9	6	1,054	3.7
99	Unspecified commodities	10	336	3.1	–	–	–	–	–	–	9	704	2.6	–	–	–	–	–	–

Data Source: UN COMTRADE

on the capital-intensive part of the chains.[12] The impact of labor costs on the competitiveness of these sectors is decidedly limited.[13]

As for the rest of the potential exports, a great number depend on agriculture (fruits and vegetables (HS08, HS20), olive oil (HS15), tobacco (HS24), cotton (HS52) and fisheries (HS03). Regarding agriculture, anybody who has visited a Greek farm in recent periods would have noticed that most of the labor consists of immigrants (many illegal) from all over the world including Asia, Africa and Albania. Practically all are paid in cash as part of the large gray economy and for them the formal wage sector and what happens to minimum wages, union contracts and so on is barely relevant.[14] As for cotton, the less said the better: cotton is a product heavy in the use of water, an input in very scarce supply in Greece, making it a product which is profitable only under very heavy subsidies, not to be used during a period of fiscal stringency. Finally, fisheries emerged recently as a major export, with Greece being the leading exporter of products of fish farms in the Mediterranean. Unfortunately, these exports also stagnated in recent periods partly as a consequence of credit difficulties of the major producers. All the adjustment in the current account occurred through the compression of imports.

The main difficulties of expanding exports in my view rest with the administrative procedures and overall business climate and fall under the general rubric of trade facilitation. Weaknesses in trade-related institutions is also the main reason for the weak Greek export performance according to a European Commission study (Bowerm et al. 2014). There was practically no discussion of the export sector in any of the lengthy Letters of Intent and MOUs in the early years. No trade expert came from Brussels to help. It was only in the later periods of the EFF that conditionality focused very lightly on these issues, and the customs regulations were improved in 2014 (IMF 2014).[15] But in 2015 exports fell significantly in part because of the imposition of capital controls and they appear to have declined further in 2016.

In the second year of the program the Troika also mishandled the conditionality regarding privatization. Given their uncertainty, proceeds from privatization are not counted in filling financial gaps of IMF programs. Yet, a figure of 50 billion euros was publically announced as a program target by the European Commission representative without prior consultation with the Greek authorities.[16] The figure is preposterously large, especially as it is intended in part to be based on the privatization of Greek public real estate assets which have never been evaluated, not the least because there is no full cadaster of the Greek economy. Whatever the origin, the number created a storm of opposition from all directions, including a number of labor unions. The communist-led union of Piraeus Port workers was especially incensed as the proposals appeared to include fuller privatization of the Piraeus port in which the Chinese company COSCO already had a substantial stake. As a result, we had the oxymoron situation in which a communist-led union in a market economy opposed the acquisition of a public asset by a state-owned enterprise of a communist country considered even today a non-market economy by the US and the EU (see Chap. 10). After many years and many false starts, the sale was finalized in early 2017. The strikes, however, resulted in significant losses of foreign exchange as for many years they made it impossible for cruise ships to make Piraeus their port of origin or part of their itinerary.

The Greek Government

Early on and throughout most of the standby, there was no questioning of the Greek government ownership of the program of fiscal adjustment. Any government which reduces a budget deficit by more than 5% of GDP must have been committed to the program. This was especially the case with the Ministry of Finance and the Prime Minister. While not all aspects of the fiscal reform were implemented on time as the situation in the Ministry and related agencies was truly chaotic, the bulk of the benchmarks were met. Major problems continued however, with tax evasion.

And as had happened in many developing countries in the 1980s, problems arose with the implementation of the reforms by the other ministries. The main problems were with privatization and labor reforms. This should not have come as a surprise given that 'socialist' is one of the initials in PASOK, the government party at the time. There were also problems with efforts to open the so-called closed professions, that is, lawyers, engineers, pharmacists and notaries. There were, and still are, two kinds of issues: either legislation would pass, but the relevant ministries would not implement it; or the 'vested interests' would block its implementation through a variety of means, including recourse to the very slow judicial system. To date and despite various legislative efforts by various governments of the Right, the Left or the Center, Greek pharmacies operate on hours determined by their guild not the relevant legislation and one cannot buy aspirin or other non-prescription drugs anywhere else except in pharmacies.

This kind of ownership problems should not have come as a surprise to the IMF—perhaps the ECB and the Commission were not aware of them because of their lack of experience with these matters, but this issue was central to all the IMF programs in Latin America, Sub-Saharan Africa, everywhere in the 1980s and 1990s. The government, meaning the Prime Minister, the Ministry of Finance and the Central Bank, would come to an agreement with the IMF (and the World Bank) on a package of reforms which would frequently not be implemented by the rest of the government (see Chap. 4). And the response should not have been what the IMF did (and to which the government agreed), which is to devise a large number of detailed steps as prior actions, but as the recent report states 'ownership could be fostered by focusing on a smaller number of reforms with a clear implementation sequencing' (IMF 2017). This was written in 2017 regarding actions that took place five years earlier. But the lessons on these aid issues were clear to the OECD/DAC of 20 years before and the Paris Declaration on Aid Effectiveness in which the IMF participated in the early 2000s (Chap. 8). They were ignored by the Troika as well as the Greek government, both of which should have known better. Regrettably, the early failures in structural reforms undermined confidence in the government's commitment and resulted in a 'short leash' detailed conditionality later on.

The government also failed in 'selling' the program to the public—partly because the main ministries involved in the program could only speak about the hardships the program would entail. There were a few voices, arguing that all the measures advocated by the Troika had to be undertaken, irrespective of whether they were part of the onerous 'memorandum' because they made sense and would strengthen the Greek economy in the long run. But these voices were drowned out by the fierce political opposition by the parties of both the Greek Left and the Greek Right. There was no consensus for reform in Greece at that time or later. The bottom line is that all three major participants in the first Greek bailout failed to heed the lessons of the past. The result was a second bailout with some of the same flaws which only partly improved the situation and the saddling of the Greek economy with a debt whose servicing is causing a major constraint on future growth.

False Dawn: The Second Bailout

About a year into the first bailout, doubts about its sufficiency started to grow: despite large progress, the 2011 Greek budget deficit continued to be in the range of 10% of GDP and the primary fiscal balance at around −2.5%. Combined with the large decline in GDP, the debt/GDP ratio deteriorated and a 'debt restructuring became inevitable' (IMF 2017, p. 8). A plan for a PSI was announced in July 2011, but it was not agreed until an EU Summit on October 26–27 in Cannes. In between there were several months of EU meetings and negotiations, considerable internal opposition and a government reshuffle in Greece as well as a casual private proposal of the German Minister of Finance Schaeuble in September that Greece should consider an orderly 'Grexit' (Papaconstantinou 2016, p. 328).

The agreement called for the Eurozone countries to provide up to 100 billion euros in new credits on softer terms as well as 30 billion euros for a possible haircut of 50% of the private debt. But the Cannes agreement was not the end of the story. The Greek Prime Minister, George Papandreou, was deeply concerned that the agreement would entail significant additional hardship through budget cuts that would involve more reductions on pensions and other areas. He also wanted to show up the opposition which had opposed the bailout but insisted on wanting to stay in the euro. Thus he proposed to put the whole agreement up for judgment in a public referendum. Papandreou's referendum proposal resulted in an uproar in the Eurozone because of its possible implications for the markets and the future of the euro. It also generated opposition within his own party, as a result of which he agreed to withdraw the referendum proposal as well as resign, to be succeeded by a technocratic government supported by PASOK and ND, the two centrist parties which with different names had governed Greece for most of the post-World War II era.

It fell upon the technocratic government headed by Loukas Papademos, a former banker and deputy Governor of the ECB, to pass the legislation needed as prior actions for the second bailout amidst extraordinary demonstrations supported by the opposition Left and Right parties. I happened to be in Greece that fateful evening in mid-February 2012 and wrote a letter to a number of friends and relatives from which I quote:

I just came back from Athens where at midnight last Sunday I witnessed live on TV what constituted possibly the next to the last act of the modern Greek tragedy: the Greek parliament voting in the affirmative, with a large majority to accept the onerous terms of the latest bailout, while on a split screen one could see several buildings burning and the police battling thousands of hooded anarchists who were throwing Molotov cocktails.

Sunday's events resulted in two sets of ruins: First a number of buildings were destroyed including two movie theaters and one restaurant, whose charred ruins I visited with sadness on Monday amidst residual tear gas fumes; these will be rebuilt. What will not be rebuilt is the second set of ruins, which consists of the Greek party political party system which (with the exception for the few years of the nasty colonels) has governed Greece for the last sixty years. After the vote almost 50 MPs from the two ruling parties (PASOK and ND) which have been supporting the government have been expelled from their parties for not voting for the bailout. PASOK is in total disarray and may not muster 10% of the vote in the next elections. The decline of the two parties may not be a bad thing in the long run: they have been responsible for the patronage and corruption that has been endemic in Greek governments. But in the short run it will force the creation of multi-party governments requiring the building of consensus for any policy action, something that Greek parties have not done for years. And it will make staying the course in implementing the commitments of the new memorandum even more difficult possibly heading into a more tragic finale.

There are no big time heroes in this play. The only heroes I can think of are the thousands of pensioners who will have to eke out an existence with as little as 250 euros a month or less; or perhaps the shopkeeper near Syntagma in Central Athens whose shop had been vandalized by anarchists on two previous occasions and who on Sunday night crashed a bat on the head of an anarchist forcing him and his buddies to scamper.

There are many villains. On the Greek side I will start with the tax authorities and personnel, the bulk of whom are either incompetent or corrupt. As of the end of the last fiscal year, the Greek government was apparently owed 8 billion euros in taxes and fines from roughly 25,000 individuals or companies; it had been able to collect only 100 million. If it had collected a bit more than half of the total, it would have had no budget deficit. A second collective villain is the thousands of doctors, lawyers, plumbers, electricians and many other members of the so-called free professions who habitually report only about one tenth of their taxable income. A third collective villain is the so-called syndicalists the trade union people whom the Greeks in a play of words call the syndicat robbers…

Competitiveness cannot increase in the short run by opening up the professions; and as inflation is low and the exchange rate fixed there is little one can do… Alas, the economy under the best of circumstances will be in a depressed state for years to come.

What is needed is for the creditors to find a way to be more generous; also what is needed is for a new Greek government to manage to behave more responsibly for a sufficient period to also ease the uncertainty. This is almost like asking for a *deus ex machina* who used to resolve problems in ancient tragedies. I end on an optimistic note not because I believe in miraculous interventions. Rather I believe in Greek ingenuity and, unlike what one hears in Northern Europe these days, Greek industriousness and work ethic. Most Greeks work hard in order to consume more and they invest a lot in the education of their children. So that even if there is a disorderly default, a few years later the economy will pick up within the euro, if there is still a euro, or with the drachma a currency whose history is much longer than the euro. (Michalopoulos 2012)

The PSI haircut resulted in a 53% reduction of the private debt. But as a great deal of the foreign bond holders had already dumped their bonds, the haircut fell disproportionately on the Greek (and Cypriot banks) which had to be recapitalized as well as on Greek pension funds. At the same time, there was continuous loss of bank deposits. The Greek banking system, which, unlike the Irish banks, had not been overextended at the start of the problem, became shakier and shakier. The ECB, which had previously purchased Greek bonds at a discount in the open market, was also excluded from the haircut, thus realizing a profit which would be the subject of considerable discussion and controversy in subsequent periods.

A new EFF agreement was requested and obtained from the IMF of 28 billion euros with a set of conditionalities involving 'rapid fiscal and external adjustment to be accompanied by politically difficult structural reforms in support of the (authorities) strong preference to remain in the euro area' (IMF 2017, p. 11). The IMF staff felt that it would have been desirable to have a slower but longer adjustment period, but were willing to give the Greek authorities a chance to implement the program recognizing that 'the new program is a bold step in the right direction but given the challenges and the track record is subject to exceptional risks' (IMF 2012).

The IMF staff report contained two 'boxes', one of which essentially said that internal devaluation was extremely difficult and rarely if ever succeeded. There is little to disagree with this judgment, especially as contrary to expectations, the internal devaluation would have had to take place in an overall deflationary international environment requiring actual declines in nominal wages and prices, a very difficult feat indeed. The other box said that leaving the euro would result in many unpleasant and unquantifiable adverse repercussions for the economy (IMF 2012). Thus, the IMF staff was protected on paper against any program outcome. But it is hard to fault them: the only alternative was even more financing from the Eurozone. And that was not forthcoming. While it is correct to argue that Eurozone financing was self-serving to a considerable extent, it is also important to consider that some of this financing had to come from Eurozone countries that were significantly poorer than Greece. And it is also true that because Greeks had to cope with inflation for so long, they channeled their savings into real estate, with the result that while their per capita income was less than the Eurozone average, real assets were significantly higher, leading to significant political opposition to the Greek bailouts by the general public in Western Europe.

After two parliamentary elections, a new coalition government was established headed by ND but including PASOK and DHMAR, a smaller left wing party. The new government started to implement the EFF program with considerable success for almost two years. It had the benefit of a new ECB boss, Mario Draghi, previously the Governor of the Central Bank of Italy, whom I had met in the 1980s when he was a lively and knowledgeable Executive Director for Italy (and Greece) at the World Bank. He calmed down the markets with his now famous dictum that the ECB will do 'whatever it takes' to support the euro and there were no more 'Grexit' discussions for a while. In November there was a softening of the terms of the Eurozone official loans and a return to Greece of some of the ECB profits on the Greek bonds.

There was long a list of conditionalities, 44 prior actions plus 43 structural benchmarks, of which 10 were converted into prior actions—compared to 9 prior actions in the Cyprus program, 5 in the case of Ireland and 17 in Portugal (IMF 2017, Figure 21, p. 28). The conditionalities contained the usual efforts to improve fiscal and general government performance, the labor market, opening up the professions and so on and for the first time paid attention to trade issues (see above). Perhaps its greatest accomplishment was the introduction of a new unified tax on real estate.

Performance was not perfect, but until mid-2014 it appeared to be slightly better than under the standby, partly because there seemed to be greater ownership of the program by the governing coalition. The review by the Troika in May 2014 said: 'To have reached a surplus on primary fiscal and current account balances so swiftly is an extraordinary adjustment by any international comparison' (IMF 2014, p. 4). The government was on track to achieve a primary surplus of 1.5% and the 'Fiscal Adjustment continues to impress' (IMF 2014, p. 22). In the spring, the government managed to return to the markets for the first time in four years with a five and half year bond for 3 billion euros at 4.95%. The GDP growth was projected to be positive and it looked finally like a turning point had been reached.

But then politics 'interfered'. SYRIZA, the main opposition party following the two elections, continued its hard opposition against the program and reform fatigue appeared to have set in. It was expressed in losses for the ruling coalition in the European elections in June. In the summer of 2014, the government took two steps that weakened its position. The first was that it forced the resignation of H. Theoharis, the

Director General for Revenue, a professional highly respected by the Troika. The other was the sudden closing down of the public television stations in order to meet its commitment for government personnel reductions. The latter action resulted in another round of massive demonstrations and the departure of the DHMAR party from the government coalition.

In the fall, S&P and Moody's upgraded Greek bonds and the banking system had started to accumulate deposits. The European program of support was ending and there was a question of what if anything would replace it, while the IMF EFF was to last until 2016. The government would have preferred to have no program at all, but probably would have agreed to a contingent credit. In retrospect, it appears that during this period the government also started to loosen the budgetary strings. A scheduled Troika visit for the fall was repeatedly postponed as it appeared that the country was headed for elections: the President's term was coming to an end and a replacement had to be approved by a majority of at least 180 MPs, a number that the government was unable to secure. In the absence of agreement on a new President, the constitution required new parliamentary elections.

The ND government had been campaigning on a platform that Greece no longer needed external support from the IMF or anybody, the hated 'memorandum' would be torn up and Greece would be able to tap the markets on its own. Given this position, the last thing the government needed was a Troika mission that would have discovered that the bulk of the structural reforms were not being put in place, that the target of a primary surplus of 1.5% GDP would not be achieved and that significant budget stringency would continue. In the event, the overall deficit for 2014 was about 4% of GDP and the primary surplus close to zero—good results but probably not sufficient to guarantee that Greece could borrow from the markets the large amounts that it needed in 2015.

We will never know. Samaras came to Washington in November 2014 to plead his case but got no takers from the IMF who thought that he will lose the election and did not wish to be bound vis-à-vis the new government. It is reported that at the December 2014 Eurogroup meeting, the Commission sided with the Greek government that it had done enough to receive the next installment of funding, but the IMF and the ECB objected (Hardouvelis 2015). As a result, the European program was extended to the end of February 2015, but no money was released. SYRIZA won the January 2015 election, formed a coalition with ANEL (a right wing party whose main interest was in securing the Ministry of Defense for its leader) and ushered a new adventure for the Greek economy and people.

A Left Turn to a Dead End

The acronym of SYRIZA in Greek means coalition of the radical left. It is headed by Alexis Tsipras, a young and charismatic leader, and includes a number of left leaning groups including splinters of the communist party.[17] For years it had argued about the unfairness of the 'memoranda' and the burdens they imposed on the Greek people. Soon after it won the election, the government had to face urgent negotiations with the dreaded Troika about extending the European program of support which was to end in February 2015. But before it did that, it announced a number of steps which helped set a tone for the upcoming discussions: all the civil servants fired with the closing of the public television stations by the previous government would be rehired[18]; and the Troika was no longer welcome in Athens. Only technical teams were welcome. The political, that is, minister-level negotiations with 'the institutions' would take place in Brussels.

The government publicly stated that it was in agreement with 70% of the memorandum conditionality—for example, that which related to reducing tax evasion and strengthened governance and administration. There were four major issues: the debt, and the related macro framework, the issue of pensions, the labor market legislation and privatization (Galbraith 2016, pp. 12–13). They were correct on the first—the prospective macro framework continued to be too restrictive because of the debt and not likely to result in restoration of growth in the near future; partially correct on pensions, and ideologically driven and hence mostly incorrect on the question of labor markets and privatization.

The macro framework continued to call for a substantial primary surplus aiming to reduce the size of the official debt, which would have undoubtedly resulted in continued GDP stagnation. It could have been achieved only in part by further reducing pensions. These had already been reduced substantially but still accounted for a significant portion of the budget, partly because earlier retirements and firing of civil servants under previous administrations had increased their rolls and the finances of the pension funds had been hurt by the debt haircut. And all this without any desire by the Eurozone for political reasons to even consider a reduction of the official debt burden.

The government's position on the labor front and privatization was less solid: there was little reason to believe that reversing the loosening up of the labor market done by the previous governments would have raised incomes for the really poor; and while it was correct that privatization should not lead to 'fire sales', irrespective of the nuanced government position, statements and actions by various government officials continuously undermined the government's ownership of the program.

The February discussions were artful in papering over temporarily the disagreements and resulted in kicking the bucket down the road: the program was extended until June 30, 2015 and in the meantime discussions were to take place to reach agreement, but no money was released in the absence of a Troika assessment which the government did not want because it would have shown the increased deficit caused by the increased spending linked to the new hires as well as reduction in budget revenues. The discussions were taking placing under the Damoclean sword of the ECB's possible cutting off credit to the Greek commercial banks, and continuing uncertainty about the government's ability to meet external payments either of which would have meant unruly Greek default.

Yannis Varoufakis, the Greek Minister of Finance during this period, has written an extensive memoire of these negotiations (Varoufakis 2017). In it he maintains that he was committed to keeping Greece within the Eurozone, providing that he would be able to reach a reasonable agreement on reducing Greek debt with its Eurozone creditors. This was critical to loosening the requirement for maintaining a large primary fiscal deficit of 3.5–4% which in turn was an essential condition for restoring growth.

He was also concerned about the progressive hemorrhaging of bank deposits which he blamed in large part to the lack of cooperation of the Greek Central Bank. In fact, the decline in deposits began pari passu with the increased popularity of Tsipras and SYRIZA's statements based on the party platform which Varoufakis himself characterized 'incoherent' as 'it promised wage rises benefits and investment paid for with resources of funding which were imaginary or illegal' (Varoufakis 2017, p. 88).[19] Varoufakis was convinced that he had a potential weapon in threatening the ECB with a loss on the Greek bonds held by the latter. In parallel he ordered the secret elaboration of a plan for Grexit in case he was not able to reach agreement in reducing the debt and the ECB stopped completely the emergency liquidity it was providing to the Greek banking system.

Schauble, the German Finance Minister, strongly opposed any talk about debt relief. He fundamentally wanted Greece out of the Eurozone because he did not trust any Greek government's commitments; and if Greece were to stay in the Eurozone, it would have to follow *his* rules, which required continued fiscal austerity, which he knew was not likely to produce any growth. Schauble was supported in all this by a number of other governments, notably the Netherlands, Finland and several Eastern Europeans as well as countries like Spain which had also faced difficulties and did not want to give Greece an easy ride. The European Commission was more supportive of the Greek position, but typically less powerful in the actual Eurozone negotiations. The IMF wanted to ensure that any new program would have restored debt sustainability.

Varoufakis' approach alienated his Eurozone partners, introduced doubts in his own party and contributed to a frigid relationship with the Greek Central Bank. Characteristically, Tsipras ordered Varoufakis to tell the IMF Managing Director Christine Lagarde that Greece will default on an IMF payment in May, although he had decided not to. In fact, the Greek government made the payment using some of its SDRs.[20]

In May, Tsipras sidelined Varoufakis from the negotiations, which continued in Brussels. In the meantime, given the increasing uncertainties, bank deposits declined as did investment, for who in their right mind would consider investing in the Greek economy under such circumstances?

Varoufakis says little about the problems introduced by the 'internal devaluation' and for the need for essential structural reforms. Yet, he was right on the need to reduce the debt, and the related fiscal austerity and on this he received the support of a large number of distinguished economists worldwide. Unfortunately, he did not know the difference between being right and getting it right or getting others to agree.[21]

I arrived in Greece for my annual vacation in early June carrying with me a substantial amount of currency in US dollars and euros for our expenses as I feared a banking system collapse. I regret that I was not wrong. Final discussions on a program were going on in Brussels in the last week of June. The Greek side put together a proposal which I thought was reasonable in many respects. Apparently the *institutions* did not think so and came back with a text full of changes. The differences were extensive but focused on excruciating details: Should the increase in the upper range of the VAT include hotels or not? Should all businesses be asked to prepay their income taxes as the creditors wanted or should business with profits over 500,000 euros pay an extra tax, and so on (Kathimerini 2015a). They showed how little confidence the creditors had in the government and how not to put together a rescue program. Tsipras canceled further discussions and returned to Athens. I predicted there will be a run on the banks.

Tsipras announced a referendum on the institutions' proposals early Saturday June 27. The referendum was vaguely drafted and ill construed—some said unconstitutional. The government recommended a NO vote hoping that this would strengthen its negotiating ability. The ballot itself had a NO vote as the first option—a telling point. A YES vote was supposed to be supportive of the *institutions*. Some interpreted a YES vote to mean staying in the Eurozone and NO, a vote to leave. There was a run on the banks over the weekend and the Bank of Greece closed the banks on Monday morning June 29. Famous liberal economists like Krugman wrote in support of NO (Krugman 2015).

I voted YES and lost as the NO votes carried the day by a large margin, 61–39%.[22] Then something funny happened. For the first time, Tsipras asked for support from the opposition parties to negotiate a deal that would permit Greece to stay in the Eurozone. Varoufakis, the Finance Minister, who had contemplated an exit from the euro and alienated a lot of his colleagues in Europe in six months of futile negotiations resigned, saying cheekily in his blog 'soon after the announcement of the referendum results,

I was made aware of certain preference by some European participants and assorted partners for my absence from its meetings; an idea that the Prime Minister judged to be potentially helpful to him in reaching an agreement' (Kathimerini 2015b). In his book he states that he was asked to stay with the government but in a different job, so he decided to resign. As Papaconstantinou has made famous, the game was truly over.

Armed with the support of the other political parties and a new Finance Minister, Tsipras went to Brussels to 'negotiate' with the Eurozone leaders the weekend of July 11–12. The road had reached a dead end and beyond it lay the cliff of Grexit. He was presented with two alternatives: either leave the Eurozone for five years according to a proposal circulated by the German government or agree to the demands of the Eurozone leaders regarding reforms and even greater austerity. And as to the needed debt reduction, he was given only vague promises that it may be discussed in the future provided Greece made sufficient progress in the agreed reform package that included all the things the government had opposed earlier, including the establishment of a new agency to handle privatization and government asset management.

Given these 'options', Tsipras turned around and a new 'memorandum' was soon to emerge.

> After five years of deep economic and social pain, in the beginning of 2015 the economy was growing again and the Greek state was spending less than it collected in taxes (aside from interest payments). What lay ahead was a promise of additional debt relief and economic and social recovery… It took five short months to destroy all this. A projected 2.5% growth rate for this year turned into a recession and the primary surplus turned into a deficit—all courtesy of the SYRIZA-ANEL government under Prime Minister Alexis Tsipras (Papaconstantinou 2015).[23]

In addition, of course, the banking system was ruined. While the banks reopened, capital controls have continued to this day, with adverse repercussions for all business activity and especially investment and exports. And at the end of the day, Greece had a larger debt burden than it started with. To top it all, during this summer of discontent, there was a mass influx of refugees from Syria and elsewhere through Turkey, further challenging the government's capacity to operate.

The government received relief through a bridge credit that permitted it to meet its obligations to the IMF whose repayment had been delayed and then obtained a new credit from the European Stability Mechanism of 86 million euros on softer terms than previously. The austerity measures imposed were much harsher than had been offered by the Eurozone earlier in the spring, partly because in the meantime the economy and the budget accounts had deteriorated. And the long-term problem persisted. As Stiglitz wrote: 'The Germans say there is to be no debt write-off and that the IMF must be part of the program. But the IMF cannot participate in a program in which debt levels are unsustainable, and Greece's debts are unsustainable' (INY Times, Stiglitz July 27, 2015). In the end, the IMF agreed to be part of the ongoing reviews but did not provide any new funding. After six months of useless acrimonious negotiations and a government 'program' that scared investors, domestic and foreign, Greece was in worse shape than a year earlier.

Tsipras, facing a revolt from SYRIZA's extreme left over the Eurozone agreement, resigned and called for new elections in September of 2015. SYRIZA won the elections, with a slightly smaller majority but was still able to form a new government in a coalition again with ANEL. It is now implementing the third memorandum which contains a number of important reforms, for example, in unifying the various pension funds. The government has had the pleasure of participating in discussions with *four* institutions, as representatives of the ESM have now been added to the Troika making it the *quartet;* and the latter no longer meets with the government in Brussels, but usually in Athens.

The government's ownership of various parts of the program, in particular privatization, is conspicuously lacking. In the summer of 2016, the agreement with COSCO for the privatization of the Pireaus port was submitted to the Parliament for final approval. At the last minute and without consulting with the Chinese firm, the Minister in charge introduced certain changes detrimental to the firm. The timing was extremely unfortunate as that very day Tsipras was about to meet with the top of China's government in a formal visit to Beijing. Following the Chinese firm's loud protests, the changes were withdrawn and the legislation passed.

In June 2017, there was a new and spectacular dose of muddling through and kicking the bucket down the road. Following the passage of legislation by the Greek parliament for the implementation of a number of agreed conditions under the program, the Euro group agreed to provide the Greek government with 8.5 billion euros bringing the total amount disbursed so far to around 40 billion euros out of 80 billion euros approved in 2015.

The Greek government committed itself to maintain a 3.5% primary budget surplus until 2022 and a 2% surplus for decades thereafter. The IMF continues to believe that the Greek debt is unsustainable without further easing of its burden by the Eurozone creditors. But the Eurozone creditors refused to commit to an easing of the debt burden until the completion of the program in 2018. They indicated a willingness to consider at that point a further extension of loan maturities between 0 and 15 years as well as the possibility of tying future debt repayments to growth performance. On its part the IMF also committed itself to consider the possibility of a $2 billion standby, when the debt burden is judged to be sustainable. The Eurozone governments also agreed to help with additional investment funds as well as to assist the Greek government reenter the capital markets at the end of the program in 2018. In the meantime, there are supposed to be four more reviews as well as another 10 billion euros or so disbursed under the program.

The recent agreement reflects two facts: the lack of confidence of the Eurozone creditors in the commitment of the Greek government to implement sound economic policies and the politicization of the Eurozone assistance program. Both are bad omens for the future and unless changes are made, they are likely to result in continued stagnation of the Greek economy and suffering for the Greek people.

What Next?

After almost a decade of stagnation, it is fair to ask, what needs to be done differently so that the Greek economy can start to grow again. After all, despite all its governance shortcomings, nepotism, tax evasion, subsidies and inefficiencies, the economy had grown at a healthy clip before the excesses of the first decade of the twenty-first century. Many mistakes had been made by all the major participants in the failed efforts of the past.

Some structural reforms have been put in place—for example, of the pension system and real estate taxes; while the ease of doing business is worse, as Greece has deteriorated a few rungs in the World Bank 2017 Doing Business rankings (World Bank 2017). But the past is what it is. The question is about the future. Can Greece stay and prosper in the euro as it is or will it better off outside it? Can the European experiment become more complete?

Let us look at the growth performance. The most striking statistic of the past eight years has not been the decline in GDP but the spectacular decline in investment—both public and private. By contrast, consumption fell less, since households used up their savings. At 75%, the decline in investment is the largest by far of all the countries that suffered the kind of original shocks that Greece suffered. How can labor productivity grow under these circumstances?

It is necessary to create the environment to increase both public and private investment, domestic and foreign in physical and human capital. On the public side, there is a need to improve the government effectiveness in using investment funds available to it from the European Commission—large amounts of these funds go unused partly for the lack of counterpart funding from the Greek government and partly because of general agency sloppiness. But there is little doubt that more is needed and that the budget constraint has to be relieved.

The budget constraint exists because of the need to maintain a primary budget surplus in order to meet debt obligations. This constraint has resulted in the establishment of an equilibrium at low levels of capacity utilization with no growth and a vicious circle: incomes are growing very slowly, if at all, and as a result government revenues stagnate, the debt has to be repaid and the only way to do this, given large expenditures on defense (other than the US, Greece is the NATO country that devotes the largest share of its GDP to defense, more than 2%), is to squeeze expenditures resulting in stagnant incomes and so on. Pensions and investment have borne the bulk of the budget cuts. I suspect that pensions cannot be squeezed much further without causing even more social unrest.

The recent deal with the Eurozone partners committing Greece to maintain a 3.5% primary budget surplus means continued fiscal stringency until 2022. At a time when the euro has strengthened further, internal devaluation is needed to maintain exports. All this amounts to a lack of stimulus to the economy. The small increase in GDP in 2016 was fueled by an increase in consumption as Greeks continue to reduce their savings.

The problem of course is that 2017 was not the best time to organize a debt deal, if there was ever a good time, given the sin of converting private sector obligations into public debt under the first bailout. Europeans are starting to breathe a sigh of relief that the populist storm has been weathered and that pro-European sentiment is on the rise. But there are still uncertainties down the road. A deal on the debt could not be done before the German elections in September 2017. There is also a fatigue of having to deal with continued extended negotiations with the Greek government and politicization leading to pettiness: Spain was thinking about attaching as a condition to participating in the Greek bailout that the Greek government agreed to pay the legal fees of a Spanish consultant who was unfairly accused of some misdeed and was facing a day in a Greek court.

What can Greece do under the circumstances? It seems to me that the only option it has if it wants to stay in the euro is to demonstrate political stability and for the government, whichever government, to stay on course and to do what it has agreed to do for the three years of the current program. Besides the rising debt burden, the only other constant of the last decade has been Greek political instability: five parliamentary elections in six years and eight ministers of finance do not promote confidence to investors either domestic or foreign. Agreements with creditors and the IFIs have typically lasted about 18 months and after that ran into trouble for one reason or another: this was true for the Papandreou government, the Samaras government and now Tsipras. Staying the course must result in a deal with the Eurozone partners to relieve the debt burden and start growing again. It will be essential for the return of foreign direct investment that has stagnated.

A stable political and economic environment will also have a salutary effect on Greek human capital. I have always argued, perhaps because of my personal experience, that Greeks have a high propensity to migrate. In the last several years, tens of thousands of Greek professionals and many businesses have left Greece to carry out activities in other parts of

Europe.[24] They represent a loss to Greece, but not a permanent one. A large number will return if the situation stabilizes and prospects improve.

Even if all goes well and at some point in the future there is a reduction in Greece's external debt burden, I doubt that growth in Greece is going to recover former levels unless there is a fundamental reorientation of Greece's production structure that favors exports. That will take time and a great deal of investment, both domestic and foreign, as well as favorable political developments in nearby places like the Balkans and Middle East where Greek firms have shown the ability to compete (Athanasoglou et al. 2010).

There are still many structural problems: university education is a mess, the justice system is sclerotic and oligopolistic structures and restricted professions are still a problem. These will take time to fix. Urgent attention is needed to address a few other major problems: for example, the banks' portfolio of non-performing loans, many of which are not performing not because the debtors cannot pay, but because they are taking advantage of the situation and are hoping for a favorable deal; eliminating the government's own payments arrears as well as the tax arrears owed to the government by rich individuals and major corporations.

A few years back I had thought that Greece should have taken whatever steps needed to be taken to stay in the euro to gain time until measures were introduced to strengthen the Eurozone's long-term viability. In its own muddling through way, Europe has taken some of these steps: the establishment of the ESM was one such step; the strengthening of the ECB's role in supervising the banking system was another. Ultimately, as many have pointed out, the Eurozone is not likely to be viable without a unified fiscal policy or something like it, common deposit insurance and possibly issuance of euro bonds. 'A fiscal expansion by the core economies of the euro area would have a large and positive impact on periphery GDP… A euro-area fiscal compact that would allow more distressed countries greater latitude to engage in deficit financing could yield substantial benefits' (Blanchard et al. 2016).[25]

Germany seems to agree that greater policy integration is needed, but is concerned that proposals on the table will result in costs to its taxpayers. I seriously doubt that a major fixing of the euro is possible in the near future because of the nationalistic, anti-European sentiment in many important countries. But something less than that could be expected from countries like Germany which has constantly expected others to change their policies while it goes its own way unperturbed by the effect of its policies on the rest of the Eurozone.

In the last decade, countries in the periphery, Greece, Italy, Ireland, Portugal and Spain, have all reduced their current account deficits as a percent of GDP—some have turned them into surpluses (see Table 9.4). By contrast, Germany has increased its current account *surplus* from 4.6% of GDP in 2005 to 8.4% in 2015. That year, while Greece was struggling mightily to achieve an internal devaluation, Germany through its own macroeconomic policies achieved a further *undervaluation* of its real exchange rate by 10–20% compared to 5–15% in 2014 (IMF 2016, p. 7).

It is not new that surplus countries like to throw all the adjustment onto the shoulders of deficit countries. In 1960–1961, there were serious imbalances in international payments under the then prevailing system of fixed exchange rates. The group of surplus countries included the usual suspects: Germany, the Netherlands, Japan and some more Europeans. On the other side were not weaklings like Greece and Portugal but the US. The latter demanded and Germany and the Netherlands agreed to revalue their currencies upward by about 5% in February 1961. 'What is necessary at this time is to have the surplus countries take further steps to make the exchange rate adjustments effective in stimulating their imports and restraining their exports. For this purpose, the surplus countries must

Table 9.4 Current account balance as % of GDP for selected countries

Country	2000	2005	2008	2009	2010	2012	2014	2015
Greece	−7.5	−7.4	−14.5	−10.9	−10.1	−2.5	−1.6	0.1
Ireland	–	−3.4	−5.6	−2.1	1.0	4.1	3.5	10.2
Italy	−0.5	−1.6	−2.8	−1.8	−3.4	−0.4	1.8	1.6
Portugal	−10.9	−9.9	−12.2	−10.4	−10.2	−1.8	0.0	0.4
Spain	−4.4	−7.5	−9.3	−4.3	−3.9	−0.3	1.0	1.4
Average	−5.8	−6.0	−8.9	−5.9	−5.3	−0.2	1.0	2.7
Germany	−1.7	4.6	5.6	5.8	5.6	7.0	7.3	8.4

Source: IMF

lower interest rates to expand home demand' (Bernstein 1961, p. 83). They did not, and soon the dollar had to float.

Exchange rates are fixed and monetary policy does not vary within the currency union. The only thing that works is a more expansive fiscal policy for surplus countries. The IMF staff report on Germany for 2016 (IMF 2016, p. 10) cautiously states 'a looser fiscal position than currently envisaged through 2016–2021 would be appropriate. This would also modestly reduce the current account gap (surplus).' Unless Germany and the other surplus countries are prepared to adjust their policies to some degree, the euro will not survive and/or some countries including Greece will leave it as their continued participation will demand indefinite stagnation. And if they leave the euro, they are not going to pay back the German taxpayers.

Grexit: A Feasible but Not Desirable Option

Eurozone exits had not been contemplated at its establishment but the European community has always been able to devise legal approaches to achieve commonly desired results. As long as Greece continues its membership in the European Union, an exit from the euro is manageable. The details of reintroducing the drachma have been discussed elsewhere and need to be repeated here (Amiel and Hyppolite 2016). There will be a need to maintain tight fiscal and monetary policy to curb inflation and capital controls for the new currency to settle at a new exchange rate. GDP will drop again and the poor will suffer the most. Official reserves of the Bank of Greece stand around US$6 billion, less than two months of imports. They would need to be augmented through support from the IMF which has done this many times before. The whole process will be painful and it would be a shame if it were to happen; but it will happen at some point unless the debt burden is substantially reduced, macroeconomic policy is loosened and growth returns. The social costs of maintaining the current muddling through cannot be tolerated indefinitely.

Greece should not get out of the euro now. But it cannot stay in the euro without substantial easing of its official debt burden. I outlined the conditions for this above. If there is a stable Greek government that adheres to sensible macro policies for a period of time—the three years of the present program, but much less than 3.5% per year thereafter, debt reduction must be secured.[26] A *New Deal* is needed for Greece without a long protracted and acrimonious negotiation by the summer of 2018.

The conditionality has to be focused on the proper issues. Between now and then, the government should not be on a short leash with the tranches of assistance dribbling in every three months or so. Visits by the *quartet* should be reduced. They only serve two purposes: to irritate public opinion and to inhibit investment through the creation of uncertainty. If these conditions do not materialize, an orderly exit would have to be prepared, not in secret but with the full involvement of the Bank of Greece which would have to play a central role.

A Greek exit from the euro will undoubtedly result in substantial domestic economic dislocation for some time. I believe that it is not desirable: Greece has suffered quite a bit in its efforts to stay in the Eurozone and does not need the additional dislocation that would result from the exit. In a way, the best time to have left the zone was some time ago—before all the costs of the attempted internal devaluation had been incurred. It was also early on and before the first agreement with the Eurozone that Greece had the greatest leverage—which it did not choose to exercise in the mistaken hope that its Eurozone partners would have extended it the needed support. They did but, as was discussed earlier, not in the proper way, so in the end the Greeks are paying a high price for European solidarity while at the same time they are criticized for their policy failures. Both European solidarity and Greek policies must improve for Greece to prosper and the euro to survive.

Notes

1. Actually, the Phoenicians preceded the Greeks as traders by a couple of centuries, but they had little impact on culture, religion and political links in the region. The Romans did far more to unify the area under their control a few centuries later including the building of a large transport infrastructure.
2. My paternal grandfather migrated from Greece to the US around 1908 and died there ten years later (see Michalopoulos 2008).
3. Ukraine's decline in the 1990s was apparently slightly longer (see Gournichas et al. 2016), except that it had the alibi that it was going through a systemic transformation.

4. Orphanides (2015) called the first bailout the original sin in his 2015 paper. But while the bailout contained a lot of sins it certainly was not the original one.

5. The replacement rate is the ratio of the pension to the pensioner's salary.

6. There was a number of other countries that attempted to adjust with internal devaluations or with fixed pegs (e.g., Latvia); but none faced the triple problems affecting Greece.

7. Although the US did provide assistance to Mexico directly.

8. I participated representing the World Bank in what was probably the first 'Troika' mission to discuss assistance to Jamaica by the IMF, the World Bank and the US in 1985. If my memory is correct, Poul Thomsen, the IMF member of the Greek 'Troika', also participated in the Jamaica mission as an IMF staff economist. Fortunately, Jamaica's problems at the time were nowhere near the problems faced by Greece. A common memorandum agreed with the government was not needed, but the experience gave me a personal taste of the complexity of such a task should it have proved necessary.

9. Or because he wanted to increase the IMF's capitalization or for his own political ambitions as some have claimed (Galbraith 2016).

10. The West African countries did devalue the West African franc in 1993, the year Trichet left the French Treasury to take over as President of the French Central Bank.

11. 'So, the internal devaluation or price reduction was supposed to make up for the fact that Greece had a fixed exchange rate, the euro. If the IMF actually thought this would work, they should be shot!' said one commentator on this paper. The IMF staff probably did not believe the program would succeed, but had no choice.

12. The Athanasoglou study says that Greek exports are intensive in the use of 'medium' technology without an explanation of what this means in terms of capital/labor intensity.

13. Yet another recent study suggests an inverse relationship of Greek exports to unit labor costs (Geronicolaou et al. 2016). The regression analysis on which this conclusion is based is somewhat suspect as it shows a rise in unit labor costs for the period 2004–2009 and a decline for 2009–2014; but Greek exports grew, albeit slowly throughout this period.

14. Loosening labor market legislation, a structural benchmark under the program, should have reduced the incentives to hire laborers in the gray

market; however, the market for agricultural labor was almost wholly outside the formal sector and dominated by immigrants since the fall of the Berlin wall, primarily Albanian and other Eastern European labor, in the early 1990s.

15. When I tried to import a used passenger car from Belgium for my personal use in Greece, I was told by a friendly moving company official that there are no customs duties, but its registration required 29 different clearances (signatures) and would take approximately two weeks; I was advised to hire a customs expeditor—apparently a regular profession, who for a fee of 500 euros would obtain the clearances on my behalf in a few days—which I did and he did.

16. One source (Papaconstantinou 2015) suggests that the number came from the IMF. It may have been used to 'fool' the markets as debt reduction was still not on the table.

17. The main Greek communist party KKE continued to obtain around 5–10% of the votes but stayed in opposition.

18. As well as the cleaning ladies of the Ministry of Finance that had also been fired.

19. An excerpt from a speech by the Governor of the Bank of Greece quoted by Varoufakis (2017, p. 106) was not helpful in dealing with the problem, but I am not familiar with the rest of the speech or the context.

20. Varoufakis says that the Governor of the Greek Central Bank called him to say that '650 million euro had miraculously been discovered idling around in some forgotten account that happened to be stuffed with funds that we were allowed to use to repay the IMF' (Varoufakis 2017, pp. 406–407). In fact, these funds constituted part of Greece's official foreign exchange reserves, whose existence is regularly reported by the Bank on a monthly basis.

21. This is a Dutch proverb 'Het verschil tussen gelijk hebben en gelijk krijgen'.

22. The polls had predicted a very close context, the first of several recent instances where the polls have been wrong.

23. Varoufakis claims that the economy was still declining when SYRIZA took over, based on a four month moving average of quarterly GNI (Varoufakis 2017, p. 126). The facts are GDP growth in constant prices was −3.24% in 2013, +0.35% in 2014 and −0.22% in 2015 (World Bank 2017).

24. A personal friend, owner of a construction company, faced with a stagnant Greek market relocated most of his company's activities in building

renovation to London. Finding that Greek producers of building fur-
nishings and materials had excess capacity due to the deep recession, his
firm is now exporting these goods to the UK. Brexit is causing him some
concerns but he believes he will weather it.

25. There is a huge number of proposals designed to ensure the long-term
viability of the euro. These will be discussed in the last chapter of this
volume.

26. The proposal to tie the debt relief with GDP growth should be approached
with caution: Greece needs private market access; what happens to the
costs of accessing the market, if it looks that for one reason or another its
growth is not sustained? Furthermore, long-term forecasting of debt sustainability is a business prone to large errors for which countries should
not have to pay.

References

Amiel, D. and P.A. Hyppolite, (2016) "Is there an Easy Way Out? Redenomination
Issues and their Financial Consequences in Case of A Greek Exit from the
Eurozone" in *A New Growth Model for the Greek Economy*, P.E. Petrakis, Ed.
(New York: Palgrave/Springer).
Athanasoglou, P., C. Backinezos and E. Georgiou (2010) "Export Performance,
Competitiveness and Commodity Composition" *Bank of Greece, Working
Paper 114*, (Athens: Bank of Greece).
Bernstein, E. M. (1961) "The New Administration and the Dollar Payments
Problem" in *The Dollar in Crisis*, S.E. Hariss Ed. (New York: Harcourt Brace
and World).
Blanchard O., C. Erceg, and J. Linde (2016) "Jump Starting the Euro Area
Recovery: Would a Rise in Core Fiscal Spending Help the Periphery/" *NBER,
Macroeconomics Annual #31*, (Cambridge, Mass.: MIT Press).
Bowerm, U., V. Mitrou and C. Ungerer (2014) "The Puzzle of the Missing
Greek Exports" Economic Paper 518 (Brussels: European Commission).
Dornbush, R., (1996) "Euro Fantasies." *Foreign Affairs* Sept/October.
Eurostat (2010) "Report on the EDP Methodological Visits to Greece in 2010"
(Brussels: European Commission, Eurostat).
Friedman, M. (1997) "The Euro: Monetary Unity to Political Disunity" Project
Syndicat, August.; http.www.projectsyndicat.org/commentary.

Galbraith, J. K (2016) *Welcome to the Poisoned Chalice*, (New Haven and London: Yale University Press).

Gibson, H., T. Palivos and G.S. Tavlas (2014) "The Crisis in the Euro Area: An Analytic Overview", *Journal of Macroeconomics* (39) B., March.

Geronicolaou, G., E. Spyromitrou and P. Tsintzos, (2016), "What Drives Greek Exports Performance: A Macrolevel Analysis" in *A New Growth Model for the Greek Economy* P. E Petrakis, Ed. (New York, Palgrave/Springer).

Gournichas, P., T. Philippon and D. Vayanos (2016) "The Analytics of the Greek Crisis" *NBER Macroeconomics Annual #31,* (Cambridge, Mass.: MIT Press).

Hardouvelis, G. (2015) "Greece: How to Undo the Damage" *INY Times* July 7.

IEO (Independent Evaluation Office of the IMF) (2016) *The IMF and the Crises in Greece, Ireland and Portugal,* (Washington, DC: IMF).

IMF (2012) "Greece: Request for Extended Arrangement Under the Extended Fund Facility: Staff Report", Country Report 12/57, (Washington DC: IMF).

IMF (2013) "Greece: Ex-Post Evaluation of Exceptional Access under the Stand-By Arrangement" Country Report No. 13/156, (Washington DC: IMF).

IMF (2014) "Greece: Fifth Review Under the Extended Fund Facility and Request for Waiver of Non-observance of Performance Criterion and Re-phasing of Access" Staff Report 14/151, (Washington DC: IMF).

IMF (2016) "Germany: Report of the 2016 Article IV Consultation" Country Report 16/202, (Washington DC: IMF).

IMF (2017) "Greece: Ex Post Evaluation of Exceptional Access under the 2012 Extended Arrangement" Country Report 17/44 (Washington DC: IMF).

Kathimerini (2015a) "Marathon Discussions in Brussels." June 25.

Kathimerini (2015b) "Domestic Backing for PM's Last Gasp Effort." July 7.

Krugman, P. (2015) "Greece Over the Brink" *INY Times* June 30.

Maisonneuve de la, C. (2016) "How to Boost Export Performance in Greece" OECD Economic Department Working Paper 1299, (Paris: OECD).

Michalopoulos, C. (1968) "Imports. Foreign Exchange and Economic Development: The Greek Experience" in P.B. Kenen and R. Lawrence, *The Open Economy,* (New York: Columbia University Press).

Michalopoulos, C. (2008) *Migration Chronicles,* (Lusby: Point of View Publishing).

Michalopoulos, C. (2012).A Modern Greek Tragedy: the Final Act? Letter to E.Herfkens.

Orphanides, A. (2015) "The Euro Area Crisis Five Years After the Original Sin" MIT Sloan Working Paper 5147-15 (Cambridge, Mass: MIT).

Papaconstantinou, G. (2015) "Re Greece over the Brink", *INY Times* July 9.

Papaconstantinou, G. (2016) *Game Over I Alithia ya tin crisi,* (Athens: Papadopoulos).

Pisani-Ferry, J. (2014) *The Euro Crisis and Its Aftermath,* (New York: Oxford University Press).

Sardelis, C. (2013).Mithi ke Pragmaticotita ya tin Ypothesi Goldman Sachs (in Greek-Myths and Reality about the Goldman Sachs Issue) Oiknomiki Epitheorisi, March.

Stiglitz, J.E. (2015) "Greece, the Sacrificial Lamb", *INY Times* July 25.

Tsoukalis, L. (2016) *In Defence of Europe,* (Oxford: Oxford Univeristy Press).

Varoufakis, Y. (2017) *Adults in the Room* (London: Vintage).

World Bank (2017) *Ease of Doing Business Index,* (Washington DC: World Bank).

Wyplosz, C. and S. Sgherri (2016) "The IMF's Role in Greece in the Context of the 2010 Standby" IEO Background Paper BP-16/02-11, (Washington DC: IMF).

10

The Twilight of Liberalism?

Introduction

Fifty years ago, it was popular to divide the world economy in three parts: the developed countries, roughly speaking, the members of the OECD; the centrally planned economies of the Soviet Union, its satellites and China; and the developing countries or the 'Third World'. The OECD group and the centrally planned economies had economic ideologies distinguished by their approach to the role of the market, while the developing countries, many recently freed from the shackles of colonialism, were experimenting with mixtures of the two systems.

Over time, and especially following the Soviet Union's demise and changes in the economic orientation of China, more and more countries worldwide came to adopt variations of a market-based system broadly characterized by the principles of economic liberalism. For me, these include roughly the following: (a) government intervention in the economy in support only of social welfare objectives (including reducing income inequality) and addressing market imperfections or externalities; (b) multilateral approaches to global economic problems; (c) aid and other kinds of support to promote sustainable development; (d) humanitarian

© The Author(s) 2017
C. Michalopoulos, *Aid, Trade and Development*,
https://doi.org/10.1007/978-3-319-65861-2_10

assistance in support of victims of conflict or other disasters; and (e) a liberal international trading system based on multilaterally agreed rules.

The deep crisis that afflicted the developed countries in 2008 affected the world economy in the next few years and ushered a new era whose implications are not yet fully understood. The prolonged but weak recovery in the US combined with stagnation in several Eurozone countries led many to agree with Larry Summers that 'growth challenges are not so much a matter of the lingering effects of the crisis as they are of structural changes in the global economy that contributed to the crisis and the problems in its aftermath' (Summers 2016). The emergence of China as a leading global power with a system which can probably be best characterized as 'state capitalism' and the reemergence of Russia with a similar system have raised questions about the prospects of liberalism. The final questions were raised by the President of the United States who in his inaugural speech stated that 'Protection will lead to great prosperity and strength.'

As these words are being written, it is not yet clear how much these changes in the world economic order will affect actual trade and aid policy and institutions. But it is perfectly clear that a new look at some fundamental tenets of the global economic system is in order. This chapter will review global aid and trade developments in the period since 2008 and identify the main emerging challenges for development. The final chapter will look ahead to explore the changes that need to be made to buttress the edifice of liberal economic order.

An Overview of Developments Since 2008

In the immediate aftermath of the crisis, world trade declined in absolute terms. But, in 2010, trade picked up again and in the next few years it appeared that, while there was some increase in protection, the international trading system had weathered the financial shock pretty well. To be sure, the Doha Round continued to be moribund, and there were rumblings that multilateralism was on the wane as a number of mega-regional preferential agreements started to be negotiated. But there were no major reversals of the trade order such as had occurred in the aftermath of the great depression. And even better, a new Trade Facilitation Agreement (TFA) and an expanded Information Technology Agreement (ITA) were signed and came into effect. In the past year, however, worries have resurfaced about global trends in trade, which has been growing at a slower pace than at any time in the last 30 years.

In 2015, the UN was able to celebrate the achievement of substantial progress in meeting the MDGs and to set up a new set of targets for 2030. But the crisis led to very large declines in international private financial flows to developing countries. Tight budgets in several European countries also resulted in reductions of their aid flows. While overall flows of ODA did not seem to be affected, its quality deteriorated and its distribution was heavily influenced by aid allocations to conflict management, peace and security activities in countries with civil strife and refugee assistance in the developed countries themselves.

Underneath this mixed set of news and relative calm, a substantial storm was brewing which is directly related to the perceived impact of globalization, not so much on the poor in developing countries, but to a slice of the population in developed countries who have been left behind. In 2016, they flexed their political muscles by voting for Brexit and by electing an apparently heavily protectionist administration in the US. In doing so, they directed attention to a problem that has afflicted some developed economies and especially the US: the lack of effective policies for those who lose jobs through technological change, including through competition from imports and foreign outsourcing, which are important elements of globalization, but often not the main source of their economic difficulties. This is an old problem which has festered for decades. Forty years ago, Schiavo-Campo wrote, 'Equally or more severe human hardships are caused by a myriad of economic changes which have nothing to do with foreign trade' (Schiavo-Campo 1978).

In recent periods, the problem has become worse for a variety of reasons of which perhaps the most important is the reduction in both occupational and geographic labor mobility. This has led to the phenomenon of whole communities in the developed world becoming wastelands of unemployed and unemployable groups full of resentment for their plight and directing their anger not to the invisible forces of technological progress but to the foreigners who have stolen their jobs.

At the same time, the EU has been deeply affected by a different aspect of globalization: the large increases in the flow of immigrants both for economic reasons as well as refugees from war-torn zones. They have generated fears that the influx of foreigners with different and alien cultures will result in a dilution of the national identity in many countries and have generated a xenophobic response in European societies as different as the UK and Hungary. With the EU and the US preoccupied with these matters, and major players like Brazil and Korea in current or recent political turmoil, the future of the global system of trade and finance appears to rest to a significant degree in the uncertain hands of China, a trade behemoth but certainly not a paragon of economic liberalism.

Development Finance

In 2015, total net financial flows from all sources to developing countries were about 40% less than in 2010. This was due to a very large decline in private capital flows, in particular portfolio investment, which turned negative, and direct investment, which while substantial, was still less than in 2010 (see Table 7.2).

ODA levels in 2015 were slightly higher than in 2010, resulting in a significant increase in its role as a source of development finance.[1] But as noted above, the allocation of large ODA amounts to countries with civil wars as well as the inclusion of assistance provided to refugees and other expenditures in the donor country as part of ODA tend to distort the actual benefits for recipients. Recipient programmable aid actually declined in absolute terms between 2009 and 2015 and even more as a share of the total. Perhaps the most positive development was the continued increase in the importance of grants by private voluntary agencies which rose both in absolute amounts and in their share of the total.

In November 2008, a follow-up to the Monterrey Conference on Finance and Development was convened under UN auspices in Doha. Coming so soon after the Lehman Brothers default, it was remarkable that it took place at all. The meeting was attended by lower level officials—that is, ministers rather heads of governments and produced another well-balanced and fully agreed document. The *Doha Declaration on Financing for Development* (UN 2009) reiterated all the donor aid commitments of the Monterrey meeting and, having the benefit of the Paris Agreement on aid effectiveness, added all the right things about donor and recipient responsibilities. It contained the by now standard recommendations regarding the Doha Round of multilateral trade negotiations in ways that would benefit developing countries and repeated the admonishment for increased coherence between aid and trade policies. The problem was that donors mired in financial crisis and recessions started to backtrack on aid commitments. Besides the deterioration in the aid quality of some donors for reasons discussed earlier, there was backtracking in the commitments they had made on increasing aid effectiveness.

Recall that the Paris and Accra Agreements had set up a system of quantitative targets on aid effectiveness to apply to donors and recipients and a time horizon for their achievement. These were monitored by the DAC and showed progress in some areas, for example, in the coordination of technical cooperation, but except in Latin America, there has been little progress in the use of country systems for the implementation of aid programs.

The Fourth High Level Forum on Aid Effectiveness was scheduled for Busan, Korea, from November 29 to December 1, 2011. This Forum was to be sponsored jointly by the OECD and the UNDP and included not only the traditional bilateral and multilateral donors but also new bilateral donors like China and Korea and the major private voluntary agencies.[2] T. Abdel-Malek and B. Koenders, the co-chairs of the working party preparing the Forum writing on the eve of the conference, posed the question as to whether aid was being delivered in a more effective way than in 2005. They said, 'The answer is clear: progress has been made, but globally donors and developing countries have fallen short of the goals they set for themselves for 2010. The findings from monitoring and evaluating the implementation of the Paris Declaration make for sobering reading' (Abdel-Malek and Koenders 2011). In fact, only 1 of the 13 targets— improving technical cooperation—had been met. The co-chairs, after noting that the targets were still meaningful, recommended that 'Busan can and should aim to ensure deeper political commitment- coupled with concrete actions to follow through' (Abdel-Malek and Koenders 2011).

The opposite happened. The meeting at Busan weakened both the commitments, especially by the donors, and the monitoring mechanism of aid effectiveness. The Forum produced a new document which reaffirmed the major principles articulated in earlier meetings such as recipient government ownership and using country systems for implementing aid programs. However, 'the new donors questioned the legitimacy of the OECD/DAC … and did not want to be shoehorned into these Western dominated institutions and agreements. Thus, the UNDP was mandated to be involved in the follow up. Alas, given the UN's "*anxiety to offend*" its rich country members, this put an end to the scrupulous monitoring of individual OECD/DAC member commitments' (Herfkens 2014, p. 60).

The commitments and monitoring were weakened in a variety of ways:

* There were no more time frames for achieving the various targets;
* Several of the donor targets were completely eliminated, including the targets for programmable aid, the target for shared analysis and joint missions and the target for mutual assessment;
* The targets for using recipient systems were combined and only averages reported for all targets, thus masking individual donor performance for each target;
* Most of the baseline information was to be obtained from recipient data; as a consequence, donor performance was based only on a fraction of their overall aid.

There was yet another conference in Mexico City in April 2014, this time labeled 'First High Level Meeting of the Global Partnership for Effective Development Co-operation: Building Towards an Inclusive Post-2015 Development Agenda', with the long title reflecting the paucity of results. The meeting was attended by a variety of bilateral and multilateral donors, philanthropic organizations, trade unions, civil society organizations and so on. Its main outcome was to request that a new study of aid effectiveness be undertaken based on the new monitoring. It produced another communiqué from which the following paragraph is quoted to indicate how unfortunately general, platitude-full and purposeless the process has become:

We encourage continued progress in ensuring that all stakeholders and voices are duly acknowledged and the necessary space is given and expanded to enhance inclusive and democratic ownership of the development agenda, including through women's empowerment, in the spirit of openness, trust and mutual respect and learning from the different and complementary roles of all partners (United Nations 2014, p. 3).

A study by Center for Global Development (CGD), based on data through 2012 for 31 donors, including many of the new ones, showed that the quality of ODA had improved in that there were 'visible and significant gains in fostering institutions and in transparency and learning. However, there has been almost no change in maximizing efficiency or in reducing the burden on recipient countries'; moreover, 'the quality of aid of non-DAC donors is less than for DAC donors' (Birdsall and Kharas 2014, p. 3). The new study of the Global Partnership was produced in 2016, but because of the problems with the monitoring noted above, it is impossible to say whether donor performance has improved or not (Global Partnership 2016).

In the meantime, aid fragmentation has continued unabated, increasing the implementation burden for recipients, especially LDCs about whose governance donors are presumably worried. The number of developing countries with over 40 official donors went from zero in 1990 to over 30 in 2012, with the average project worth slightly more than half a million euros (Herfkens 2014).

And new donors are continuously being created. China has been at the center of the establishment of two new multilateral financial institutions outside of the BWI. First, in 2012, with the participation of Brazil, India, Russia and South Africa, it set up what was originally called the BRICS Development Bank, which later was renamed New Development Bank (NDB) with an initial capitalization of US$50 billion, distributed equally among the five founding members, with headquarters in Shanghai (www. ndb.int). China was also behind the establishment of the Asian Infrastructure Investment Bank (AIIB), which was launched in late 2015 with a capital of $100 billion and membership of 57 countries, including several from the OECD but not the US and Japan.[3] Its new global initiative 'Belt and Road' promises to expand funding for transport infrastructure through both Asia and Europe.

The new institutions reflect both the changes in the global economic importance of China as well as some of its frustration and that of other emerging powers about the lack of progress in changing the power structure of the BWI, which continue to be dominated by the US and the EU. An agreement was reached in 2010 to reallocate some of the IMF quotas away from Europe and in favor of developing country constituencies but the agreement was held up for six years(!) in the US Congress until it was finally approved in 2016. The power distribution in the BWI appropriate 50 years ago cannot be appropriate today as so much has changed. Absent change, the system would tend to lose legitimacy and the emerging powers will try to go their own way.

It is far too soon to assess the effectiveness of these new institutions in delivering assistance to needy developing countries. Undoubtedly, they offer new opportunities to developing country recipients. But they obviously also increase their burden in coordinating implementation.

Financing for development was the subject of yet another UN conference held in Addis Ababa, in 2015. It is fair to say that very little progress was achieved. There was yet another document referring to the earlier commitments. But, since 2008 nothing much has really happened either to increase the level or improve the quality and effectiveness of development assistance or strengthen the coherence between trade and finance. Perhaps the only positive step is that for the first time the BWI combined with the WTO would produce a new report on world trade (IMF, World Bank, WTO 2017).

International Trade

Overview

In October 2008, with the world gripped by financial panic, WTO Director General Lamy decided that the WTO Secretariat would monitor trade restrictive measures taken in response to the crisis using the WTO Trade Policy Review Mechanism. In November 2008, just after the US presidential election, leaders of the G-20, fearing a repetition of the experience of the great depression and its transmission across frontiers by trade-restricting beggar-thy-neighbor policies, promised to refrain from imposing new import barriers, export restrictions and WTO-inconsistent measures. Subsequently, the G-20 also promised to minimize the negative impact of stimulus measures on trade and asked the WTO to monitor and publicize the extent to which they adhered to their promises.

In this manner, a new reporting system of trade measures taken by both developed and developing countries has emerged. Since then, the WTO has produced these reports on a semi-annual basis.[4] The novel feature of the reports is that they extend the definition of trade measures far beyond the traditional border actions involving tariffs or other restraints and include, for example, measures that aim to provide general economic stimulus or strengthen the financial system, especially as such measures may discriminate against foreign suppliers or banks.Their main shortcoming is that they count the number of 'actions', which may have a very different effect on total trade. Giving the same weight to a German 'Rescue aid scheme for the manufacturing industry' (amounting to a grand total of €5 million for six months) and to the US Trade Adjustment Assistance Act (which affects tens of millions of workers for years) makes a mockery of any quantitative analysis of this information. Still, the reports provide a sense of direction: how policy is changing over time in the biggest trading nations (WTO 2009).

Early on, in 2009, the changes were not as bad as people had feared: 'to date we have not observed large scale increases in the level of discrimination by major trading states' (Evenett 2009, p. 5). Another writer concluded that the great collapse of trade in 2008 was not due to any failings in the trading system and that 'the amount of trade affected in relation to actual trade flows was trivial' (Wolfe 2011, p. 13).

Unfortunately, the situation appears to have worsened over time. The latest WTO report shows that the share of world imports covered by import restrictive measures since October 2008 and which are still in place covers 5% of world trade and 6.5% of G-20 trade. The initiation of trade remedy investigations primarily for anti-dumping and countervailing accounted for 72% of the actions (WTO 2016). The report prompted Roberto Azevedo, the Director General of WTO, to state that 'The continued introduction of trade restrictive measures is a real and persistent concern… It is clear that the financial crisis has had a long tail and that the world economy remains in a precarious state' (Azevedo 2016).

In addition to these issues, there is a rising concern that Chinese state enterprises continue to be subsidized and thus are provided with an unfair competitive advantage. The WTO disciplines on the subject are embodied in Article XVII and they are not very elaborate. They involve requirements to report government entities 'which have been granted exclusive or special rights and privileges including statutory or constitutional powers in the exercise of which the level and direction of exports and imports' (WTO 1995). China has duly provided such a report (WTO 2015) which provides information on a large number of enterprises involved in international trade, primarily of agricultural commodities and raw materials. It has blithely asserted that they are all functioning on the basis of market principles.

The problem does not arise with the enterprises designated as 'state trading'. Rather, the problem arises with the lack of transparency in the relations between the state and all state-owned enterprises, whether formally engaged in trade or not. This has been and continues to be a problem with Russia and other formerly centrally planned economies. Neither the EU nor the US has relied on Article XVII to deal with problems of state trading. Rather, they have used the WTO provisions on countervailing and antidumping to raise a large number of complaints against China (as well as Taiwan, and other developed and developing countries) using the WTO's DSM on most of which they have prevailed. China has abided by the DSM decisions and has raised a number of complaints itself (Michalopoulos 2014). Moreover, the EU and the US have used the designation of China as a non-market economy for a period of 15 years from its accession during which they were able to use far more arbitrary methods in determining anti-dumping than would otherwise be the case. The period ended in December 11, 2016, but neither the EU nor the US dropped the 'non-market economy' classification, whereupon China raised a complaint with the DSM, which is where the issue stands at the moment.

In the years since the 2008 crisis, three major developments have jeopardized the future of world trade, justifying Azevedo's concern: (a) the failure to conclude the Doha Round; (b) a proliferation of regional PTAs; and (c) major uncertainties on the future of the international trade policy that will be pursued by all major trading powers—the EU, which would be involved with Brexit; an overtly protectionist US administration; and China's future international trade policy. On the other hand, the new WTO agreement on trade facilitation and an expanded Information Technology agreement point the direction for future cooperation.

The Death of Doha

The failure to conclude the Doha Round has shaken WTO's first leg: its usefulness as a forum for multilateral trade negotiations aimed at liberalizing trade. Despite continuing discussions on various aspects of agriculture, and other topics that were central to the conclusion of the Round, at this point, there is little expectation that a Round covering the Doha Development Agenda will be put together.

The world cannot engage in fruitless negotiations for more than a decade without somebody to blame. In the Doha Round there are many countries large and small, developed and developing, which can be blamed for the failure to reach agreement.

The negotiations were launched soon after September 11, 2001, when there was a large amount of international goodwill in support of the US following the terrorist attacks. Developing countries agreed to the Doha Agenda despite a lot of misgivings about what they saw as lack of implementation of developed countries' Uruguay Round commitments and the agenda contained the Singapore issues on which developing countries were not interested in negotiating.

The US failed to see an advantage in the negotiations: its benefits from liberalization in manufactures would have been modest, especially as there was no agreement on initiatives to eliminate all tariffs on sectors of interest; the offers for prospective service liberalization were also miniscule; and the potential benefits from agricultural exports would have been threatened by the proposed Special Safeguards Agreement.[5] The EU saw limited benefits in both NAMA and services, and its main stance was driven by efforts to safeguard its agricultural policies. In both the US and the EU there was a failure to mobilize the private sector, which had in the past played an important role in supporting trade negotiations.

Developing countries asserted themselves in the negotiations as they never had before, especially concerning their prerogatives to seek special and differential treatment in all aspects of the negotiations. On the Indian side, it became clear early on that there were no prospects of using the negotiations to achieve liberalization in the movement of natural persons. This was also combined at the last moment with narrow political concerns by its main negotiator resulting in a rigidly defensive stance. China was not interested in further liberalization, as it had just gone through a large amount of liberalization in connection with its accession—although it was likely to benefit significantly from the NAMA liberalization. Brazil was the country which at the end was the most supportive of the deal that was put on the table by Director General Pascal Lamy at the last set of negotiations.

The developed countries have blamed the main developing countries in the negotiations—Brazil, China and India—for not showing proper leadership commensurate to their large and rising importance in international trade. The fact of the matter is that the WTO negotiations were a clear example of the rising strength of emerging powers such as China and India, which do not accept the legitimacy of the US and EU-led international trade and finance system while they continue to seek greater power within it. Brazil is closer to the OECD countries in its approach to trade and finance but is still fiercely protective of its industrial policy. All three countries, as well as South Africa, insist on a greater voice in the functioning of the system while continuing to benefit from SDT.

The SDT principle is enshrined in the WTO and earlier GATT agreements. There are many legitimate reasons for providing substantial and meaningful SDT as well as technical and financial assistance to lower income developing countries and LDCs which do not have the institutional capacity to implement WTO rules. Policy space is needed for these countries to build capacity and transform their economies to meet the challenges of the twenty-first century. But the rising power of developing countries in the WTO resulted in proposed agreements for treating developing countries arbitrarily and in ways, which, if implemented, would have had deleterious effects both on the countries themselves and the WTO as an institution.

The only way that developing countries could have overcome the entrenched protectionism in developed countries in agriculture, textiles or maritime services was to take advantage of the pressure that export interests in the developed countries would have brought to bear on their own governments to negotiate in order to open up developing country markets. But this presupposed a willingness to reduce their own applied tariffs and protection in agriculture and services. This they did offer—but either because protectionism in developed countries was too entrenched or because the offer was not sufficiently attractive or most likely a combination of the two, the result was no deal.

Finally, the loading of the negotiations with too many topics as well as the principle that nothing is agreed unless everything is agreed was also in part to blame for the Doha Round failure. Before the start of the Doha Round I had warned (Michalopoulos 2001, p. 226), using the old bicycle analogy that the momentum of a new Round is needed to push the bicycle forward, but that the bicycle should not be loaded with so much baggage that it collapses under the excess weight. Unfortunately, the bicycle was overloaded, and although the developing countries succeeded in lifting the weight of the Singapore issues from the agenda, the remaining burden proved too much, and the bicycle collapsed.

At this point, it has been impossible to even agree to give the Round a decent burial. But one thing is clear: the chances are that a Round with all the complex undertakings involved in Doha Development Agenda is not going to happen. The future lies in specific agreements such as the one reached in 2013, at the Bali WTO Ministerial, on Trade Facilitation (TFA), which went into effect in February, 2017; and the expanded ITA agreed at the Nairobi Ministerial in late 2015, which went into effect in July 2016.

Trade Facilitation

As formal trade barriers decline, the importance of the environment and procedures for the conduct of international trade increases. This is not simply the logistics of moving goods through ports or customs. It relates to the whole set of activities, practices and formalities involved in collecting, presenting, communicating and processing information both at the border and behind the border regarding the movement of goods in international trade as well as the procedures for adjudication of disputes regarding this movement.

On average about 60 documents are used in an international trade transaction, and they often differ from country to country. This is compounded by antiquated official clearance procedures. Lack of transparency and predictability is a major source of uncertainty in terms of the costs and time incurred for delivery of commercial transactions. The problems are typically much greater in developing countries with weak or non-existent automated procedures in customs administration.

In several years of negotiations, a number of studies have concluded that what was included in the proposed agreement would result in large gains to developing countries, amounting to $131 billion compared to $94 billion for developed countries (Hufbauer et al. 2010). Much larger estimates of gains have been claimed by the WTO (WTO 2016).

There is little doubt that adherence to standardized and transparent rules and procedures would be of great benefit to developing countries by reducing transaction costs and delivery times both for their exports and their imports. Developing countries have wanted to avoid repeating the mistakes of the Uruguay Round, wherein they committed themselves to a variety of agreements, which they lacked the capacity to implement and relied on vague promises of technical assistance which did not materialize or transition periods which had little to do with the time it takes to implement institutional capacity. They also wanted to avoid being found responsible for violating WTO rules in the context of a dispute proceeding when they had been unable to fulfill an obligation because of inadequate capacity.

These legitimate developing county concerns have led to a variety of special and differential treatment rules in the agreement. The commitments made by developing countries and LDCs have been organized in three categories: 'A', 'B' and 'C'. Category A commitments involve rules that the developing country or LDC have accepted to implement at the time the agreement enters into force; category B includes provisions that would be implemented after a specified transition period; and category C relates to provisions that could be implemented only after the country has received technical (or financial) assistance that would enable it to meet its commitments.

A number of developing countries with strong trading performances, such as South Korea and Singapore, have chosen to accept all of the commitments under the agreement up front, at the time the agreement enters into force. Unfortunately, China, the number one exporting country in the world, has chosen to delay acceptance of certain important provisions much the same as those by a country such as the Kyrgyz Republic with miniscule share of global trade.

In order to deal with the potential costs in implementing the TFA by developing countries, yet another small 'aid for trade' facility, the Trade Facilitation Agreement Facility (TFAF), was established in the WTO with resources so far amounting to about $4.3 million (TFAF 2016). The TFAF is intended to carry out a new set of 'needs assessments' much like the original needs assessment that were to be carried out by LDCs 20 years ago (see Chap. 7). It is difficult to understand why such a new facility was created when several small such facilities already exist focused on LDCs in the WTO. It is likely to increase primarily the benefits that accrue to foreign expert consultants and impose additional management burdens to poor developing countries, thus continuing the trend of aid fragmentation. It seems to reflect only the priorities of LDC representatives in Geneva who hardly have any link to the realities of implementing and coordinating assistance in the countries themselves.[6]

Information Technology Agreement (ITA)

A plurilateral agreement was signed in 1996, eliminating tariffs on a group of information technology products. After extended negotiations, a new agreement covering more countries (over 50) and more products was signed at the Nairobi Ministerial in December 2015 and put into effect in July 2016. Given the large increases in the amount of trade in these products, the new agreement is expected to reduce tariffs in covering products worth more than $300 billion annually.

Preferential Trade Agreements

The unfettered proliferation of regional and other PTAs—'termites' in the language of Bhagwati (2009) ostensibly consistent with WTO provisions—is undermining the edifice of WTO rules based on the MFN principle, and thus weakening the second leg on which the WTO stands, that of the institution in which the rules governing international trade are made. More and more trade is subject to rules made in Brussels, Washington and the myriad other centers of preferential agreements in developed and developing countries alike, scattered throughout the globe. These agreements also threaten the third leg on which WTO stands: dispute settlement, as disputes arising from rights conferred by PTAs are extended only to their members and may be adjudicated by them rather than the WTO: 'Can the WTO save itself from irrelevance?', *The Economist* asked in early 2013 (*Economist* 2013, p. 74).

It is well understood that under certain circumstances preferential arrangements can have a net positive effect on international trade. While they are never going to be better for global welfare than multilateral trade liberalization on an MFN basis, they could be better than no liberalization at all. But their dynamics are protectionist and discriminatory: they are designed to gain advantage against a competitor in a third market, or to safeguard a value chain and the related investment. Their multiplicity results in a fragmented trading system with rising global inefficiencies.

Agreements between smaller developing countries and developed ones such as those pursued by the US and the EU pose an additional major problem for developing country participants: the developed country partners propose and usually obtain through these agreements commitments which they have not been able to obtain in WTO negotiations. These include commitments on intellectual property rights, which go beyond TRIPS, as well as in areas such as labor standards, environmental considerations as well as capital account controls and protection of investments. Developing countries correctly blocked consideration of many of these issues in the Doha Round. But this has not stopped developed countries from obtaining similar objectives through preferential arrangements by dangling preferential market access in exchange.

Bilateral agreements typically involve much deeper tariff concessions from the developing countries and make demands on issues like intellectual property rights that go far beyond what WTO members require of each other and can threaten the health and livelihoods of the poor. Many countries would do well to resist the immediate temptations of a bilateral embrace and build up slower but ultimately more productive multilateral relationships that can lead to more durable human development outcomes (UNDP 2006).

Preferential agreements existed before the WTO and have been pursued in parallel with multilateral trade liberalization for many decades. Their supporters have always argued that they could be used as stepping-stones for broader multilateral agreements. And indeed the efforts to rationalize the overlapping preferential arrangements in Africa, involving 26 countries, members of Common Market for East and Southern Africa (COMESA), East African Community (EAC) and Southern African Development Community (SADC), are a step in the right direction.

Starting in 2012 the US and the EU launched a number of preferential initiatives: (1) an agreement in services among 46 countries, which includes the US, the EU, Canada and many developing countries in the WTO; (2) Transpacific Partnership (TPP), a free trade agreement involving the US, Australia, Mexico and Canada but also Malaysia, Vietnam and Japan—12 countries altogether; (3) a US/EU trade and investment agreement—the Transatlantic Trade and Investment Partnership (TTIP); and (4) an EU/Japan and an EU/Canada free trade agreement. The Regional Comprehensive Economic Partnership (RCEP) launched earlier with the participation of both India and China appears to be an effort by Asian countries to hedge their bets by promoting their own preferential trade relationships against the rest of the world.

These agreements moved forward in large part because the Doha Round negotiations had stalled. The earlier concern was that if they were successful, they would result in a very significant fragmentation of world trade with a large number of important developing country trading nations such as India and China being left out; and they would provide an alternative to moving forward in the WTO negotiations to the detriment of the WTO and of the large developing nations being left out of the agreements.

Brexit and the new US administration have changed the landscape for international trade cooperation in ways that would have been very difficult to predict in early 2016. To begin with, Brexit means that the EU would be occupied with the negotiations for its future trade relationship with the UK, an important trading partner along a very large range of issues including trade, migration and the movement of natural persons.

It is hard to visualize the EU engaging and concluding a serious trade negotiation at the WTO while this is going on.

The attitudes of the US administration pose even greater dangers for the future of international cooperation on trade. The administration has canceled US participation in the TPP and served notice of its desire to renegotiate NAFTA. Discussions with the EU on TTIP appear to be frozen as both sides are otherwise preoccupied. The US has made many loud noises about 'buying American'. It has launched two studies on US trade relations with ill-defined objectives and has made clear that it prefers 'bilateral deals' to regional or multilateral ones. Most ominously, the administration has launched investigations on steel and aluminum based on the rarely used GATT Article XXI permitting the imposition of controls for the protection of essential security interests. This is a thinly disguised protective initiative aimed to deal with the global excess capacity of these products, in a way that will cause serious damage to the US economy. It is likely to be opposed by the users of these products who in the past have argued effectively that protecting jobs in steel and aluminum, both industries where employment has been declining for decades in large measure because of technological change, is likely to hurt badly employment in much larger industries like automobiles, in which these products are used as inputs.

At the point of this writing, it is not clear how much of these loud protectionist noises will be translated into action. But combined with the slowdown on world trade, they have created a pall on global trade discussions and pose serious perils for the future. This is in part because they also appear to reflect a resurgent xenophobic anti-globalization protectionism on both sides of the Atlantic. This protectionism has roots in economic, social and cultural problems which both Europe and the US have neglected to address in the past and which, unless addressed, will threaten liberalism and the principles of international economic relations on aid and trade that have evolved over the last half century.

On the other hand, there is economic dynamism in Asia led by China and to a lesser extent by India. But China's economic model of state capitalism does not fit well with these principles: support for state enterprises is inconsistent with WTO provisions and the tied aid for infrastructure it provides harks back to 50 years ago when the US and the rest of OECD also used aid to help promote their own commercial interests.

The MDGs at 2015

The post-2008 slowdown in trade, finance and growth of the world economy did little to slow down the developing country progress in achieving the MDGs. Building largely on the momentum gained in the early 2000s, when globalization was galloping forward, developing countries achieved great progress in meeting the MDGs (UN 2015). The overall poverty reduction goal was achieved, as did the goals in improving gender equality in education, reducing child mortality and reversing the spread of AIDS. Considerable progress was made in meeting most of the goals—a first for the UN, which reported that 'As we reach the end of the MDG period, the world community has reason to celebrate' (UN 2015, p. 4).

At the same time, major development challenges remain. Although there was significant progress on overall targets, millions of people were left behind. Sub-Saharan Africa probably made the biggest relative gains, but large numbers of people are still living in extreme poverty without basic services. Inequality has increased in many countries globally and big gaps still exist between the poorest and the rich households, between rural and urban areas and between men and women.

In the fall of 2015, the UN adopted a new set of goals for the world community to achieve by the year 2030 (UN 2015). The Sustainable Development Goals (SDGs) include reducing income inequality, are many in number (17), extremely ambitious—eliminate poverty, hunger and illiteracy for all—and, as they include 169 targets many of which are non-quantifiable, they will be less measurable and more difficult to monitor than the MDGs. There is no campaign organized for their achievement and thus no obvious pressure on governments. In 2017, the developed world is starting to look ominously inward. Combined with the slowdown in the world economy, international trade and the flow of resources to developing countries, the prospects for achieving the SDGs look quite uncertain.

The Rise of Anti-globalization

What happened between the fall of 2015, when the world was celebrating poverty reduction for hundreds of millions in developing countries and the achievement of the MDGs, and a year later when the clouds of inward looking populism darkened the prospects for global cooperation? Much has been written about the rise of anti-globalization forces in Europe and the US during this period, but no single event is held to blame. Everybody is speaking of a process with cumulative effects over time.

Critics speak about the excesses of 'super-globalization' (Rodrik 2016). Subramanian and Kessler (2013) developed this concept originally to alert the economic community to the convergence of a number of factors—seven in all, including the very rapid growth of trade relative to GDP, the emergence of a 'mega trader' in China and the negotiation of a number of 'mega' PTAs—that required a new look at the role of China and the rules governing global trade. Soon after, many of the factors they had identified started to change. Some started to speak positively of 'de-globalization', referring to the fact that in the last decade or so growth in trade has been less than growth in GDP (Schillinger 2016). Most recently, the 'mega' PTAs seem to have stalled and China started to emphasize domestic growth.

Altogether, these developments suggest caution about the future. Everybody agrees with Stiglitz that governments have not dealt well with those left behind (Stiglitz 2002). Nobody has easy answers.

There are commonalities and differences in the rise of anti-globalization populism in the US and Europe. There is an anti-immigration element in both, though the immigration issue is very different in each case; and there is a common desire of wanting to restore control over policies that affect local communities which have been handed to 'Washington' or 'Brussels'. There is a far greater anti-trade sentiment in the US than in Europe, focused on the loss of manufacturing jobs and partly explained by the lack of a decent system of social support. The challenge is to develop constructive responses to real problems as opposed to appealing solutions which may help a small minority at the great costs to the majority, the global economy and to addressing worldwide inequalities. The policy challenges relate to trade, immigration and capital flows, including aid.

Trade

As noted earlier, there are some indications that merchandise trade is declining as a share of global GDP. This is variously attributed to long-term factors such as that the rapid changes taking advantage of the benefits of global value chains are being exhausted. Also, as incomes rise globally, services increase relative to goods as a share of GDP. But services are less tradeable and much more subject to restrictions than merchandise trade. Thus, it could be expected that merchandise trade would fall as a share of GDP—and that is as it should be—in fact it should fall even more if services trade were to be liberalized further. Of course, this is not an answer to people who have currently or recently lost their jobs and cannot find another and thus are unemployed or drop out of the labor force.

The essence of capitalism is creative destruction. But if it appears that manufacturing jobs are created in China or Mexico and destroyed in the US or the UK, then there is a political economy problem. The problem is exacerbated if it appears that, in the case of China, state-owned enterprises continue to be subsidized—an issue on which the WTO disciples are not that strong.

The fact is that the US has been losing manufacturing jobs for since 1953, when they peaked at 30% of the labor force, at a time when Europe had not fully recovered from World War II.[7] In 2015, manufacturing accounted for only 8.6% of total US employment. The decline has been faster at some times than others and recently the absolute numbers have steadied, though as a share of the total, jobs in manufacturing are still falling.

Until 2000, as noted in Chap. 7, the conclusion was that trade was not a significant contributing factor in the decline of manufacturing jobs and workers losing their jobs tended to find jobs in other regions. Still, during 1990–2007, the US lost roughly 7.3 million jobs in manufacturing in the decade, of which 21% was estimated to be due to competition from imports mostly from China and the rest due to productivity improvements (Autor et al. 2013).[8] The losses, close to a million jobs, were greatest in the period 2000–2007. Let us say then that the US lost 100, 000 jobs a year for almost 20 years to competition from China at a time when in the US there are roughly 1.7 million layoffs *a month*. And of these 100,000, how many actually could not find any job and dropped out of the labor force or remained unemployed? A significant number did, but whatever the number, it is tiny compared to the US labor market.

In the US, there is a steady decline of men in the workforce, especially those with less education and skills as well as an increasing differential in wages between low skill and skilled workers. There is also a measurable reduction in labor mobility both professional and with respect to localities, all of which contribute to feelings of alienation and exclusion and give rise to increased drug use and lower life expectancy. Protection is not the answer for many well-known reasons:

* The total cost to the US economy far exceeds—from 6 up to 20 times—the benefits to the workers protected: in the 1970s, tariff protection of the nut, bolt and screw industry cost $550,000 per job saved—average wage $23,000; in the 1980s, voluntary restraints on Japanese car imports cost $193,000 per job saved—six times the average wage; in 2012, stopping a surge of Chinese import of tires cost $900,000 per job saved or more than 20 times of the average wage in the affected industry.

* In a global economy where world trade is to a significant extent based on value chains organized by multinational firms, blocking some imports is like shooting oneself in the foot; the recent action by the US administration to launch an investigation on subsidies allegedly involved in imports of lumber from Canada has been met by strong resistance from US building industries that use it as an input in construction, much as the US auto industry has consistently opposed restrictions on steel imports.

* The costs of protection are borne more heavily by the poor in the US and developed economies as well as some higher income developing countries because a larger share of their income is spent on imports of items like shoes and clothing.

* Retaliation by affected countries would hurt US jobs and exports: Retaliation by China on US exports in the tire case cost the US exporters of chicken parts sales of $1 billion.

The US Trade Adjustment Assistance Program is supposed to help individuals and communities adversely affected by import competition. Workers who have lost their jobs tend to be older, less educated and take longer to return to work. The program, however, has failed to address the problems in the last several years for a variety of reasons: the training provided did not improve earning and employment outcomes; workers are often not aware of its existence as demonstrated by the fact that only 40% of eligible workers signed up for it and in any case it was too small to make much difference (IMF et al. p. 32). Perhaps most important is the fact that the program's benefits are too small to matter much. Indeed the evidence is that other US programs, including the social security disability benefits and unemployment benefits, are far more important in offsetting earnings losses from people losing their manufacturing jobs. But even all these together make up only a small part of the earnings losses.

In studies of the same issue in Europe, the results were mixed: in Spain apparently, they found jobs in non-manufacturing, in Germany they found jobs in export industries, while in Norway and the UK they tended to stay unemployed longer than others (Economist 2016). In general, the anti-trade voices in Europe have been less strident in part because the social support systems have been far more effective.

Migration

The WTO contains very few provisions that permit the cross-border movement of labor and that only for temporary workers. Long-term immigration has been controlled in both developed and developing countries although economists have always argued that freedom of labor movement would contribute to increasing world welfare.

The impact of migration on receiving and sending countries' wages, employment, fiscal burden and overall welfare is an extremely complex

subject and varies by country of origin and destination, the age and quali-
fications of the migrants and a variety of economic and social policies in
the host country. A detailed assessment of the migration issue in the US
and Europe is clearly beyond the scope of this volume. A few impressions
are presented below colored no doubt by my own experience as an immigrant, which I have detailed in my book *Migration Chronicles*
(Michalopoulos 2008).

At present, both the US and Europe are struggling to control their border against the influx of new migrants. But there are many differences:

* Actual net migration of illegals into the US is at present negative,
  meaning more illegal immigrants are leaving than are coming in, partly
  as a consequence of increased border security and deportation. Inflows
  of immigrants, mostly refugees have been large, though recently
  declining in Europe.
* The influx of refugees into Europe stems from war-torn countries in
  the middle-east and Sub-Saharan Africa; but there are some illegal economic migrants as well from Sub-Saharan Africa as well as South Asia
  and elsewhere; a large portion of illegal immigrants into the US come
  from Central America, many seeking a better life, others to avoid local
  conflicts.
* In the US, there is a major issue about the treatment of the large stock
  of illegal immigrants; this has not been an important issue for Europe—
  although it will be growing in importance over time.

The freedom of labor movement within the EU has resulted in significant flows of laborers across borders. The recent dramatic expansion of
inflows of refugees, many from Syria, has increased the burden to receiving countries which have been unable so far to establish either effective
border controls or an agreed upon distribution of the migrants for settlement among the various EU countries. In the UK, the anti-immigration
sentiment in the Brexit campaign was highest, not where the number of
immigrants was the largest, but where it had grown the fastest. In the US,
the anti-migration sentiment was drummed up in the same areas where
jobs were lost through technology change or import competition—not
where the immigrant population was the largest.

In both the US and the UK, economic issues have been raised about the potentially adverse impact of immigrants on wages and welfare benefits. The evidence is mixed: the overall effect of the influx of immigrants on wages may be insignificant, but there may be a localized impact on certain groups of low-skilled workers—farmers, in the UK, service industry personnel in the US. But it may well be that a lot of the low-skilled immigrants are really complements to the domestic labor force which does not want to do certain jobs—take for example the immigrant farm workers from Asia and Sub-Saharan that dominate farm labor in Greece; or immigrants that dominate the dairy industry of Wisconsin. Immigrants may not be substitutes for native workers. New immigrants are substitutes for old immigrants (from different nationalities and waves) as older immigrants move on and get better integrated in the economy: the Greek immigrants who dominated the cheap diners of yesterday have moved on to the professions and their place in cheap fast food places has been taken by immigrants from Central America.

On welfare, the impression in the US is that immigrants pay more in taxes than they get in public services. This is apparently not the case in the UK where 'centralized budgets make it difficult for local authorities to respond flexibly to local conditions and strict planning rules limit the construction of new homes when demand surges' (Economist 2016).

The anti-immigration sentiment surfaced most vehemently for cultural not economic reasons in a number of CEE countries, notably Hungary, which have not been exposed to significant inflows of foreign workers for any reason in recent periods. On the contrary, the population of countries like Greece, which have had to bear a large share of the burden of dealing with refugees, especially at their point of entry, have shown little anti-refugee sentiment—possibly because they themselves have had a history of acceptance and assimilation of workers from foreign cultures.

In the long term, the aging population in Europe can use a significant influx of migrants to add to its shrinking labor force. Similarly, the US economy has used and will continue to use immigrant labor for various sectors and regions of its economy. The economy of a large portion of the US Southwest region, which borders on Mexico, is critically dependent of immigrant labor. The issue has to do not with the benefits of migration, but how to deal with desperate refugees fleeing war or crime-ridden societies; and how to organize significant legal migrant flows that would be mutually beneficial both for sending countries—usually developing ones—and receiving countries in the OECD. Neither of these long-term objectives are served by the anti-immigrant hysteria dominating the populist movements in the US and some parts of Europe today.[9]

Capital Flows

The populist movement has not yet gained enough political power globally to affect aid flows. But the signs are ominous: the US administration proposed a reduction of one-third in the FY 2018 aid budget of the State Department; and it has made the point that it will seek reductions in the US contribution to various UN activities. It has apparently also recommended the termination of USAID's 'Development Assistance' program, the oldest and only traditionally 'pure' development assistance program in the US collection of aid programs; a sad end, if it happens, to a program launched in 1961 by President Kennedy as one of the original USAID programs (Konyndyk 2017). The extent to which these proposals will be enacted into legislation remains to be seen. But it is highly likely that US ODA flows will decline in the near future. At the same time, many European countries are devoting increasing amounts of assistance to refugees which they count as ODA. These resources are not likely to be additional to previous ODA commitments, thus leading to the ironic situation that refugees are being supported more than their usually poorer and more destitute compatriots left behind. While the prospects for ODA levels from traditional OECD donors are not bright, the new multilateral aid institutions in Asia are only now starting operations, providing another source of development finance, which however is not likely to qualify as ODA. Even if it does, its tied nature is a serious defect, which over time is bound to reduce developing country enthusiasm for its provision.[10]

The anti-globalization movement in the US has sought to reduce the outflow of private direct investment primarily through what Americans call 'jaw-boning' by the US President, who has claimed some success in this area: a number of US auto firms have announced significant domestic investments for a number of new projects. But it is doubtful that their decisions were in response to the pressure put on them by the US administration or by general economic forces which have seen the return a number of foreign-based operations to the OECD. In addition, it appears that the US is planning a reform of its corporate tax system aimed at reducing tax incentives. Both of these factors suggest again a reduction of future foreign direct investment flows to developing countries.

Finally, bank and portfolio lending to developing countries has fallen significantly primarily because of global economic conditions rather than political developments. The abrupt changes in these flows in response to factors unrelated to developing country performance suggest that developing countries need to be extremely careful in the management of these flows and the degree to which they rely on them for long-term development finance. The Greek debacle as well as recent experience with capital controls in Chile, Brazil and China suggests that countries need to consider a variety of approaches to regulate the flow of these resources.

The Challenges Ahead

The evolution of the world economy since the 2008 crisis poses a large number of challenges to the future relations between developed and developing countries—the modern designation is 'emerging and developing market economies' (EDMEs). There are several major global economic trends: there is a slowdown of both trade and growth and there is an increase in intra-country inequality of income in most developed and developing countries alike; and there is a shift in the balance of economic power away from the US and Europe toward China and Asia.

It could be argued that developed countries did not do too badly in crisis management in terms of restoring and maintaining GDP levels, although growth rates declined in both developed countries and emerging powers. Employment trends however were a different matter: labor force participation rates plunged and unemployment rose to very high levels for various reasons—due to cyclical factors, increased 'churning' and structural reasons, including increased offshore investment and the impact of long-term labor-saving technology. Leipziger in a prescient article (Leipziger 2009, p. 7) writes: 'The political economy consequences are inevitably going to be on the side of creating and preserving (through whatever means) domestic jobs. Even more important to the future is that, whether this will be seen as formal protectionism or not, globalization will no doubt be put at odds with national economic goals in a highly politicized fashion.'

The long tail of the 2008 crisis has hit in the form of the highly divisive politics of 2016–2017 in the US and Europe which create tremendous challenges for the global economy. I cannot possibly address all these challenges in this volume. I will attempt to address those linked to issues of aid and trade in support of development. Some of these issues, such as policy coherence and protectionism and differential treatment of developing countries in trade are issues that I have traced throughout this volume. Others, such as the rise of state capitalism and what to do about the losers from globalization, have been around for many years but have risen in importance in more recent periods.

According to a recent letter to the *Washington Post* (May 12, 2017), Supreme Court Justice William O. Douglas warned that 'As nightfall does not come at once, neither does oppression. In both instances there is a twilight when everything remains seemingly unchanged. And it is in such twilight that we all must be most aware of change in the air, however slight—lest we become unwitting victims of the darkness.' I do not agree that current events in the US and elsewhere signal the onset of political oppression. Despite the rise of authoritarian regimes in places like Russia, Turkey and Venezuela, there are far more democratic regimes today in the developing countries than 50 years ago. But change may be in the air regarding the liberal values that have dominated the workings of the international economy in the last half century.

There are different issues for developed and developing countries and for the system as a whole. Europe and the US face different challenges which I cannot address in detail either. How the issues are addressed, especially in light of other exogenous technology and demographic trends, will help determine in part whether what I called at the beginning of this chapter key elements of economic 'liberalism' will survive. Many actions are needed to prevent being engulfed in darkness.

Notes

1. Preliminary estimates of ODA levels in 2016 suggest few changes in the totals or their components (OECD 2017).
2. A major objective of bringing in the UNDP was to provide a forum for the involvement of new donors especially China, an important objective of DAC Chairman Brian Atwood.
3. A new fund in support of the new Trade Facilitation Agreement was also set up in the WTO (see below).
4. Originally, quarterly reports were prepared. The sources for the reports are official notifications as well as press stories and third-party complaints. The Secretariat attempts to verify each measure and reports, both those that it has been able to verify—which are the vast majority—and those it has not (WTO 2009). In parallel with the WTO, a private database has been developed by Global Trade Alert (GTA), an independent group of experienced analysts who have published regular reports on trade measures (Evenett 2009).
5. This involved the establishment of a new mechanism that developing countries could use to increase agricultural protection at times of import surges.
6. Twenty years ago when Eveline Herfkens was chairing the WTO LDC sub committee which had agreed to support the undertaking of the original LDC 'needs assessments', a WTO representative from a Sub-Saharan African country approached her and asked how soon should his authorities expect the consultants to come to identify what their needs are to which she replied: "why don't you check first with your private sector, your exporters or your chamber of commerce to determine what your needs are?"
7. The share was even higher, 39% in 1944 when Europe was still in ruins (Autor et al. 2016).
8. It appears that, despite the current US administration's complaints about NAFTA, adding NAFTA to China does not add much if anything to US job losses in manufacturing (Autor et al. 2016).
9. Another issue deserving global attention involves the plight of refugees and displaced persons in developing countries, all living in infernal conditions.
10. See the recent reaction of Kenyans to the opening of the new Chinese financed railroad in which the railroad staff was wearing uniforms with the Chinese flag colors (INY Times, May 9, 2017).

References

Abdel-Malek, T. and B. Koenders, (2011) "Progress towards More Effective Aid: What does the Evidence Show?" 4th High Level Conference on Aid Effectiveness, http://www. Busanhlf4.org.

Autor, D.H., D. Dorn and G. H. Hanson (2013) "The China Syndrome: Local Labor Market Effects of Import Competitions in the United States" *American Economic Review* 103 (6), pp. 2121–2168.

———— (2016) "The China Shock: Learning from Labor to Market Adjustment to Large Changes in Trade" *Annual Review of Economics.*

Azevedo, R. (2016) "The WTO's sixteenth Monitoring Report on Group of 20 (G20) Trade Measures", Press Briefing 10 November. https://www.wto.org/English/thewto_e/dg_edg_e.htm.

Bhagwati, J. (2009) *Termites in the Trading System: How Preferential Agreements Undermine Free Trade* (New York: Council of Foreign Relations).

Birdsall, N. and H. Kharas, (2014), *The Quality of ODA, Third Edition* (Washington DC: CGD and Brookings).

Economist, the (2013) 'Can the WTO Save itself from Irrelevance?.' 16 March.

Economist, the (2016) 'The World Economy' Special Report., 1 October.

Evenett, S. J. (2009) *Global Trade Alert 1st Report* (London: CEPR).

Global Partnership for Effective Development Collaboration (2016), *Making Development Co-operation more Effective* (Paris and New York: OECD/UNDP).

Herfkens, E. (2014) "Aid Effectiveness: Lessons Learned- and Forgotten (in Dutch)" S. Vermer, L. Schulpen and R. Ruben Eds. *Hoe nu Verder* (Arnhem: LM Publishers).

Hufbauer G. et al. (2010) *Figuring out the Doha Round* (Washington, DC: Peterson Institute for International Economics).

IMF, World Bank, WTO (2017) *Making Trade an Engine of Growth for All,* (Geneva: WTO).

Konyndyk, J. (2017) "Our First Peek at Trump's Aid Budget: Big Changes but Will Congress Play Along", www.cgdevelopment.org 28 April.

Leipziger, D. (2009) "Globalization Revisited" in D. Leipziger and M. Spence *Globalization and Growth,* (Washington DC: World Bank).

Michalopoulos, C. (2001) *Developing Countries in the WTO* (Houndsmills: Palgrave).

Michalopoulos, C. (2008) *Migration Chronicles* (Lusby: Point of View Publishing).

Michalopoulos, C. (2014) *Emerging Powers in the WTO* (Houndmills: Palgrave).

OECD (2017) "Development Aid Rises in 2016 but Flows to Poorest Countries Dip" DCD-DAC (Paris: OECD).

Rodrik, D. (2016) "Deglobalization is a Chance to Make Good an Imbalance" *Financial Times* Oct.16.

Schiavo-Campo, S. (1978) *International Economics: An Introduction to Theory and Parctice* (Cambridge, MA: Winthrop).

Schillinger, H.R. (2016) "In Need of Rethinking: Trade Policies in Times of De-Globalization" (Geneva: Friedrich Ebert Stiftung).

Stiglitz, J.E. (2002) *Globalization and its Discontents* (New York and London: W.W. Norton and Company).

Subramanian, A. and M. Kessler (2013) "The Hyper-globalization of Trade and Its Future" Working Paper WP13-6, (Washington DC: Peterson Institute for International Economics).

Summers, L. (2016) "Weak economy, angry politics", *Washington Post.*, October 10.

TFAF (2016) "The Trade Facilitation Agreement Facility, 2015 Budget" www. tfat.org.

United Nations (2009) *The Doha Declaration on Financing for Development,* (New York: United Nations).

United Nations (2014) "Mexico High Level Meeting Communique", The Global Partnership for Effective Development Cooperation and the Post 2015-Development Agenda., 16 April.

United Nations (2015) *The Millennium Development Goals Report 2015,* (New York: United Nations).

UNDP (2006) 'Trade on Human Terms', *Asia and Pacific Human Development Report 2006, Overview* (Macmillan India for UNDP).

Wolfe, R. (2011) 'Did the Protectionist Dog Bark?' Policy Report, (Stockholm: ENTWINED).

WTO (1995) *The Results of the Uruguay Round of Mulitlateral Negotiations* (Geneva:WTO).

WTO (2009) *Report to the TPRB from the Director General on the Financial and Economic Crisis and Trade Related Developments*, WT/TPR/OV/W/1, (Geneva: WTO).

WTO (2015) "State Trading: China" G/STR/N/10-15/CHN (Geneva: WTO).

WTO (2016) *WTO Report on G-20 Trade Measures (mid-May 2016-to mid-October 2016,* (Geneva: WTO).

11

The Future

Introduction

Globalization has changed the economic realities in all of humanity. The impressive gains in income and the improvement in global income inequality noted by Milanovic would never have been possible without it. But the institutions within which developing countries have achieved great progress in the last half century have changed very little. They continue to reflect the economic power distribution of the past 50 years. As a result, they are in danger of losing legitimacy, which would undermine the validity of the principles of economic liberalism on which they were founded. And at the same time, within country inequalities have increased in many if not most countries.

Change is needed. As the OECD Secretary General, Angel Gurria recently said, quoting Lampedusa, 'Much has to change for everything to remain the same' (Gurria 2017). China and the other emerging powers have to play an increasing role and accept greater responsibilities in global economic management. But for the OECD democracies, change typically takes place at a glacial pace unless there is war. Muddling through

© The Author(s) 2017
C. Michalopoulos, *Aid, Trade and Development*,
https://doi.org/10.1007/978-3-319-65861-2_11

has been the preferred option, even in periods of crises, such as the oil price increases of the 1970s and the financial disaster of 2008.

Violent conflict cannot be excluded given the unstable leadership in Washington and Pyongyang. And there are some who say that China and the US are on a long-term violent collision course as the transition from one leading world power to another has usually involved war. But as Nobel laureate Daniel Kahneman said, 'When action is needed, optimism, even of the mildly delusional variety may be a good thing.'[1] I am an optimist in the sense that I believe that economic liberalism reflects fundamental human values that will win out over time, and that humanity will take the necessary steps to avoid catastrophic events as well as introduce necessary changes despite the dark clouds emanating from Washington these days. It will take a while to do, so it has to start now.

The actions proposed below fall into five main groups: (a) *Globalization: Addressing the Problems of Those Left Behind;* (b) *The WTO and International Trade;* (c) *Aid;* (d) *Private Capital Flows; and* (e) *Challenges of the Future.* Throughout the discussion, special attention is directed to actions needed to address the rising importance of China and the other emerging powers. The proposals are not designed to address all of world's economic ills; only some of those are related to aid, trade and development.

Globalization: Addressing the Problems of Those Left Behind

The highest priority should be given to the development of policies and systems to address problems of individuals and communities adversely affected by globalization or technological change, or a combination of the two. The first thing to acknowledge is that trade liberalization can have local victims as well as general benefits. Unless the problems of the victims are addressed, trust is eroded in the economists' arguments about the benefits of globalization. 'It is rarely in the interest of those in the right to pretend they are never wrong' (Economist 2017, p. 66). Next is to decide that the victims' problems cannot be overcome through protection. It is a temporary palliative for the few while causing great harm for everybody else. It would make the solution worse than the original problem. But what has to follow is a diverse set of policies that address the plight of those left behind.

There is no one-size-fits-all strategy. There is usually a need for a combination of passive labor market policies such as unemployment insurance and social protection policies with active labor market programs. Trade Adjustment Assistance in the US and the European Globalization Adjustment Fund are often not enough. In most developing countries, they do not exist at all.

Active labor market programs require early and frequent engagement with displaced workers, requiring them to participate in interviews with employment counselors, formulate individual plans, accept offers of suitable work and attend training programs, if necessary. This is best done on the job and involves establishing strong ties between the programs and the private sector, which has been done more effectively in Europe than in the US. Regional development policies may also be needed in some cases when job losses in manufacturing affect the rest of the community and lead to the creation of newly depressed areas.

A variety of other policies are needed to address problems of geographical and functional mobility and its impact on employment. First, of course, is the need to maintain a stable and growing economy with increasing employment opportunities. The angst about the impact of globalization has increased since the 2008 crisis and the subsequent slow economic recovery which was accompanied by anemic employment growth. In the US and some other developed economies, house ownership is high among older workers, but housing prices are depressed in communities where unemployment is soaring due to technological change or to competition from imports: a housing allowance may be needed as an incentive to relocation. Education policy as a whole may need to be reconsidered in order to equip individuals with skills which increase flexibility in getting jobs in the face of rapid technological change which destroys jobs. And if trade is going to decline as a portion of GDP, governments need to consider what kind of pro-competition policies they need to implement to make up for the loss of competitive edge that trade introduces (Leipziger 2016).

The WTO and International Trade

Following the actual, though not formally acknowledged, death of the Doha Round, the WTO is facing several challenges. In the short term, the challenge is to identify some pieces of the Doha development agenda which could be promoted and result in a multilateral agreement. In the longer term, there are several other challenges: how to ensure that the mushrooming preferential trade agreements contribute rather than undermine the multilateral trading system; what to do about the increase in state trading; and how to change the existing rules regarding special and differential treatment to ensure that they reflect the needs of low-income developing countries and LDCs but exclude emerging powers that do not need special treatment. The establishment of an openly protectionist administration in the US; China's proposed 'Made in China 2025' import substitution program and to a lesser extent Brexit will affect how and when these challenges are met and add further challenges to the system.

The Buenos Aires Ministerial

At the time of this writing, a number of initiatives pertaining to agriculture and food security as well as fisheries were being discussed for possible agreement at the WTO Ministerial in Buenos Aires in December 2017. The EU, Japan and a number of developing countries have in the past been at the forefront of agriculture protection. Japan appeared ready to liberalize its agriculture in the context of the TPP agreement scuttled by the US. And the EU may have been ready to reduce agriculture supports for budgetary reasons. Given the upcoming negotiations on Brexit, however, it is unclear how much leeway the EU will have to commit itself on trade matters until the arrangements with the UK are finalized. The US, the world's largest exporter of agricultural products, has obvious interests in broader trade liberalization, but also provides significant supports to its agriculture. It has also initiated a review of NAFTA, a highly visible political matter with a great number of agricultural issues. Again, it is highly unlikely that it will be prepared to engage in a serious multilateral agreement in agriculture, fisheries or anything else in the near future.

Services

The other area of great potential international liberalization is services. A preferential agreement involving 23 countries accounting for about 70% of world trade in services, but not China, has been in the works for years. The US, Australia and the EU were among those driving the negotiations, which had moved sufficiently to schedule a Ministerial for the end of 2016. Regrettably, however, it was canceled. An agreement in services, even if it does not cover all of the WTO membership, would be an important step forward given the rising importance of services in global GNP and the much greater restrictions against services trade in place in all countries. The agreement would be in keeping with the principle of different groups of countries joining to liberalize in a specific sector, as happened recently with the ITA. There were some preliminary discussions on questions of services facilitation in the context of the upcoming Ministerial. However, given that the US is just starting to think about this agreement and that there are obvious uncertainties in Brussels, the timing may be too short for anything substantive to happen in Buenos Ayres.

Preferential Trade Agreements

While the prospects are limited for moving forward with significant multilateral agreements in the next few years, the danger to the multilateral system from the mega-regionals has temporarily abated as both the TPP and the TTIP have been shelved for the time being. This means that it would be possible to take a few steps to strengthen the prospects that existing and future RTAs support rather than undermine the multilateral system. A number of useful proposals have been made in this connection by the E15 initiative, such as simplifying and standardizing the conduct of business across the 400 or so existing RTAs; providing for extended cumulation in the rules of origin, affecting LDC exports—as is done by Canada; or providing 'multilateral impact' statements which estimate the effects of RTAs on third countries and in particular low-income developing countries and LDCs (Melendez-Ortiz and Samons 2016).

It could be that the TPP would move forward without the US or be combined with RCEP in Asia, which itself could be expanded to include deeper integration. Perhaps the best development would be a PTA between China and the EU that includes services but excludes the US. This could take a long time to negotiate, but it could create a significant leverage on a protectionist US that could later be translated into a global agreement that includes services and other issues.

State Trading

Continued opaque links between the state and state enterprises in China and elsewhere are going to be a problem for years to come. The outcome of the pending DSM case involving China's designation as a non-market economy is of considerable importance in setting the stage for considering more restrictive WTO rules on state trading. It will take time before a definitive ruling China's complaint is made (see Chap. 10). But unless the protagonists reach an agreement, the case could result in significant cleavages and risks for the WTO as an institution, in particular if any of the three main protagonists feels that it cannot abide by the decision.

Special and Differential Treatment

As the WTO governance structure and rule making is formally based on the principle of unanimity, the organization in practice works on the basis of consensus. Over time the emerging powers including Brazil, China, India and others have asserted themselves in the WTO, and there is no question of the new economic powers wielding too little influence. The opposite problem has emerged: the principle of special and differential treatment has been imbedded so deeply in various forms in the various agreements that the emerging powers are permitted too much flexibility in adhering to the rules embodied in the basic WTO texts. Developing countries, including China, bear less responsibility in the system than their economic status warrants.

In December 2015, while attending a conference in Beijing, I asked Chinese officials why China, the world's largest trading nation, claimed as many exceptions from the recently concluded Trade Facilitation agreement as tiny, landlocked Kyrgyz Republic. Their response was that China too is a developing country, as some of its western regions are relatively backward. Of course all countries have backward regions. But it is absurd that, for example, EU members Bulgaria or Romania are supposed to provide preferences to trade powerhouses like Brazil, China, Korea or Singapore, all considered 'developing countries' based on WTO's self-selection principle. There is an obvious need to rationalize the system through the use of income, size or similar criteria used effectively for many decades by the IFIs as well as the UN in deciding aid terms. Developing countries have opposed this in the past because of fears that such an approach would dilute their political influence in the organization. But their rising strength reflected in all of WTO's deliberations, and decisions should permit them to develop a system which makes more economic sense and is focused on the less advantaged developing countries whose institutional weaknesses continue to prevent them from maximizing the benefits they could obtain from international trade. In such a system, higher income emerging economies would be excluded from SDT and they themselves should provide SDT to low-income countries and the LDCs. The same principle should apply to the GSP, which contains a hodgepodge of eligibility criteria applied by individual countries, the EU's EBA and the US AGOA, all of which are often provided on political grounds, having little to do with the capacity of eligible developing countries to compete in international trade. I had made detailed recommendations for the cleaning up of the SDT system and global preferential arrangements a few years back when the prospects for a liberal economic order based on multilaterally agreed rules appeared much better (Michalopoulos 2014). They are still needed, but they would probably have to wait for a more cooperative international environment.

Dangers to the Open Trading System

The US and the EU have been at the forefront of global rulemaking on trade for the last 70 years. The rise of China and other emerging powers has changed the global balance in trade. However, the US size and global trade reach not only in goods but especially in services makes it an indispensable country for global rule making. It is unlikely that another combination, for example, EU and China, could substitute for US leadership, especially in the near future. Thus, the most important priority over the next several years would be to protect the multilateral system from being damaged.

At present the biggest potential danger to the multilateral system derives from the possibility that the US or another major power would openly defy an adverse decision by the DSM, such as the one involving China's 'non-market economy' issue. Despite the protectionist rhetoric, the US so far has worked within the system both in the case of NAFTA and on WTO issues. As long as it continues to do so, the damage to the system would be limited to its inability to move forward and address pending problems or conclude new meaningful agreements. Fortunately (!), the DSM works slowly, so by the time all appeals are exhausted on present cases, a new less protectionist regime may be in charge in Washington.

Aid

ODA

Global ODA needs have declined and will continue to decline as more developing countries are able to obtain and service private capital flows. But ODA must continue for a number of low-income developing countries and LDCs especially in Sub-Saharan Africa. After many years of trying, the DAC/OECD has only been able to nudge traditional bilateral donors toward providing increasing amounts of assistance to the LDCs. Beyond that achievement, donors continue to allocate assistance based on a variety of economic and political self-interests; and even for LDCs, they continue to tie some procurement to donor sources despite an explicit agreement not to do so.

The problem may be worse with the new donors with the exception of private philanthropy; but it is hard to say. China, the largest new bilateral donor, continues to hide its assistance operations under the mantle of

'South-South' cooperation; does not publish annual assistance data which outside research institutes (Kitano 2016) and the DAC have to estimate—probably because the Chinese government itself does not know what it spends[2]; and continues to tie practically all its bilateral aid to procurement in China. China will not join the DAC. As the UN approach, starting with Busan, has failed to yield results, probably the only palatable new approach to dealing with aid questions would be to introduce them in the deliberations of the G-20, a group that more accurately reflects global economic realities. This would require an expansion of the role and membership of the G-20 as an institution, which would be desirable for a number of reasons discussed below.

Aid Effectiveness

Several major changes are needed in order to increase aid effectiveness of donors: first, to increase the use of innovative aid instruments such as 'Cash on Delivery', which rely more on recipients' systems and receiving aid after they have accomplished certain targets rather than providing aid based on advance conditionality and detailed monitoring.[3] There was progress in providing aid in the form of budget support in the early 2000s, but there has been retrogression recently despite the fact that recipient systems have been strengthened.

Second, many bilateral aid programs are replete with donor pet-areas of interest, such as disease A or B, while the health systems, especially of low-income countries, lack fundamental financing, governance and delivery. The aid delivery model was supposed to have been changed with the Paris Agreements. But although some progress has been made, it has not fundamentally changed in many countries.

Monitoring the effectiveness of aid and using the information to improve aid practices is an issue that has occupied both developed and developing countries for a long period of time. In the last several years, this effort has languished. The best way forward could be for expanded responsibilities for multi-stakeholder initiatives such as the International Aid Transparency Initiative (IATI), through which NGO efforts in combination with a coalition of the willing donors is making a difference in providing information about projects worldwide. Alternatively, NGOs such as the CGD in combination with a developing country NGO or think tank could take on a properly funded global responsibility in this area much like Amnesty International and Transparency International have done in areas where formal government collaboration has been lagging.[4] While political will may not be present at the moment, this may change and widespread publicity on relative effectiveness of aid practices may help bring about that change.[5]

IFIs and the New Banks

There is a need to reduce the demands placed on aid recipients by merging donors and better donor cooperation and coordination locally. This has been continuously stressed by all finance-for-development meetings and conferences, but the reality has been more and more donor entities functioning in an already crowded field. Some is due to frustration by new donors about the continuation of arrangements in the IFIs that do not reflect current economic realities. Others reflect the lack of coherence between aid and trade officials at the national level.[6] Changes are needed in the existing structure and organization of multilateral institutions which have been established a long time ago and which have been resistant to change.

Globally, there is a need for a fundamental change in the representation of China and to a certain extent of the other emerging powers in the IFIs. The shares of the different countries and groupings in the IMF determine their shares in the World Bank. Both require changes to increase China's and emerging countries' representation and decrease those of the US and Europe.

Multilateral institutions need to merge. The most obvious example involves the Asian Development Bank (ADB) and the newly established AIIB. The ADB has many different programs but 70% of its lending is in infrastructure and the country coverage of the two institutions is very similar. The only difference is that one is dominated by Japan and to a certain extent the rest of the OECD; the other by China, with OECD membership (with the exception of the US). What is logical may not be politically feasible, given the long-term leadership competition between China and Japan. An even more interesting alternative may be to merge AIIB with a restructured World Bank. The World Bank needs recapitalization. Instead, what about merging the AIIB, the NDB and the World Bank to form a new Global Development Bank which reflects more accurately the economic importance of China and the BRICS?

On a smaller scale, there is an extremely urgent need for consolidation of aid agencies in the field of aid for trade. The only reason that at present there are three very little aid agencies in the WTO—one for LDCs, one for SPS and TBT and a new one in support for Trade Facilitation—plus a separate technical assistance budget for the WTO, a separate one for UNCTAD as well the ITC, is that developing countries want to have more control of the aid allocation process. I had earlier proposed an integrated aid for trade fund (Michalopoulos 2014).[7] It is more urgently needed now that we have a new tiny trade facilitation aid fund with a total capitalization of around $4 million—a ridiculously small amount to address developing countries' needs in this area.

Aid and Trade

I have avoided so far to mention the old bromide 'trade not aid'. I firmly believe that both public concessional assistance, ODA in short, and international trade have played and can continue to play a positive role in development and poverty alleviation when accompanied by a host of other policies discussed in earlier chapters. But whatever their relative importance in the past, in the future, there is no question but that trade will be far more important simply because developing countries have made so much progress that rather few of them, mostly LDCs and a few other low-income countries, need continued access to ODA. And there will always be some fragile states as well as countries that face catastrophic natural events that would require assistance.

Little can be expected in the near future on question of coherence of aid and trade policies, as aid practices tend to reflect more donors' interests than recipient needs. WTO participation in the IFIs has been mostly cosmetic, while developed countries have resisted developing countries' initiatives to introduce serious discussion of financial issues in the UN or the WTO. In any case, coordination of this issue is primarily a domestic matter, and on this, recent experience is also discouraging: The UK and the Netherlands combined aid and trade policies in one ministry. Alas, in both cases trade interests tended to drive the agenda and in the case of the UK, the Ministry of Trade was separated again in anticipation of Brexit. Nevertheless, the EU is one hope for the future, if a new spirit of European-wide cooperation and deeper integration succeeds following political developments in France and Germany. This would require strengthening European-wide institutions more generally as well as the reestablishment of the EU Development Council.[8]

Internationally, and for the longer term, the G-20 is the one group that has the proper balance of representation of global economic interests to have the potential for meaningful discussions of trade and aid policies and their linkages. For the G-20 to play a more meaningful role, it will require changes to reflect the interests of low-income countries and Sub-Saharan Africa, as South Africa, its only current member, does not represent aid and trade interests of the other Sub-Saharan African countries. It will require an institutional strengthening, through more staff and responsibilities in bringing together global leaders. This in turn will require greater commitment to international cooperation for development, which is not on the horizon for the near future but could be in the offing as political changes occur in major countries in the EU as well as the US and China. This year, Germany's effort to focus G-20 on Africa is a welcome beginning.

Private Capital Flows

As the role of aid has declined and will likely decline further in the future, the importance private capital flows play in development will rise. In this regard, there are trends which need to be encouraged and issues to be addressed.

The first trend to be encouraged is the development of public-private initiatives, especially needed to address large-scale infrastructure and energy projects. The World Bank and the MDBs are quite active in this area and should be encouraged to do more, especially in Sub-Saharan Africa. The application of new instruments such as Development Impact Bonds could be expanded. These bonds provide upfront funding for development programs by private investors who are remunerated by donors or host country governments and earn a return if evidence shows that the programs achieved pre-agreed outcomes.[9]

The other positive trend is the expanded role played by private philanthropy, especially in the area of global health. It is important to recognize in this connection that the driving force in this sector has been the Gates foundation, which alone accounts for over 50% of all global private philanthropic flows for all sectors combined. While the rise in private philanthropy extended on grant terms is a welcome offset to declines in official aid, the very large number of small private donors increases the difficulties faced by local administrations to coordinate their activities.

Developing countries face two other major challenges that need to be addressed, one for each major capital flow: first, foreign direct investment and second, short-term capital flows, primarily bank lending and portfolio investment. With regard to foreign direct investment, the key issue is how to ensure a fair distribution of the costs and benefits from FDI. This has been based on thousands bilateral investment treaties which tended to reflect the interests of the exporting country investors.

> If you wanted to convince the public that international trade agreements are a way to let multinationals get rich at the expense of ordinary people, this is what you would do: give foreign firms a special right to apply to a secretive tribunal of highly paid corporate lawyers for compensation whenever a government passes a law to, say, discourage smoking, protect the environment or prevent a nuclear catastrophe. Yet that is precisely what thousands of trade and investment treaties over the past half century have done, through a process known as "investor-state dispute settlement", or ISDS (Economist 2014).

Many of these treaties are expiring. This is the time to replace them with new ones that reflect a more balanced approach to the rights and responsibilities of the sending and receiving country. A new initiative in this area by UNCTAD to develop a model treaty should be of significant assistance to developing countries (UNCTAD 2017).

The key concern with capital flows other than FDI is their volatility, which often depends on considerations completely outside the control of recipient developing countries. The issue received prominence during the East Asia financial crisis in the late 1990s and again in 2008–2009. It has finally been accepted that some form of controls of the capital account in developing countries should be used to dampen the impact of external developments that adversely affect domestic economic performance—especially surges followed by large outflows (Ostry et al. 2010). Several countries especially in Latin America but also Malaysia and Thailand have used various types of controls to dampen capital flow volatility and especially to try to lengthen the maturity structure of the flows. The IMF cautions that 'there is no surefire one-size fits all way to deal with the impact of potentially destabilizing short term capital inflows.' Still, as ODA declines as a source of development finance and developing countries turn more to private sources, managing the capital account through some type of capital controls is 'a legitimate part of the toolkit to manage capital inflows in certain circumstances' (Ostry et al. 2010, p. 15). A key requirement is effective bank regulation, which may not be present in a number of less developed countries entering the private capital markets. Great caution is needed especially as debt sustainability issues appear to be re-emerging in a number of developing countries of Sub-Saharan Africa.

New Global Issues

As US leadership declines, it may be possible in certain areas for a combination of Europe and China to provide an alternative. The obvious case is on climate change where there is a need to take steps to fill the vacuum left by the US in providing funds to developing countries. Cooperation with China may extend to other areas as well—but there will be limits, sometimes self-imposed by the lack of coherence in EU's own policies. The petty example of Greece scuttling an anti-China EU resolution on human rights is the kind of thing that has to be avoided in the future.[10]

Global demographic trends involving the aging of population will require increasing attention to issues such as migration, which require cooperative action at the regional or global level. Europe has to play an important role in this partly because it is a recipient of large inflows and partly because its focus is on economic assistance programs in Sub-Saharan Africa, the one developing country region with substantial future population growth.

Another global trend is the emergence of megacities in the developing world. These offer opportunities for increased employment and income but also create different kinds of challenges in addressing poverty: as rural poor employed in subsistence agriculture move to the cities, agricultural productivity needs to rise while more resources are needed to address problems of urban poverty and agglomeration. The rapid urbanization of Africa is a case in point. Donors, combined with private capital, need to help countries build urban infrastructure.

All this requires the elaboration of coherent development strategies, not simply the kind of large, one-shot infrastructure projects which characterize China's assistance. It is the kind of thing in which the World Bank, the MDBs and developing country-based institutions such as the Africa Center for Economic Transformation (ACET) have a comparative advantage. The past 50 years have demonstrated that for such strategies to succeed, there are three essential ingredients: the developing country must be in the driver's seat with full ownership of the program; the program should be coherent; and it must never be based on one-size-fits-all approaches.

China, Europe, the US and the Developing Countries

In June 2017, as this is being written, there were celebrations commemorating the launching of the Marshall Plan 70 years earlier, perhaps the greatest act of public generosity in recent history. At that time, the US also urged Europe to move toward greater trade integration fully aware that such a step would have resulted in discrimination against its own products. It was generosity balanced by self-interest. The net result was a growing Europe which became a partner in setting up the global institutions within which development has occurred and poverty has been reduced worldwide.

But the project is unfinished. Poverty still afflicts more than a billion people worldwide. There are 60 million refugees often living in horrid conditions. A lot more needs to be done. Unfortunately, the US today is run by a xenophobic, isolationist, protectionist administration whose head seems to confuse government with personal business. It appears keen to abandon the leadership role it has played globally, notably in trade. China is the rising global power, run by an authoritarian regime, fraught with human rights abuses that has espoused state capitalism as a means for greatly increasing prosperity of its people and has already established economic leadership in Asia.[11]

Can China be persuaded to operate a more open market, less statist system in exchange for having a greater role as well as greater responsibilities in the operation of a new global system? How would such an increased global role track with its apparent desire to move toward a more domestic-oriented growth? Will China want to play a global role commensurate with its economic strength or will it be content to consolidate its leadership position in Asia, with limited economic links to developing countries in Latin America and Africa centering on its continued needs for raw material imports? It is hard to have a clear answer, but a protectionist, isolationist US is pushing China to go its own way, not to engage more actively in the global institutions the US has helped create.

In this uncertain setting, can Europe, a bastion of the liberal economic order which for many decades had balanced the provision of social protection and economic justice for its people[12] with support for eradication of global poverty, provide an alternative pole of attraction for the developing world? And can it reign in the xenophobic sentiment that is emerging in some of its own member states? I believe it can, provided it sets its own house in order. This requires action in three areas of ascending order of economic significance.[13]

The first is in the area of trade, and it is a small matter in the grand scheme of things: it must terminate its effort to sign preferential trade agreements with its former colonies in Africa. The Sub-Saharan African countries do not want them and they interfere with the rationalization of their own preferential trade schemes which itself is urgently needed.

The second is Brexit, a complex and unpleasant business which will occupy the EU in the immediate future; but which will be sorted one way or other in the next few years. At the end of it, both the EU and the UK are likely to be worse off than at present, but it is highly likely that the UK will continue its commitment to a liberal international economic order, as has been its policy for many decades and consistent with its announced commitment to maintain EBA for LDCs after it leaves the EU.

The third area is strengthening the euro. Continued trouble within the Eurozone weakens Europe's capacity to play a role in global issues. The only way to strengthen the euro is to develop deeper European integration. Without it, the currency union is unworkable as it imposes too many hardships on its weakest members. It will be very difficult to accomplish and it will take time and leadership by the combination of France and Germany, whose governments appear to be moving toward greater degree of cooperation. The main elements for strengthening the euro have been discussed for years: the need to establish a Eurozone-wide deposit insurance; the establishment of some kind of a Eurobond. Most importantly, it is necessary to have a new deal between creditors and debtors, starting with the Greek debt in 2018. Such a deal would require an actual haircut of the existing debt or the equivalent in exchange for the establishment of an effective supervisory system to prevent debt accumulation in the future. Debt relief on official debt should be extended to other members of the Eurozone that need it. The devil will be in the details, which will take a long time to figure out. One of the most difficult problems would be the impact of this on lower income Eurozone members. Here, Germany has to play a role: an unquestionable leader in the Eurozone and a global economic power, it has to take on more of the obligations of leadership. Leaders have to be generous because of the self-interest they have in strengthening the economies of the group they lead. Germany has to learn from the example of the US 70 years ago. It will also help if its citizens and government spent a bit more so that it stops running huge current account surpluses. But this may be too much to ask at least for this German generation!

Concluding Comments

This volume has documented the great progress developing countries have made in reducing poverty and increasing the well-being of their people during the past half century amidst great changes in the global political and economic environment. These included the brief rise and subsequent decline of OPEC, the dissolution of the Soviet Union, the changing economic model and subsequent steady and rapid increase in the economic importance of China, the increasing importance of rising economic powers like Brazil, India and Korea and the relative decline but still very large role played by the US and Europe in a multipolar world.

This progress has taken place in the context of globalization, which has involved increasing economic integration through trade, aid, capital flows, technology, culture and a variety of other ways by which global interconnectedness has increased. It has been supported by institutions reflecting in large measure the liberal values espoused by US and Europe, which have spread through most of the developing world.

In recent periods, both liberalism and globalization have come under attack: the growth of China under a model of state capitalism and a one-party communist system and the re-emergence of Russia with a similar system combined with a new US administration mired in isolationist and protectionist tendencies have eroded confidence in the institutions that have formed the foundations of the global economy in the post-World War II years. This last chapter presented a number of suggestions of things that can be done to prevent a further deterioration of the liberal economic system.

Moving forward will be a slow and difficult process. The international community is excellent at muddling through, which has seriously adverse consequences for the weakest countries and people. But this same community can mobilize itself surprisingly quickly in response to major events such as the dissolution of the Soviet Union.

A lot of the priority in the next few years should be devoted to holding actions, especially in the area of trade, to avoid undermining the international trading system for a few years, until hopefully, a less protectionist US emerges. At the same time, more attention should be devoted to approaches that limit the distortions that state capitalism introduces to international trade. More action is needed to bring about changes in the global institutions that affect multilateral economic assistance so that they can reflect better the relative economic importance of emerging powers, especially China. Several aids for trade institutions should be combined to avoid duplication and reduce the burden to recipients. Public-private sector investment initiatives need to be encouraged. And consideration should be given to how to expand the role of the G-20 especially in promoting coherence between aid and trade.

By far there are two most important tasks in preserving the liberal economic order: first, to develop systems of social protection for those left behind as a result of globalization and/or automation in all countries; and second, to continue to provide support to developing country efforts to eliminate poverty, reduce inequality and achieve the other sustainable development goals agreed at the UN.

Development depends on the efforts of the developing countries themselves. The external environment, aid, capital flow and trade can only help or undermine these efforts. Liberalism offers a supportive approach that combines economic progress with individual freedom and respect for human rights. If it does not deliver on economic progress for all, it gives rise to alternatives that endanger individual freedoms and human rights.

China's state capitalism offers a seductive alternative much like Soviet central planning did in 1930s. It may have a more lasting value or it may morph into something else, or it may collapse under the pressure of democratization spread by information technology—an eventuality with unknown consequences. But India with a very pluralistic system has also done pretty well in recent years. The US and Europe must recognize that the threats to liberalism derive partly from their own shortcomings in addressing the needs of those left behind. The current US administration, having come to power on the strength of the votes of the disaffected, is promoting domestic policies likely to exacerbate inequalities and do nothing to increase social protection, while ignoring the plight of the poor worldwide. It may fall on the shoulders of Europe to rise again in defense of liberalism. As this is being written, there is a flicker of light suggesting a new tomorrow based on stronger Franco-German collaboration. If it comes about, the benefits will accrue not only to Europeans but to everybody.

Notes

1. No Date. Retrieved June 25, 2017 from Azquotes.com.quote/684175.
2. A study of China's aid for the period 1956–2006 (Dreher and Fuchs 2015) suggests that it was no more prone to allocate ODA based on political considerations than other DAC donors; but apparently was influenced in the allocation of non-ODA loans by commercial access to raw materials considerations. Given uncertainties about actual aid levels and the large recent increases of China's aid to Sub-Saharan Africa, it is unclear whether this conclusion still holds.
3. *Cash-on-Delivery-Aid* (COD) implies that donors offer a fixed payment to recipient governments for each additional unit of progress toward a commonly agreed goal, for example, $200 for each additional child who takes a standardized test at the end of primary school. This approach provides funders with an opportunity to deliver identifiable and visible results to their taxpayers. It enables the donor to pay only for an outcome, not for inputs, while the recipient has full responsibility for and discretion in using funds (Herfkens 2014).
4. CGD is well positioned having already produced a significant report on this subject a few years back (Birdsall and Kharas 2014).
5. Peer reviews of donor practices have in the past been an effective mechanism used by the DAC to improve aid effectiveness. It was emulated in the WTO through the establishment of the Trade Policy Review Mechanism. Both have languished in the recent past because of the same lack of political will in donors and the anxiety of not to offend by the recipients.
6. In part this is also the result of the mushrooming of small private philanthropic institutions.
7. See also an earlier proposal I made to DFID (Michalopoulos 2005).
8. The Development Council was abolished because it was argued that only a few EU countries had Ministries of Development Cooperation and the development cooperation questions could be addressed in the Foreign Affairs Council. The justification was flawed as the EU has separate Councils on issues typically addressed by Ministries of the Economy.
9. See www.cgddev.org.
10. Of course the Greek government action may have been a childish tit-for-tat coming a few days after its Eurozone partners failed to provide it with the kind of debt relief that it so eagerly sought.
11. A recent example is that when the US Federal Reserve raised interest rates recently, China's central bank did not follow and neither did the rest of Asia or Europe.

12. Arguably sometimes too much and unsustainably so: There are 35 social benefits in Greece, *even excluding unemployment*, including the infamous benefit for the blind, which resulted in the case of an island having a large portion of its population declared blind, as well as something called 'social tourism' (Kathimerini, June 25, 2017).

13. There are obviously many other challenges faced by Europe which are beyond the scope of this volume. To name a few: addressing the refugee crisis, working on climate change, strengthening Europe-wide security systems, dealing with terrorism etc.

References

Birdsall, N. and H. Kharas, (2014), *The Quality of ODA, Third Edition* (Washington DC: CGD and Brookings).

Dreher, A. and A. Fuchs (2015) "Rogue Aid? An Empirical Analysis of China's Aid Allocation" *Canadian Journal of Economics* 48 (3) August.

Economist the (2014) 11 October.

Economist the (2017) 17 June.

Gurria, A. (2017) "Globalization: Don't Patch it up, Shake it up" OECD *Observer*, June.

Herfkens, E. (2014) "Aid Effectiveness: Lessons Learned- and Forgotten (in Dutch)" S. Vermer, L. Schulpen and R. Ruben Eds. *Hoe nu Verder* (Arnhem: LM Publishers).

Kathimerini (2017) 25 June.

Kitano, N. (2016) "Estimating China's Foreign Aid II 2014 Update" JICA Research Institute Working Paper No. 131 (Tokyo: JICA RI).

Leipziger, D. (2016) "Trade is Slowing Down: What does this Imply for Globalization?" The Growth Dialogue www.growthdialogue.org, November.

Melendez-Ortiz and R. Samons (2016) "Strengthening the Global Trade and Investment System in the 21st Century, Executive Summary" (Geneva: ICTSD and World Economic Forum).

Michalopoulos, C. (2005) "Enhancing the Integrated Framework: A new Approach" mimeo., Prepared for UK Department for International Development.

Michalopoulos, C. (2014) *Emerging Powers in the WTO* (Houndsmills: Palgrave Macmillan).

Ostry, J.D. et al. (2010) "Capital Inflows: the Role of Controls" IMF Staff Position Note SPN/104 (Washington DC: IMF).

UNCTAD (2017) "Phase 2 of IIA Reforms: Modernizing the Existing System of Old Generation Treaties" IIA Issues Note #2 (Geneva: UNCTAD).

Biographical Appendix A: Constantine Michalopoulos

Date of Birth: March 16, 1940, Athens, Greece

Education

1950–1957   Athens College, High School Diploma, 1957
1957–1960   Ohio Wesleyan University, BA, 1960
1960–1966   Columbia University, MIA, 1962; PhD (Economics), 1966

Academic Work

1965–1967   Trinity College (USA), Instructor, Assistant Professor
1967–1969   Clark University, Assistant Professor
1993–1996   American University, Adjunct Professor
2012–2017   Johns Hopkins University, SAIS, Adjunct Professor, Visiting Scholar

© The Author(s) 2017
C. Michalopoulos, *Aid, Trade and Development*,
https://doi.org/10.1007/978-3-319-65861-2

Public Service

1969–1982   US Agency for International Development (AID)
1969–1972   International Economist
1972–1974   Chief, Trade and Payment Division
1977–1981   Director, Office of Economic Affairs
1981–1982   Chief Economist

1982–1997   World Bank, Washington
1982–1983   Senior Advisor, Economic and Research Staff
1983–1987   Director, Economic Policy and Co-ordination, Economic and Research Staff
1991–1997   Senior Advisor for Operations, Russia and Central Asia

1997–1999   World Trade Organization, Geneva, Special Advisor

1999–2001   World Bank, Brussels, Senior Economic Advisor

2001–2008   World Bank, IMF, DFID, GTZ, SIDA Consultant

Statistical Appendix B

There is no formal 'developing country' definition in any of the major international organizations such as the World Bank or the WTO. The former uses for statistical purposes per capita income and regional groupings which do not distinguish between developed and developing countries and which are used in Tables 4.1 and 7.2. The WTO has no official breakdown of developed versus developing countries. For operational purposes, 'developing' countries use the principle of self-selection. The breakdown between developed and developing countries used in this analysis follows roughly the breakdown used by the WTO for statistical purposes with a few changes to be noted below.

Developed countries in my analysis include 49 countries (of which 42 in Europe—28 in the EU, plus Iceland, Norway, Switzerland—all the Balkans—plus Belarus, Kazakhstan, Russia and Ukraine, but not Armenia, Azerbaijan, Georgia or Moldova) plus Australia, Canada, Israel, Japan, New Zealand, Turkey and the US. This is pretty close to the WTO definition with the exception that South Africa, which the WTO classifies as 'developed', in our case is in the developing country group—while Turkey, classified by the WTO as 'developing', is in our analysis in the developed country group, as it is applying for association with the EU. Also, Armenia, Georgia and the Kyrgyz Republic classify themselves

© The Author(s) 2017
C. Michalopoulos, *Aid, Trade and Development*,
https://doi.org/10.1007/978-3-319-65861-2

in the WTO as 'transition' economies—a category that had been used in the past but which is of doubtful usefulness in this analysis. All three countries are classified as 'developing', as are Moldova, Tajikistan, Turkmenistan and Uzbekistan.

All remaining countries and territories are considered 'developing'. For merchandise trade, the analysis has data for 142 countries. Forty-nine are in Sub-Saharan Africa, 37 in Asia, 35 in Latin America and the Caribbean and 21 in Europe, the Middle East and North Africa. The latter region includes the five North African countries (Morocco, Algeria, Tunisia, Libya and Egypt) and stretches all the way east to include Iraq and Iran (but not Afghanistan, which is in Asia). It also includes Armenia, Azerbaijan, Georgia and Moldova. LDCs are the 48 countries in the UN list, shown as a separate category.

Index[1]

[1]Note: Page numbers with "n" denote footnotes

© The Author(s) 2017
C. Michalopoulos, *Aid, Trade and Development*,
https://doi.org/10.1007/978-3-319-65861-2

Printed in the United States
By Bookmasters